STRANGE, INHUMAN DEATHS

STRANGE, INHUMAN DEATHS

MURDER IN TUDOR ENGLAND

JOHN BELLAMY

SUTTON PUBLISHING

First published in the United Kingdom in 2005 by
Sutton Publishing Limited · Phoenix Mill
Thrupp · Stroud · Gloucestershire · GL5 2BU

British Library Cataloguing in Publication Data
A catalogue record for this book is available from the British Library.

ISBN 0-7509-3863-3

Typeset in 10.5/15pt Photina MT.
Typesetting and origination by
Sutton Publishing Limited.
Printed and bound in England by
J.H. Haynes & Co. Ltd, Sparkford.

CONTENTS

LIST OF ILLUSTRATIONS

ACKNOWLEDGEMENTS

My debts are to the Social Sciences and Humanities Research Council of Canada, whose funding assisted in the research for this book, and to my wife, Annette, for her enduring support, her assistance in preparing the text, and her salutary advice.

J.G.B.

INTRODUCTION

Murder in the sixteenth century, which to English men and women of that time meant planned slaying, usually with an element of stealth or with the victim taken unawares, was not then a common crime; rather the reverse. For example, Sir Thomas Smith, the knowledgeable Tudor legal commentator, tells us murder by poisoning was virtually unknown in his day. Also writing in the reign of Elizabeth I was William Harrison, who, in a contribution to Holinshed's *Chronicles* that dealt with the criminal law, its penalties and its impact on society, stated that, although manslaughter and 'bloudie robberies' occurred 'now and then', 'we do not often heare of horrible, merciless, and wilfull murthers'.[1] Nor do other writers of the period who touch on criminal law or on crime and public order indicate anything different. These brief indications of a relatively low murder rate are borne out by statistics to be garnered from the extant assize records of the later sixteenth century. Because of the existence of victims' corpses, murder may well have been among the most reported of felonies (that is, reported to officers of the law), yet in Sussex and Cheshire in Elizabeth's reign only about 5 per cent of all persons put on trial for felony were suspected murderers, while the relatively high rate of 8 per cent in Kent has to be set against the trivial 1 per cent in Essex. The overall impression is that probably about one in every twenty indicted felons was believed to be a murderer.[2]

Noticeably absent from our sources is evidence of sixteenth-century persons who committed murder on more than a single occasion. Multiple and serial murderers, and there must have been some, do not seem to have been brought to book for their plural slayings. Certainly these are almost entirely absent from extant legal records. This may help to explain the fact that contemporary writing offers no portrayal of an English sixteenth-century murderer as a monster. Although murder was regarded by most Tudor commentators on the law as being, with the exception of treason, the most reprehensible of offences and much more heinous than the crime of killing in 'chance medley' (that is, killing in hot blood, usually after an altercation, which was deemed to be manslaughter) there was relatively little rhetoric in official documents about its villainy.[3]

As might be expected, there was a big difference between the number of men and the number of women arraigned for murder – that is to say, for murder proper – with so-called witchcraft slayings and infanticides excluded. Surviving court records of four south-eastern counties indicate that about 73 per cent of those put on trial for the crime, either as principals or as accessories liable to the death penalty, were male, and thus women accounted for nearly 27 per cent of the total. This involvement by women was, apparently, considerably greater than in the later medieval period. Evidence from mid-fifteenth-century Yorkshire suggests a female rate of only about 4 per cent. In Elizabethan Sussex, infanticide and witchcraft killings apart, women murdered half the number of persons that men did. Their victims were usually male rather than members of their own sex; the ratio was 2:1. In Essex in the same period women committed a mere quarter of the murders that men did, and the number of women arraigned was just over one sixth of the number of men put on trial for that crime. The sex of the victims, whether the deed was done by male or female assailants, was male rather than female, but only in the ratio of 5:3. In Elizabethan Kent men were arraigned for 3.5 times as many murders as women. In contrast with Sussex and Essex, Kentish men murdered members of their own sex rather than women, and in the high ratio of approximately 10:1. Kentish women, for their part, murdered just over twice as many males as females.[4]

The total number of men of whom we have record from Elizabeth's reign as being arraigned for murder in the three counties of Kent, Essex and Sussex is 190, just under four times the number of women similarly arraigned (52). Seven of these women had to answer for the slaying of their husbands (13.5 per cent), and eleven men for the death of their wives (5.8 per cent). Killing one's spouse was obviously not a common type of murder. Murdering other family members was also uncommon. Women slew only eight such in the three counties (including four sons), and men killed a mere four (three were children). Only one victim was a sibling and none a parent of the murderer. As we might have expected to find, the conviction rate for murder differed according to the sex of the perpetrator. In Sussex 86 per cent of men arraigned for the crime in Elizabeth's reign, of whom we have knowledge from the extant assize records and on whom a trial jury is known to have rendered a verdict, were found guilty. In Essex the figure was 71 per cent, in Kent 67 per cent. In regard to women murder suspects, the figures were noticeably lower in two counties: 38 per cent in Sussex and 30 per cent in Essex. In contrast, Kent juries were very hostile to murderesses: the conviction rate was a notable 75 per cent. How far socio-economic conditions and belief systems, on the one hand, and jury control by law officers, on the other, affected these rates historians have not yet determined.

There can be little doubt that the coming of Protestantism had a considerable effect on murder. It did not lead, as far as we know, to increasing or decreasing incidences of the crime; nor was it connected with changing fashions in how murders were committed. Its impact was felt through the publicity given to particular murders, by a number of writers of Protestant or assumed Protestant inclination, through the revelation of details of the more distinctive examples of murder and the behaviour and fate of the murderers. These 'in-depth' studies, which fed a growing public interest in murder, contrast sharply with the passing references to instances of the crime in late medieval historical sources.[5] The first murder case of the sixteenth century to be reported in more than a few lines occurred early in the reign of Henry VIII and undoubtedly owed its notoriety to its having an important religious dimension. Richard Hun was a wealthy London merchant-tailor and suspected Lollard. Between 1511 and his death late in 1514, he dared to quarrel with the Church in the courts: first, over a piece of London property; then, with the Rector of Whitechapel over a mortuary, over the bearing sheet of his dead infant son. Subsequently, he had the temerity to sue the rector's chaplain for slander in the Court of King's Bench, and then to issue a writ of praemunire through the same court against the offending rector and his abettors. This litigation provoked ecclesiastical wrath and accusations of heresy against Hun.[6] Hun was arrested by the Church authorities and imprisoned at St Paul's in the Lollards' Tower, where he died on the night of 3/4 December 1514, a death that appeared to many to be no less than murder on the part of the Chancellor of the Bishop of London and his underlings. The circumstances of the death were recorded at some length, first in a pamphlet dating from about 1538, and then ten years later, in virtually the same words, in the chronicle of Edward Hall.[7] The account and supporting documentation of the Hun case in this chronicle, which appears without introduction or indeed any apology for the inclusion of such a lowly matter, are placed in between a description of the festivities that celebrated the marriage of Henry VIII's sister to Louis XII of France and the New Year celebrations at the English Court. This testifies to the great impact of the case on the public mind.[8]

A London coroner's jury, 'a verie substanciall' one (that is, the jurors were of substantial wealth) 'elected by greate dyscrecion' (that is, after careful consideration), was sworn in to enquire into the suspicious death, for Hun had been found hanging by the neck in his place of confinement.[9] We know that the jury was 'laboured' (that is, lobbied) by law officers of the Crown and that a little later the case was taken up by the King's Council. There the circumstances of the death were debated at length, with the King himself hearing much of the argument. Hall's chronicle tells us that the clerical members of the Council were particularly vehement. Their concern was that the coroner's inquest would find, unfairly as they saw it, that Hun's death had been a murder on the part of his ecclesiastical jailers, and that there would probably then be some sort of confrontation between the London citizenry and the Bishop of London, which might fuel an attack on the Church in the forthcoming parliament.[10] Of particular interest is the fact that the Council seems to have called before itself one of the leading suspects, Charles Joseph, a summoner. It must have been on the Council's orders that he was held in the Tower of London, where he eventually provided a confession. The Council sent the case, and doubtless the confession, back to the coroner's inquest.[11] A set of law reports dating from fairly soon after the event tells us that a considerable time elapsed between the first meeting of the inquest and the announcement of a verdict. The writer called it 'a great and long deliberation'.[12] Whether this was because of the time it took the jurors to complete their own investigations or because they had to await the results of the Council's intervention is not clear.

The importance of the Hun case in the history of sixteenth-century murder, apart from the light it throws incidentally on the workings of a coroner's inquest, lies in the survival of depositions provided by suspects and witnesses. This rare series of documents allows us to benefit from detailed information, not only the evidence provided by the victim's corpse but also that concerning the movements, roles and even motivation of the players in the drama; thus we can obtain a fairly clear picture of what actually happened. Particularly striking are the careful recording and shrewd interpretation by the jury of the evidence discovered at the scene of the death: 'Hun hanging upon a staple of iron in a girdle of sylke', 'his eyen and mouth fayre closed, withoute any staring, gapying or frownyng', 'without any drevelyng or spurgyng in any place of his body'. The jury also noted that Hun's hands had been bound and his neck broken; that blood had been shed in copious quantities some distance from where his body was hanging; furthermore, that the short length of the girdle and the lack of a suitable stool or similar object would have made it impossible for Hun to have hanged himself, as the Church authorities claimed.[13]

The jurors in their verdict also referred to the confession by Charles Joseph, whom they named as one of Hun's murderers. He had admitted how, following behind John Spalding, a bell-ringer, and with Dr William Horsey, the Chancellor, coming last, he had gone up the stairs to Hun's prison cell in the Lollards' Tower. Then when 'all wee came up we founde Hun lyenge on his bedde, and than Mayster chauncellor sayde, lay handes on the thefe and so al we murthered Hun, and then I, Charles, put the gyrdell aboute Huns necke and then Ihon Belrynger and I, Charles, dyd heve up Hun and Master Chauncellor pulled the gyrdell over the staple and so Hun was hanged'. Joseph's admission of guilt received confirmation in a deposition made by his female servant, who stated that her master had told her he had murdered Hun: 'I put a wyre in his nose', he had said, adding, 'I had lever than hundred pound yt were not done.' The coroner's jury made a point of showing that Charles Joseph's original defence, which was that he had been out of town visiting a harlot at the time of the murder, was quite false, and to demonstrate this the jurors appended to their verdict depositions by five witnesses.[14]

The only evidence that suggests Hun's death might have been other than murder came in a second-hand report. A servant of the Bishop of London was stated to have said that the prisoner had asked to borrow a knife, remarking that he would rather kill himself than suffer additional ill-treatment. However, since a knife had been left with Hun by accident or design on the evening before his death without his attempting suicide, the inquest obviously had reason to discount such a form of death. More perplexing for the modern reader of the case is the fact that Hun was reported as having been set in the stocks in his place of confinement on the night of his death yet found hanging on a staple in the wall there in the morning. That Horsey, the chancellor, was a murderer himself or gave orders for the murder, as Joseph deposed, is also suggested by his visiting Hun and praying his forgiveness for 'all that he had done to hym and must do to hym', very much as official sixteenth-century executioners were wont to ask of their more illustrious victims.[15]

The verdict that the coroner's inquest returned was that Horsey, Joseph and Spalding had strangled, smothered and broken the neck of Richard Hun, and hanged his body, when dead, on a staple. 'Immediately,' says John Foxe, the Protestant martyrologist, 'certain of the bloody murderers were committed to prison'; he does not state which ones. The verdict of a coroner's jury normally became an indictment of the accused in a court of criminal law, the assize court, but whether this happened in the Hun case is unclear. The King's minister, Thomas Wolsey, Archbishop of York, seems to have come to the assistance of the embarrassed Bishop of London and his miscreant underlings. As requested by the prelate, he persuaded the King to instruct his Attorney-General to declare the verdict of the inquest untrue – a very rare occurrence – and thus allow the accused to be discharged. Foxe implies that the foreman of the jury was either bribed or pressured, but to what end he does not make clear.[16]

A law report, happily, provides us with a little more detail about the aftermath of the inquest. It states that when the popular outcry over Hun's death was dying down Dr Horsey, who although technically a prisoner had been living at Lambeth Palace, a residence of the Archbishop of Canterbury, came privately into the Court of King's Bench, where he was actually arraigned of the murder. He pleaded not guilty, the King's attorney 'confessed it' – that is to say, he admitted the indictment was erroneous or deficient – and Horsey was then discharged.[17] Joseph and Spalding, his fellow indictees, are not mentioned in this report, but Thomas More states that Horsey and 'the other' escaped trial this way. He notes also that Horsey, in addition to being dismissed *sine die*, had obtained a pardon for the crime, but one with condition. Hun's goods, which were 'of no little value', and which must have been seized by the Church when *post mortem*, he had been condemned for heresy, were to be restored to his children.[18]

There exists comment on the case, though not a description of Hun's death, in another literary source. In his *A dialogue concerning heresies* (1529) Thomas More devoted the fifteenth chapter to the Hun case, an episode in which he claimed personally to have played a small part. He said he knew it 'frome toppe to too [toe], that I suppose there be not very many men that knoweth it moche better'; for he had been present at 'certayne examynacyons thereof' and had talked to almost all those involved or who gave testimony. Despite this advantageous position, all More was able to do to shift the guilt from Horsey, his obvious aim, was to poke fun at three of the persons examined before the Council. Scornfully he referred to a man who, when he appeared, related how a gypsy woman, a necromancer, had told him Horsey was the guilty party. Secondly, More mentioned an underling of several King's almoners who, on what turned out to be actual acquaintance with a single suicide by hanging, claimed Hun could not have hanged himself. Thirdly, More argued that Horsey would never have obtained a pardon from the King, a monarch with the highest principles as he saw it, if he had in fact been guilty of Hun's murder; furthermore, Horsey was never required to sue out the pardon in court. These weak, almost flippant, arguments were all the defence More could muster on the Chancellor's behalf apart from a general statement that he personally had never heard of anything to make him think Horsey guilty. Then, as he moved into intimations of Hun's heretical leanings, More suggested that the latter hoped to make a name for himself through his praemunire suit, but when things began to go awry he began to 'fall in fere of worldely shame' and so 'rydde hym selfe' from this life 'for werynes'.[19]

It may have been that when More was writing, in around 1528–9, his recollection of the events of 1514–15 was fading, even if that memory had been refreshed in 1523. That was when Hun's daughter and her husband sought the return of her father's goods, which put at risk John Rastell, More's brother- in-law, who had obtained some of them. The most striking aspect of More's comments on the Hun case is his failure to mention the findings of the coroner's jury and the depositions that it obtained, particularly the confession of Charles Joseph. All More provides about that inquest is the patronising comment that the jurors were probably 'ryght honest menne' who followed their consciences.[20]

Modern historians have tended to view the Hun case as a test of strength between the London citizenry and the Church, with the King and his Council asking the occasional question but in the main standing by as observers.[21] Yet this interpretation of events is open to debate. A crucial piece of evidence against it is Charles Joseph's confession, which comes, as the pamphleteer and the chronicler Hall set it down, at the end of the investigations, deductions and findings of the coroner's jury, an account compiled by the jurors themselves, as the use of the first-person plural indicates. Joseph, we should notice, had fled after the crime to sanctuary in Essex where he was registered as a sanctuary man, though without confessing to Hun's murder. From there he was moved, presumably on the orders of the Council, to the Tower of London. The jurors stated that in the Tower Joseph recorded the heresy charges that the Church had laid against Hun. 'Also Charles Joseph sayeth . . .', their statement continues, and they then give his confession to the murder.[22]

The fact that Joseph made his confessions in the Tower, and that the jurors state that it was 'of hys owne free wyll and unconstreyned', is probably significant. Murder suspects in London would probably be incarcerated in Newgate, the Fleet or one of the two Counters. The Tower was for persons committing great crimes, offences of particular interest to the Crown. The Council sent prisoners there when the offence fell into that category. The Tower was also a place where prisoners made confessions. In the correspondence of officials dating from the first decade of Henry VIII's reign there are several references to admissions of guilt being obtained there by the threat or actual use of torture – 'put to some pain', as it was called. Joseph's affirmation that he deposed 'of hys awne free wyll' and in 'hys awne hand' was doubtless intended to convey the impression, whether true or false, that he had not been tortured. The crucial evidence that established that Hun had been murdered was thus obtained by the Council, whose spiritual members, keen to protect their turf, were temporarily discomfited, we may assume, by their secular colleagues.[23] Yet, as we have seen, the Council's dispatch of Joseph's confession to the coroner, while producing an inquest verdict against Horsey, Joseph and Spalding, was ultimately to no avail, probably because of the intervention of Thomas Wolsey. An attempt to prosecute the case further in parliament also came to nothing.[24] The impact of the Hun case in both the history of religion and the history of murder is not in doubt, although admittedly the second was largely the outcome of the first. There was an account of the case in Richard Arnold's *Customs of London* (1521) and comments on it appeared in the writings of Simon Fish (1528), Thomas More (1529), William Tyndale (1531) and Charles Wriothesley (1562).[25] Sometime between 1536 and 1540 there was published an anonymous tract on the murder. This short piece, the introduction to which implied that the killing of prisoners in its jails was a not uncommon practice of the Church, was probably the basis of the account that appeared in Hall's *Chronicle* when it was published in 1548.[26] In 1563 and 1570 respectively there appeared in print the first and second editions of John Foxe's *Acts and Monuments*, which each contained a substantial section on the Hun case. The pamphlet literature on particular murders, which flourished from the 1570s, must have received some inspiration from these writings, even if more obvious models for the authors were the short entries on such crimes in chronicles.

When the topic was murder, the chroniclers and pamphlet writers of the later sixteenth century, even those pamphleteers who were bent on using their writing for religious purposes, had a good idea of what would attract a readership. They knew very well what was newsworthy and what would sell. One very desirable element in any reported case of murder was an active role by a woman, preferably young and attractive ('faire'). As victims, women were in demand, but by no means as much as when they were principals or accessories in the crime. A domestic situation as the background to the murder was also considered an asset, especially if it was one in which a wife could be shown to have betrayed her husband sexually. There were erotic undertones in several Elizabethan murder pamphlets. Class bias, however, seems to be virtually absent from this type of literature.[27]

Historians have drawn attention to what they perceive as a debate on the qualities of womanhood and the status and role of women in society, which commenced in the 1540s, a time when new religious ideas were arriving in England. Such debate could not have occurred without the benefit of the printing press and thereby a new-found access to literature for many people. Printers appear to have profited from the trend and to have welcomed works both in defence of women and against their 'deceyte', works that they seem to have found much better sellers than the relatively plentiful writings on moral wisdom.[28] A notable feature of sixteenth-century murder literature is the prominence within it of the wives of men of the middle classes. Then as now people seem to have preferred to read about murder in the wealthier segment of society rather than among the members of the labouring classes. Heinous crimes by women in the higher strata of society may have stimulated popular interest in female misbehaviour in general. The misfortunes of Henry VIII's queens, the adultery of two of them being found to be no less than high treason, and the statute of 1543, which entailed the Crown and gave rise to the thought that a woman might rule England in the not-too-distant future, must have given an edge of political relevance to the debate.[29] How far women had the ability to read the writings on the qualities of womanhood for themselves is not clear. The argument is sometimes offered that the female part of the population of the period was considerably less literate than the male, yet it seems unlikely that those who took the female side in their writing expected an entirely male readership. It is obvious that literacy did not remain at the same level throughout the sixteenth century. In the last thirty years or so of the Tudor period, there was a large increase in the number of felons who gained benefit of clergy by reading a proffered text, but these by law were only male felons. Yet the fact that Protestantism promoted a desire in members of both sexes to read the scriptures for themselves, and the patent intent of murder-pamphlet writers to engage the attention of women as well as of men, suggest that the ability to read (as distinct from being able to write) among women of the middle class at least was relatively common.[30]

The history of English criminal justice in the mid-sixteenth century has been taken as showing a desire on the part of male office holders, who made and administered the law, to bring more women before the courts for felony. This was for categories of crime hitherto unprosecuted in secular courts, namely infanticide (the murder of newly born children) and witchcraft (sometimes rated as murder). Both of these offences, the first prosecuted only from the beginning of Elizabeth's reign and the second from the mid-1560s, have been regarded as essentially women's crimes. Whether we should interpret such prosecutions as part of a male desire to put women in their place, or as an understandable attempt to remedy the slackness of the ecclesiastical authorities within whose purview these crimes had fallen in earlier times, is not yet clear. Neither cases of infanticide nor those of 'murder by witchcraft', a very real crime to Tudor people, have been included in what follows.[31]

Besides the appearance of a woman or women in a murder case, there was another class of person whose presence both chroniclers and pamphlet writers found desirable. This was the servant. Servants who turned against their employer were a not-infrequent ingredient both as assistants to the murderer and as the actual assassins, although not as the original designers of the deed. Usually, it seems, they were ready to assist in the killing for their personal gain rather than because of any hatred of their employer, and the accounts are quick to provide detail as to the profit they arranged for themselves in return for their homicidal services. The sums of money range from the very small to the excessively large. The marked willingness of these servants to assist in a murder, their lack of hesitation in joining the chief conspirators, at least as the writers tell it, is very noticeable.[32]

The method of the slaying in a case of murder, as we might expect, is rarely omitted by the commentators. The instrument of death varies. Shooting with a firearm is a rarity, as is death by sword or rapier. The most common method of murder in the accounts appears to be a severe blow to the head followed by the cutting of the unconscious or semi-conscious victim's throat, a method in which many persons must have been proficient in an age in which the consumer often slaughtered his own beasts. Second in popularity was probably stabbing with a knife or dagger. Poison, definitely a woman's instrument of death, was considered the most reprehensible, and the method of poisoning, the progress of the poison and the eventual demise of the victim were usually given extended coverage.[33] Corpses of murder victims also drew comment on occasion. As we might expect, dismemberment, when it occurred, was given special attention, but the spilling of blood, except where a small amount was a clue to finding the killer, is rarely mentioned. The body of the victim was a focal point for commentators in scenes where the perpetrator of the crime came near the corpse again sometime after the murder. Then the corpse might bleed, or change colour, or the eyes might open (in one case even stare at the miscreant), indicating to sixteenth-century men and women that the guilty party was close by.[34] A confession might then be forthcoming from the dumbfounded murderer.

While the chroniclers who describe murders give little indication of emotional involvement with the sad tales they tell, other commentators, dramatists as well as pamphleteers, are sometimes less detached, as we might expect. In what is a pamphlet written in dramatic form, sympathy is shown for the sister of a murderer who was convicted of being an accessory to his crime simply because she 'received' him: she got him his food and failed to report the crime. In another pamphlet we can also detect a measure of pity for a woman, asleep in bed at night, stabbed by her husband twenty-five times on a thought that had occurred to him while he slept, who asked for God's forgiveness on him before she dropped dead. In a third case the pamphleteer seems to be so involved that he partially conceals the guilt of an adulterous wife, who was a co-planner of her husband's death, probably because she tried to provide for her children and sought the forgiveness of her husband's relatives after she had been convicted of the crime.[35] At the other end of the spectrum, in a Worcestershire case that obviously raised the writer's ire, a wife who persuaded her servant-lover to murder her husband is called a devil and a 'gracelesse strumpet'. The greatest hostility any pamphlet writer displays is that directed against a Catholic gentleman who stabbed to death a co-religionist while in the Queen's Bench Prison: 'Papists are like madde Dogges and ever ready to kill and imbrace forraine jurisdiction.' The reason for this denigration is clear enough. The murderer failed to make a good Protestant end at the gallows, hurling abuse at ministers, crowd and the Reformed faith. Any similar papist needed to be 'well cougeled' like a 'sheepwerier', states the writer venomously. One emotional account of a murder in a pamphlet manages to combine sympathy and condemnation for the principal murderer in equal measure. The duplicitous and treacherous manner in which Anne Welles murdered her husband by poison at her lover's instigation in 1590 is described in graphic detail, but so also is the way the latter mistreated her after the crime had been committed.[36] The pamphlet writers were economical in their sympathy for murder victims, even female or child victims. One wife-victim is described *tout court* as being left 'weltering in her owne goare'. Of another, who was deliberately poisoned in the vagina by her husband while on a conjugal visit to his prison, the only comment is the laconic statement that it 'was the dearest nights pleasure that ever woman had'.[37]

Children figure in only a few of the sixteenth-century murder accounts. In one instance, involving three children, it is as victims; in another, involving a boy, it is as a witness to his father's slaying of his mother. In a third case children receive the blessing of their mother after she has been sentenced to death.[38] The pamphlet writer who tells us about the son who testified against his father gives a most laudatory account of the child's calm and clear voice. He spoke, we are told, 'without any blushing feare (as commonly is seen in Children)' and refused to be moved from his statements by his father's denials. It was his adult-like behaviour, and the fact that his testimony achieved his father's conviction, that moved the writer and was expected to appeal to his readership. There was no sympathy, expressed in print at least, for a child in a tragic and traumatic situation. In the case involving the death of three children, two boys and a girl were killed by a servant following a plan concocted by their widower-father so that he might remarry without the burden of offspring. Despite the extremely cold-blooded nature of the murders, all that the pamphlet writer feels obliged to tell his readers is that the slayer knocked them on the heads with a hatchet and then cut their throats. Clearly there were few tears and thus no market for the sufferings of children.

The only admonition in Tudor murder accounts about the protection of the lives of offspring is in regard to stepchildren. An Essex man who had married a widow, when about to be executed for murdering a stepson, warned all such as he and the widows who had married them to care for their stepchildren as they would children of their own begetting. Elsewhere in his pamphlet this writer uniquely dwells on the misery created for parents, wives, children and even servants when a man is murdered. The only comparable expression of concern for the consequences of murder is by a pamphleteer writing about a newly wedded woman in Worcestershire, who was visiting relatives when her husband slew the man who lived next door. 'Women will know', he laments, 'what a greefe it was to her when first she heard of these unhappy newes.' These comments, like the murders, date from the second half of Elizabeth's reign, but whether we should attribute them to a rising sensitivity in society to the repercussions of murder, or merely to the idiosyncrasies of the writers, is not clear.[39]

When it came to the detection of the culprit in murder cases, writers, particularly pamphleteers, preferred that the establishment of guilt should be by confession rather than by the accumulation of evidence and actual trial. A confession meant a plea of guilty by the suspect on arraignment and thus no trial by jury. This helps to explain why there is so little mention of trial procedure or description of courtroom scenes in sixteenth-century murder literature. We should not forget, however, that many of the writers wore a Protestant religious mantle and that a confession was attractive to them not only because it removed any doubt as to who was the guilty party but also because confession was often accompanied by that religious desideratum, open repentance. Murder commentators knew that the desired confessions did not come readily and unsolicited; rather they had usually to be obtained by confronting the suspect with strong incriminatory evidence. Thus there are a good number of references to useful clues and pieces of proof discovered by investigators, the latter being mayors and their officers, justices of the peace and village constables, members of coroners' juries, and even concerned neighbours. A discovery that a piece of earth had been dislodged from a cellar floor, or that the rushes had been recently replaced in a particular house, or that a corpse without obvious wounds had a broken neck, or that words of a minatory nature had been uttered against the victim, were clues recognized as being of vital importance in the unmasking of the murderer and diligently sought for.[40]

Indeed, it seems fair to say that a number of these murder accounts deserve to be regarded as members of the first crop of detective stories in the English language – especially as a number of the persons appearing therein, who recognise the clues and use a moderate amount of deductive reasoning, are portrayed with favour by the writers. Other elements of the modern detective story also make an appearance. There is the alibi as to time and place, and the attempt of the murderer to cover his tracks. In one case we have the tracking of a utensil, believed to have been used by the killer, back to the original seller. Elsewhere, someone who has once met the suspect is sent to try to identify her among a group of neighbours. Perhaps this intelligent approach to crime detection should not surprise us.[41] The men of the later Middle Ages knew a lot about successful interrogation, and an Elizabethan commentator on the role and duties of justices of the peace sets out in detail the lines of investigation, some amounting to psychological assessment of the suspect, that such an officer should pursue when questioning persons supposed to have committed felony.[42]

Again suggestive of more modern times, there is in one account (as there are in governmental records) reference to forensic medicine. A dead woman's body is 'ripped' by surgeons, who are said to discover within it the ratsbane and glass with which she had been poisoned – evidence that apparently helped to secure a conviction. In another pamphlet and also in an account of murder in dramatic form there is, deliberately rather than inadvertently, an element of mystery. In the former, the conspiratorial role of a woman in the murder of her husband is concealed by the writer in his narrative until a point just before she goes to the gallows. In the second the guilt of another woman, sister of the murderer and an accessory to the crime, is cloaked throughout the account. In general, however, the writers of Tudor murder accounts were loath to complicate their tales and add mystery by suggesting there were murder suspects other than those eventually arraigned.[43]

Domestic murder – that is to say, murder committed by a member of a household or family against another of the same – was exciting news in Tudor England but was by no means as common as in recent times. In the printed accounts we have been considering, less than 50 per cent of the murders fall into the domestic category. Where they do, there is virtually no mention of prior abuse of the eventual victim. Whether this means that it was uncommon or, on the contrary, such an everyday occurrence that it was not worthy of mention is not clear. More certain is that it was not something the readership wanted to be told about, unless perhaps it was of spectacular proportions.⁴⁴

What the readers were particularly interested in was the discovery, arrest and punishment of the murderer. Although they may have metaphorically doffed their hats to the God who ensured that eventually murder 'would out', they took pleasure and found pride in the discovery of murderers by human agency. The English murder report and its cult were essentially the outcome of the English system of criminal justice. This was an open and popular system compared with the contemporaneous continental equivalents, in which prosecution by officials through their examination of witnesses and the suspect in private, and perhaps the use of torture, were dominant. English coroners' juries might operate like detectives if they chose, more so it seems than indicting jurors in other types of felony cases; moreover, the whole inquest process was local, not conducted at a privy sessions or county assize sessions. As Thomas Smith notes, much of the inquest's business was done 'commonly in the streete in an open place'. A sixteenth-century murder enquiry was thus in many ways a community event, capable of arousing the interest of a substantial local audience, its curiosity stirred when the members of the coroner's inquest went among them to collect evidence, as Smith notes, for sometimes twenty or thirty days.⁴⁵

Richard Hun's suspicious demise was recorded first, the actual coroner's report apart, in a pamphlet, and later in Hall's chronicle. It is these two types of source, pamphlet and chronicle, whose idiosyncrasies are examined below, that provide most of the information about the cases of murder appearing further on in this book. The relevant court records that survive, apart from those of coroners' inquests, are largely the files of the south-eastern (home) assize circuit for the Elizabethan period. They provide us with murder indictments containing the names of murderers, accessories and victims, the social status of the same, the home towns or villages, the location of the crime, occasionally the names of potential witnesses and the nature of the verdict. The main value of this material for the modern historian is in providing a profile of the incidence of the crime of murder, the social status of miscreants and victims, and the type of verdict, on a county scale. Such record evidence, unfortunately, is of only marginal assistance in the longitudinal study of particular murders, usually through the confirmation of the more obvious features as recorded in the literary sources. In regard to the current study, only a single difference has been noted between legal records and literary accounts, and that can possibly be explained by the damaged state of the legal document. Coroners' inquests, the verdicts of which commonly served as indictments at the assize sessions, have left records that provide information similar to that given in assize records, but without the accused's plea, the final verdict and sentence, or trial witnesses' names. Both coroners' inquests and assize sessions utilised depositions obtained from suspects and witnesses. Unfortunately, very few have survived from the sixteenth century, which deprives us of what would have been a prime source of information. Ballads, of which a fair number were written about the more notorious murders of the late sixteenth century, are another source but a poor one, since they are usually too vague, or inaccurate.

It might be thought that the very few plays that were written about particular murders would similarly be of little use in the reconstruction of those crimes. This is not in fact the case. The three examples we possess turn out, on inspection, to be historically quite accurate, and even provide details and insights, which appear to the historian to be quite valid, that are not to be gleaned from the chronicles and pamphlets. For this reason we should be grateful that the dramatists wrote at times when the details of each crime were still strong in the popular memory and historical accuracy was necessary in order to provide credibility.[46]

There is little surviving sixteenth-century correspondence between private persons that throws significant light on the notable murders of the Tudor period. On the other hand, official correspondence in the form of instructions to local officers given by the Privy Council in regard to a number of murders considered in some way to be dangerous to public order provides a good deal of information about methods of investigation (even the value of forensic medicine) and the handling of the murderer at law. In each of the four murder cases examined at length below, the Privy Council helped to discover the miscreants. In one, possibly two, of these cases, and in others not the subject of this book, the Privy Council, or probably its torture committee, recommended that murder suspects should be threatened with torture, or even put to it. Murder thus had the distinction, with treason and a very few cases of exceptional criminal activity, of being a torturable offence, albeit not, theoretically, under the common law.[47]

The murder cases that are the subjects of the pamphlets and plays have middle-class victims or at least persons above the lowest ranks of peasant or urban dweller. Only one deals with the slaying of a nobleman and none with a member of the gentry. Nearly all the victims are male, and the crimes are committed in southern England, largely in the south-east. Most of the cases have a connection in some way with London, which is probably where the pamphlet writers and playwrights were based.

The murders of the Tudor period, especially those of the second half of the sixteenth century that found a contemporary commentator, have been the subject of considerable attention in recent times on the part of writers whose speciality is English literature, as well as of social historians. Much of this comment has been enlightening, but occasionally we are left to wonder what exactly was the scope of murder under the Tudors: that is to say, how was it defined, and further, how was the crime handled under the law? Detection, investigation, the laying of charges, actual trial, verdict, sentence and aftermath: these were all elements that helped to decide if a murder was newsworthy, and determined its impact on society. We must therefore next consider the functioning of the criminal law and the situation of the suspected murderer.

Chapter 1

MURDER AND THE LAW

Murder was a particularly reprehensible crime even in the Anglo-Saxon period; it was also quite distinct in law from other forms of killing. The twelfth-century legal tract known as *Glanvill* offered the first clear definition of the crime: it was slaying done secretly, out of sight of everyone except the killer and any accomplice he had with him. Writing in the earlier part of the thirteenth century, the author known as Henry Bracton was the first commentator to use words that demonstrate that premeditation or malice aforethought was to be considered a key element in murder. The author of *Britton*, writing half a century later (*c*. 1290), made a clear separation between murder and other forms of homicide.[1] Court records and official instruments of the early fourteenth century show that, by then, murder, as secret killing, was regarded as taking the victim unawares so that he or she was unable to retaliate. Despite some debate about the matter among modern historians there can be little doubt that murder was, and had been from the Saxon period, quite distinct from manslaughter in the legal lexicon.[2] Manslaughter normally took the form of killing in hot blood and usually occurred when an altercation resulted in the participants immediately assaulting each other, with one being slain in the *chaude melle* (hot conflict) that followed. In the sixteenth century *chaude melle* became translated into 'chance medley', the emphasis being on the involuntary nature of the encounter in which the death occurred.[3]

Murder was mentioned quite frequently in sixteenth-century legislation. General pardons apart, there were, in the years 1509–59, for example, twenty-two statutes promulgated that referred to murder. Unfortunately, neither these nor the pardons help to demonstrate how murder was being more closely defined in the Tudor period. For this we have to scan the reports of relevant court cases of the period that provide opinions of the professional judges. Here we find that the definition of what passed for murder was made more precise in several ways. These concerned the position in law of those responsible for the planning of the crime; of those who commanded others to commit the crime; of those who embarked knowingly on a criminal enterprise in the course of which one or several members of the group used violence that resulted in a slaying; of those involved in attempts at murder that failed or that resulted in a death that was not that of the intended victim; and of those who killed suddenly without any altercation or expectation, or killed law officers or their deputies when they were enforcing the law. As we might expect to find, the interpretation of the law in these matters by the judges tended to widen the boundaries of the crime, although it cannot be said that there was any unexpected or illogical extension.

In an age when lordship and the master–servant relationship were still dominant, to make accessories (and therefore persons liable to the death penalty) out of procurers and commanders of murder – those who instigated or ordered other persons to slay but were not present at the committing of the crime themselves – was to close a notable gap in the criminal law. This was achieved by no later than 1555. Procurers of murder, who took no part in the slaying themselves but were present at the scene, were, according to Anthony Fitzherbert (1515), classified as principals like the actual slayers from the reign of Henry VII.[4] Thomas Marowe, at the beginning of the sixteenth century, claimed there were medieval precedents for regarding mere attempt to murder as a felony. Indeed, we might also add, there was a recent example of a restricted sort. The statute 3 Henry VII c. 14 in a discursive manner made it felony to 'compass' the death of the King or his councillors. Marowe supported his argument by pointing to the reign of Edward II: a servant who tried unsuccessfully to cut his master's throat as he slept, and a woman and her accomplice who ambushed and tried to slay her husband but failed, were all sentenced to death.[5] These cases differed from the crime dealt with in the Henrician statute in that their perpetrators committed an overt act, whereas the statute was intended to rectify the fact that currently, where there was no actual deed done, there was no remedy for such 'compassing'. Whether despite Marowe's opinion failed attempts at murder were treated as anything more serious than assault (a misdemeanour) in the Tudor period seems doubtful. Such a crime, if guilt was proven, would probably result in a fine.

Another area of improved definition was where slaying occurred in the committing of some other illegal deed, one that was not necessarily a felony.

Thus the violent death of a person whom the assaulter was intending only to beat, or the killing of someone who opposed an attempt to disseise or hunt illegally, were crimes categorised as murder by a late-sixteenth-century legal commentator.[6] Not only the beaters but the person who ordered the assault, disseisin, or hunt, were to be held as murder principals just like procurers of that crime. Indeed all 'abettors' in cases of murder, Crompton tells us, were to be regarded as principals. Such liability to be charged with murder seems even to have extended to a servant who, accompanying his master to an affray with an enemy, threw a stone at the latter that unfortunately killed a woman trying to mediate the dispute. Here there was obviously no malice against the victim, merely an agreement to engage in an illegal activity.[7] Yet increasingly in the sixteenth century the distinguishing feature of murder was reckoned to lie in the *mens rea* – that is, whether or not the slayer acted with malice aforethought or not. Thus the bringing of an old-fashioned criminal appeal against a person later slain by the appellant was found sufficient to indicate malice prepense and make the crime murder. Should A strike B with malice prepense and then B flee but subsequently turn and kill a pursuing A, this, according to Crompton, was murder. Presumably this was because B, since he was struck, had borne malice against A and in turning to face him demonstrated this. It was also murder by a person with malice if the person he slew was not the one intended. Thus should X shoot an arrow at Y with malice aforethought and the arrow kill Z, then the death was murder by X despite the fact that he had no animosity against Z.[8] Plowden records a similar case tried at Warwick assizes in September 1572 in which a husband, to kill his wife, gave her a poisoned roasted apple, but she passed it to their daughter, who ate it and died. The husband was found guilty of murder although he had no malice against his child.[9] Yet, despite this emphasis on malice aforethought as the prime requisite in defining murder, the Tudor judges were ready so to label certain slayings where there was no evidence of premeditation. The most notable category in this respect was the sudden killing, as, for example, where a man without warning drew a weapon and struck down a person at his side, there being no known enmity between them. In these cases, unless the attacker was deranged, the judges probably argued that there was concealed hatred, which, indeed, may have been discovered at the suspect's examination. We cannot say that this category was a new invention since the Pardon Act of 1390 defined murder as being to kill from malice prepense by 'agait' (ambush), or by 'assaut', the latter being surprise assault, one that could not be anticipated and thus caught a man off his guard.[10] Indeed, a crucial element in the concept of murder right from the Anglo-Saxon period seems to have been deadly assault on a person by any means that, taking him unawares, did not allow him to defend himself or evade the danger. Only in the reign of James I was this put into a statute, namely 1 James I c.8 (possibly in part as a result of the murder of William Storre by Francis Cartwright, which is discussed below).

Was a mortal attack on a law officer seeking to arrest a suspect or perform his duty in another way automatically murder? That such an offence was not uncommon and was causing the government considerable concern is demonstrated by a proclamation of 1538.[11] Dyer, in his *Reports*, mentions a case of 1558 where a sheriff and his posse went to serve a writ of restitution in a case of forcible detainer and one of his company was slain. There is no comment. Dyer merely asks, 'Is this murder or not?'[12] Coke, in his *Reports*, is much clearer. He tells us that it was agreed in the Queen's Bench at Trinity Term 1586 that the slaying of sheriffs, bailiffs or other officers of the law (including constables, their assistants and watchmen) executing the process of the law or doing their duty, such as by seeking to arrest a person or stop an affray, was to be adjudged murder. Coke implies that until the middle of Elizabeth's reign the nature of this type of killing had yet to be decided. By the time Michael Dalton wrote *The Countrey Justice* in the subsequent reign, this dictum had been supplemented with the rider that, should a person who was slain while executing a royal command 'be not an officer known' or have failed to show a warrant, the death would be but manslaughter.[13]

In the mid-sixteenth century the matter of concealment of felony, and thus of murder, arose. The issue was whether it was an offence to know of the committing of a serious crime yet fail to report it to the authorities. Staunford, Chief Justice of the King's Bench, writing in 1557, stated that those who knew of deeds of treason or felony and concealed them by failing to report them to a law officer were committing misprision, an offence but only a finable one. Concealing treason was, indeed, at this time recognised as misprision, but misprision of felony, at common law at least, appears to have been Staunford's own invention. Richard Crompton, writing in 1584, is more helpful. He notes Staunford's comments and also provides a fifteenth-century *Year Book* reference. The relevant section, although Crompton gives no indication, would seem to be the remarks by Chief Justice Prisot to the effect that each man who is sworn to the King at a leet, if he knows any felony or treason, should report it.[14] Crompton implies that such men are the adult male population as a whole, but in fact this is very doubtful. The men so sworn were most probably only those selected and empanelled to report local crimes to indicting juries at a leet or a sheriff's tourn. It rather looks as if, in including this novel crime of misprision of felony, Crompton was deferring to Staunford and adding what he took to be a supporting reference. If we seek Staunford's motives in developing this new misdemeanour, two possibilities suggest themselves. First, he and his political masters may have wanted to ensure that all who knew of heresy (the 'high profile' crime of the Marian period), which was a felony, reported it. Secondly, he may also have been intent on mitigating the penalties incurred by justices and their clerks for the so-called concealment of erasing legal records and mishandling indictments. By the time when Dalton wrote, the scope of concealment/misprision had been extended, for it had been decided that knowing felony (and thus murder) was to be committed at some future date and failing to report it (that is, pre-facto concealment) was also misprision and thus a finable offence.[15]

'Murder will out' was a traditional English maxim dating from at least as early as Chaucer and figuring in similar if not exact words in several of the Tudor pamphlets concerned with particular murders. One significant emend-ation to this adage in the sixteenth century was to the effect that it was God who would ensure that murder was revealed, and this we can attribute to the Protestant inclinations, real or assumed, of many of the pamphlets' com-pilers.[16] Behind this observation about the discovery of murder we notice that, among those who wrote on the subject in the later Tudor period, even those who did so in dramatic form, there was an interest in the detection of the miscreant through human agency, even if no writer went so far as to make heroes out of those who achieved this. It is one of the features of writing that most clearly distinguishes the Elizabethan compilers of murder literature from late medieval and early Tudor chroniclers.[17] There were two ways in which a murder investigation usually commenced in the sixteenth century. One was when a person was discovered recently slain by human hand, the body, so to speak, still warm, and perhaps the assailant observed in flight. The other was when the body of a murdered person was discovered a fair time after the crime had been committed. In the first instance it was the rule, as with crimes of theft, robbery and burglary, for the hue and cry to be raised and all able-bodied men in the township to go in pursuit of the suspect, handing over the same duty to the next township when its bounds were reached. Although such pursuits did occur and were occasionally crowned with success, as the Randolph case shows, they were reckoned by William Harrison to be a failing instrument by the late Tudor period.[18] They were supposed to be mounted by the township constable, but he probably did not have sufficient authority or prestige to persuade the local inhabitants to join in in many localities.

Because murder was a secret crime usually committed out of the sight of third parties, it was frequently undiscovered for some time. Then a passer-by, a servant or a house visitor inadvertently came across the corpse. In such cases the correct procedure was for the first finder, as he was called, or the local constable to whom the finder reported his discovery, to summon the coroner. Some murders, of course, did not take the form of sudden death, and the crime was not revealed until quite a while after the deed had been committed: a dose of poison might take weeks to kill; a person badly wounded by a sudden assault intended to slay him might succumb to his injuries only considerably later; the death of a man or woman thought to be by mis-adventure might be revealed as murder by a deathbed confession years later. Such delayed-discovery slayings became the subject of indictments at the quarter sessions in preparation for the upcoming assizes. In the cases that involved the coroner, his usual role was to swear in an inquest of twelve to fourteen men, who did some detective work themselves and before whom finders, witnesses, neighbours and associates of the deceased were called to testify. The findings of the inquest to the effect that the crime was indeed murder would then serve as an indictment at the arraignment of the suspect at the assizes or urban court. The Meaphon case demonstrates that the coroner could investigate in the same manner as a justice of the peace conducting an examination: interrogating so as to discover in particular the movements of the suspect on the day of the murder; checking the ownership of the weapon used; even eliciting the testimony of the suspect's five-year-old son, or in the Abel Bourn case that of a cast-off mistress.[19]

Until the reign of Edward I a person suspected of committing a felony could be arrested only if he was a notorious criminal, was 'caught in the act' (though probably after a hue and cry), or had been indicted or appealed, or charged by a coroner's jury. By the end of that reign, after some govern-mental vacillation, the arrest of felony suspects not yet formally accused was permitted, although a perfunctory, post-facto yet pre-arraignment inquest was often employed as a form of justification by the time of Edward III. By the later fourteenth century, arrests of suspected but unindicted felons, of which there were many, were justified in the records by reference to the statute of Winchester of 1285 and the act 5 Edward III c. 14, despite statutes like 25 Edward III c. 4 and 42 Edward III c. 3 stating clearly that no person should be arrested or imprisoned without presentment or indictment.[20] In the late fifteenth century a professional judge gave it as his opinion that a person of bad fame could be arrested without cause, but not someone of good fame.[21] Being of bad fame, we may suppose, included a person who had been observed committing a felony. But how might a person of good fame, not in flight, not observed as an agent in a felony, not indicted or appealed, yet nevertheless suspected of committing murder, be arrested? In the sixteenth century it was on instruction by a magistrate or on a constable's, or similar law officer's, own judgement.

In order to arrest a suspected murderer, or any other type of felon, law officers sometimes took it upon themselves to enter private premises. There was no statute or ordinance that authorized them to do so; they conducted searches doubtless because of the absence of any official prohibition. As will be shown in a later chapter, when in 1583 Robert Greenoll disappeared after setting off to visit Thomas Smith, the Evesham town authorities decided to search Smith's cellar and eventually discovered Greenoll's buried body. In a case of suspected murder at Bildeston, Suffolk, in 1538, the manorial bailiff and the village constables searched the buildings of Philip Witherick. Witherick had earlier given sureties for his future appearance before the local magistrate but does not appear to have been under arrest, although his family had been interrogated. The searchers took away with them some bones found in Witherick's kitchen.[22] Searches for suspected murderers and for evidence of their guilt were sometimes conducted by neighbours rather than by law officers. According to a piece of factually based drama about the murder of Robert Beech and Thomas Winchester in London in the late 1590s, neighbours organised their own search for clues and evidence in 'every place where blood may be conceald', 'To see if we can finde the murther out'. These places, we note, included 'sinkes', 'gutters' and 'privies'. When a bag of body parts came to light, the neighbours led the bag seller from door to door to see if he could identify the purchaser. We notice, however, that the neighbours, in the course of their enquiries, never sought to enter any house themselves. This task was left to a constable and three watchmen, who performed it after the suspect had been arrested.[23]

If the criminal law was vague on the arrest of suspected felons, it was just as omissive on what, by the late Middle Ages, was the next step in discovering guilt. This was the examination of the suspect and those who could give evidence about the crime; it was usually undertaken by one or more of the justices of the peace or by the coroner or his inquest. The only reference of an official sort to pre-trial examination in felony cases before the Tudor period seems to be a comment in the *Year Books* of Edward IV's reign. The practice must have been well established by then, even if it received statutory confirmation and external (though not internal) regulation only in Mary's reign.[24] Very few examinations have survived from the sixteenth century, which partly accounts for the lack of comment about the mechanics of examining, on the part of both contemporary writers and modern historians.[25] Another reason may have been distaste for the topic, despite the fact that examination, like interrogation today, was at the heart of proving guilt. It has been seen as a dirty business. From hints we may take it that sixteenth-century examiners in their interrogation of felony suspects tried to elicit confessions; and that they did so not only by using searching questions but also, on occasion, by feeding the suspect with half-truths, even outright lies, mixed with threats covert and overt, and the suggestion that there would be benefits for him if he admitted to the crime.[26] If more than a single person was responsible for the murder, then the examiner might untruthfully tell each separately that his associate in crime had put the blame entirely on him; therefore, he should tell all and show who was really responsible. From Henry VIII's reign onward, some of the felons who confessed their crime and accused confederates (turned 'king's evidence' in modern terminology) were able to obtain a pardon, although where the offence was murder those who so benefited were likely to be accessories rather than principals.[27]

What did the sixteenth century examining magistrate seek to discover in the interrogation? What did he consider to be incriminating? Luckily for historians, an Elizabethan legal writer, Richard Crompton, made a list of things such an investigator should assess when he interrogated any suspect felon. Thus for murder there would be the probable cause of the misdeed, who would profit from it and how, whether the suspect had killed before, whether he came from a lawless part of the country, what was his trade or profession, and whether he was a 'gamester' and given to ruffianly companions. His personality was also to be investigated: was he 'hasty' and ready to quarrel; did he suffer from violent mood swings; did he dress in a flamboyant fashion? The investigator was to concern himself with the suspect's opportunity to commit the crime: where was he at the time of the murder, and who saw him there? Evidence of flight and concealment of the misdeed were to be looked for, as was blood on clothing. His general demeanour at the time of arrest, and whether he was distraught, with contradictions in his speech when he first told his excusatory tale, were to be noted and considered. Even the relative strengths of suspect and victim were thought relevant. Clearly the basic elements of criminal investigation were well understood in Elizabethan England.[28]

To elicit confessions physical duress seems to have been employed against murder suspects from time to time. Witchcraft cases of the period provide examples of the accused being kept in solitary confinement, interrogated and 'walked' to exhaustion, and being deprived of sleep for the same purpose. Treason cases reveal suspects imprisoned in the foulest dungeons without sustenance, and put to the rack, the brake or the manacles. There is less evidence of the threat or actual use of torture in murder cases, but there is some. The employment of 'the tortours' in the Tower of London had been ordered on two suspects in a case of 'haynous murder' late in Edward VI's reign, but it is unlikely that the practice was novel at that time. In Elizabeth's reign, in June 1570, Thomas Androwe was ordered to be taken from the Marshalsea prison to the Tower and 'offered the torture of the racke' when being examined about an unsavoury murder recently committed in Somerset. Androwe, it was noted, was 'vehemently' suspected but had confessed nothing at earlier examinations.[29] The Privy Council had no doubt that this procedure would result in the desired confession. Lord Stourton's role in the murder of the Hartgills in January 1557, as well as the location of their corpses, may have come to light through torture threats to his servants, who at that time had been imprisoned in the Tower, a sinister move. In April 1573 George Browne, suspected of the murder of the London merchant George Saunders, was sent by order of the Privy Council to the Tower to be examined by two judges. They were to put Browne 'to the tortures' if they found cause – that is to say, if he would not confess his guilt and supply the names of his associates in the crime.[30] In 1579, one of the judges who had examined Browne was instructed, with three others, including the Lieutenant of the Tower, to re-examine two murder suspects, Robert Wintershall and Henry Mellershe, from whom nothing, to that point, had been elicited. They were to get answers by putting the pair in the Tower dungeons and 'obscure places', seeing they had 'little diet' and showing them the rack. In a case in 1597, because surgeons were of the opinion that the body of a Gray's Inn lawyer discovered in the Thames showed evidence of murder, the Privy Council ordered that one of his sons and the porter of the Inn be strictly examined, and if no confession could be obtained that way then they should be put in the manacles in the Bridewell so the truth could be discovered and accomplices named.[31] These few cases provide the only clear instances of the Privy Council suggesting torture where the crime was murder, although there may well have been other examples where the authority was either the Council of the North or the Council of Wales and the Marches. Why the suspects in all these cases should face torture is unclear. The crimes may have been heinous, but so were many other murders. Torture was threatened or used, we may surmise, because relatives of the victim had influence at court or with members of the Privy Council, or the murder somehow damaged the Crown's finances. Was the threat or use of torture generally known, and, if it was, did this knowledge help to produce confessions in other murder cases? This we shall probably never know. The government on one occasion explained why torture was used in treason cases, but the very argument used (that the crime was manifest but the suspect refused to name accomplices or confess the full nature of the conspiracy, thereby endangering the sovereign's life) was not relevant to murder.[32] A Henrician law (33 Henry VIII c. 23), which stipulated that when a person examined for the Council was found 'vehemently suspect' of murder he might be tried in any allotted place by commission of oyer and terminer (that is, without waiting for the local jail delivery/assize sessions), is the only statutory acknowledgement of the Council's very significant role in handling that crime.

Subsequent to examination there came the indictment stage of the judicial process. As we have seen, there was no need for this in murder cases that had been the subject of a coroner's inquest, since the record of the latter, naming the suspect, was itself normally used as the indictment at the trial. In other cases the jurors of the indictment, frequently referred to in sixteenth-century felony cases as the grand jury, probably had before them, as they began their task, the examination of the suspect. This had been certified to them by the examining magistrate together with, in written form, testimony from those who had brought the suspect before him.[33] Very likely any witness or person knowledgeable about the murder might appear before the grand jury in person. By this point in the process a relative of the murdered person, or his or her lawyer, had usually submitted a bill of indictment (a short accusation in proper form and detail) to the justices, who vetted it for errors and then passed it to the grand jury. Having considered the examination, depositions and any oral evidence for the prosecution, the jury then decided, apparently by majority vote, to confirm or throw out the bill. We cannot say for sure that the members of the jury made enquiries of their own about the suspect. For one thing, only a small minority of the jurors must have lived in the same locality as the accused; secondly, they had limited time to do so. Yet, since a contemporary commentator very much expected grand jurymen to be active investigators in witchcraft cases, the safest conclusion is that they may have played detective on occasion.[34]

Investigation of the murder did not cease with the decision of the grand/indicting jurymen to confirm or refuse the charge laid before them. The actual trial was frequently a scene of further probing and discovery. The justices presiding – that is to say, the justices of jail delivery and assize – when they arrived in a county twice a year or so to arraign those indicted of felony, would have had put before them written matter in the form of the findings of coroners' inquests, 'true bills' from grand juries, and examinations and depositions sent up by justices of the peace. If the justices of assize bothered to read this documentation before the trial began, which is by no means certain, they were reasonably prepared to conduct the arraignment. The actual prosecution of most murder cases (that is, those where there was no Crown prosecutor employed) seems to have relied a great deal on the efforts of court clerks. Crown clerks, perhaps in conjunction with the judges' own clerks where these were not identical, coordinated indictments with examinations and depositions, ensured bound-over witnesses were on hand, and may well have provided background information about the cases to their masters both before and during the trials. The latter were each likely to be of short duration, since the justices of assize hoped to get through all the felony cases, sometimes as many as thirty or more, in the course of a morning.[35]

The trial began with the clerk for the Crown reading out the Latin indictment and explaining it in English. To this the accused person had to offer a plea. Should he or she respond 'guilty', as did, for example, Lord Charles Stourton, there remained only to allow the prisoner to make a plea in arrest of judgment. If he responded 'not guilty', a petty jury was empanelled. This trial jury was frequently composed of office holders at the manorial level and lower-class men financially better off than their neighbours, although late-sixteenth-century complaints indicate that relatively indigent bystanders were sometimes employed.[36] In the trial proceedings the justices normally played a dominant role, one that was at the same time censorious and hectoring, but also investigative. In a small number of felony cases, exceptional because of their importance to the government, a Crown prosecutor was used. For the trial of Ann Saunders and Ann Drury the prosecutor, according to the play *A Warning for Fair Women*, was 'Master Geffrey', probably John Jeffrey, who at that time was a Queen's serjeant. Although Jeffrey is praised by the playwright for the keenness of his intellect, his role in the trial is not dwelt on. In contrast, the part played by the justices is clearly delineated and it is an overbearing one. When Trusty Roger was brought into court as a witness for the prosecution, the justices themselves put questions to him about the crucial letter: who wrote it, who gave it to him, whether his employer, Ann Saunders, knew of it, where the £26 given to George Browne (the actual murderer) came from – questions that caused an altercation between Ann and Roger. The bench then asked Saunders's co-defendant, Ann Drury, about the letter and the ownership of the plate used to raise the £26. When, later, Ann Saunders denied receiving a message in the form of a blood-soaked kerchief on the grounds she was in 'childbed chamber' at the time, one of the justices told her she was lying and that it was well known she had been unfaithful to her husband.[37] That the bench was so interfering simply because a Crown prosecutor was in court is possible but unlikely.

To our eyes the sixteenth-century criminal trial process appears to have been weighted against the accused. The person arraigned was not allowed a copy of the charge against him and thus until he heard the clerk utter it in English he may have been unsure whether he was being accused of murder, petty treason or manslaughter. Since there was no rule against it, much of the evidence against the accused may have been only hearsay. The Witherick case shows that the testimony of children, even his own, and that of his spouse against a man, was both allowable and welcome. Unless, perchance, the person on trial was able to raise a moot point of law during the proceedings, he was not allowed legal counsel, the Crown's argument against such assistance being that the accused was the one who knew his 'fact' or 'cause' the best and that counsel would make him 'covert' in his speech. There was also the problem of responding. Might the accused offer a defence to each piece of evidence as it was presented or must he wait until all had been put forward before he gave his explanations to the points raised? The latter was a most difficult task, but whether the court insisted on it is not known.[38] When the justices had heard what they considered to be sufficient evidence in the case, they would curtly terminate proceedings and, normally, give a strong admonition to the petty jury to convict.

Cases of felony were seemingly tried in batches. After a number of accused had been arraigned, 'three or four' or even 'seven or eight', so historians tend to believe, the justices ordered a petty jury to find verdicts for each of the group in a single interlude of deliberation, one that may not even have involved retiring temporarily from the courtroom.[39] While this was occurring, the justices, to assure the conviction of a particular accused, might communicate with the jurors in some manner: for example, by sending a messenger, or summoning the foreman to talk with them, perhaps on the pretence of explaining a legal point.[40] The degree of independence of mind of trial jurors in the later sixteenth century has been a matter of debate among historians. Were they dominated by the justices, who controlled the evidence from examination, indictment sessions and witnesses, who interjected remarks and questioned freely, and who provided a summation of the evidence and a final direction? Were the jurors usually persons of such small importance in society that they were easily intimidated by the bench, especially since virtually all must have lacked any personal knowledge of the crime? In answering these related questions we need to notice that the justices who tried criminal cases, even in the medieval period, had always played an active and dominant role at the arraignment.[41] Similarly, the quality of the jurors was little changed; they had been and were still, for the most part, better-off men of the lower class in the locality.

Yet this judicial domination does not appear to have succeeded in obtaining convictions in a majority (that is, over 50 per cent) of felony cases tried until the earlier sixteenth century and then probably only in certain areas of the country. In Elizabeth's reign, as we have seen, murders amounted to about 1 per cent of felonies tried in Essex (infanticides and so-called murders by witchcraft excluded), under 5 per cent of those in Sussex, and about 5½ per cent of those in Cheshire. Conviction rates of persons arraigned for the crime of murder are somewhat deceptive, since a good number of those found guilty were convicted, either at the jury's or the justices' whim, not of murder but of manslaughter. Such verdicts allowed those convicted, if male and qualified in other ways, to claim benefit of clergy; furthermore, anyone found guilty of manslaughter had a much less difficult task than a murderer in gaining a pardon. Thus the percentage of those indicted of murder who were found guilty of murder was considerably less than those indicted of murder and found guilty either of that crime or of mere manslaughter. In Essex, for example, in Elizabeth's reign, the conviction rate was about a scant 35 per cent and in Sussex about 49 per cent (even though in Kent it was 68 per cent), rates much lower than those for robbery. If 'guilty of manslaughter' verdicts are included, the conviction rate rises to 62 per cent for Essex and 68 per cent for Sussex but stays about the same for Kent. Was later Tudor justice soft on murder? The best thesis is probably that jurors and judges often found it difficult to decide if the crime was premeditated and/or really took the victim unawares.[42]

The judicial process in regard to sixteenth-century murder might occasionally be corrupted. Those who chose to do so, usually members of the upper classes intent on protecting servants, tenants or clients, appear to have preferred to make their move at the coroner's inquest stage rather than at the arraignment. The reason seems to have been that coroners were susceptible to pressure because of their relatively modest social status, one inferior to that of the justices of the peace. They were also well down the ladder of the legal hierarchy. To ensure a verdict that the crime was manslaughter rather than murder, or the reverse, coroners might be persuaded to pack their juries with tenants of the patron of the suspect, or, conversely, of the victim. There were also other ways. A Lancashire coroner in Henry VIII's reign refused to allow a King's serjeant to give evidence for the Crown at the inquest, but he allowed four maintainers of the murderer to do so and even read out a letter from the murderer to the inquest excusing his crime. Lobbying the inquest jurors with threats and promises ('labouring') might be done by both the suspect's and the victim's supporters, even at the same inquest. In Elizabeth's reign murder could still involve the paying of blood money to the victim's family. Thus in 1602 a Northumberland coroner's inquest would give no verdict until the parties were agreed on the payment. Then the inquest found a particularly brutal murder to be but manslaughter.[43] Because some victims of ambush had opportunity to draw their weapons and fight back before being murdered, powerful friends of the accused might be able to pressure the coroner's inquest into finding the crime was but manslaughter; conversely, as another case demonstrates, if the slaying was done in hot blood, influential supporters of the victim might badger the inquest into deciding there was premeditation and the crime was murder.

Should a person be convicted of murder, there was virtually but one punishment, death. This was by hanging in the vast majority of cases, but if the perpetrator was female and spouse or servant of the victim she would be burned at the stake, the murder being rated as petty treason (that is, the slaying of one's 'master').[44] There was no possibility of appeal against verdict or judgment to a higher court, as occurs in modern times. Influential friends of the accused might get the case moved to the Court of King's Bench, where acquittal was very likely, but this had to be done before the arraignment ended. Otherwise supporters had quickly to seek a reprieve (hanging sentences tended to be carried out within a few hours) so that the purchase of a pardon could be negotiated.[45] This was a common course of action for any felon with money or wealthy friends and was not regarded as an anomaly. The way to get these personal pardons, so a fifteenth-century statute tells us, was by 'brokerage, grants, and gifts to divers persons'. This meant getting a courtier to find an important nobleman or office holder who would obtain the pardon from the king. At each of the three stages bribes varying in amount according to the heinousness of the offence had to be given, in all a great expense and beyond the means of anyone below the rank of gentleman or substantial merchant. There were also general pardons, periodically granted by statute, available to all at a token charge. However, such statutes at the outset of the fifteenth century had excluded murderers from their benefits, and this became a standard feature in Tudor general pardons from early in Henry VIII's reign.[46]

In the second half of the sixteenth century individual pardons were obtained for a wide variety of murders, many of which, by the standards of the time, must have been considered particularly obnoxious. These include one where a woman killed her husband by putting arsenic in his ale, one involving the murder of a householder and his wife in the course of a burglary, one where the crime was the ambush and killing of a wealthy Yorkshire squire by a large gang, and one where the murder was of a wife in her sickbed by her husband.[47] Some of these grants of pardon suggest there had been further investigation into the murder after the trial or that evidence had come to light that cast doubt on the verdict. Others suggest the person convicted had given the Crown assistance in bringing his associates to justice. In another instance the pleas of the murderer's wife to the queen, and the testimony of several magnates as to his current penitence, brought about the desired result. Such interest in the moral state of the murderer is also demonstrated by a pardon that notes that the authorities now acknowledge the murder was committed after provocation.[48] We must conclude that, if the murderer, or his friends, had sufficient money and approached the monarch in the right way a pardon would be forthcoming in almost all cases. Frequently the Crown saw to it that a justification for awarding the royal grace was appended.

Another way for a murderer on trial to escape the gallows, up to the middle of the sixteenth century at least, was by asking for benefit of clergy. This privilege was available if the murder and the murderer were each of the right type. The latter had to be male, to have married no more than once, and to be in holy orders or able to read. If the justices and the bishop's represent-ative allowed the claim, the convicted man would probably be sent to the bishop's jail for an indeterminate period. The Tudor kings whittled away at the privilege from the start of their dynasty. A statute of Henry VII's reign prevented it from being claimed by the same man a second time and instituted branding for successful claimants. In 1512, benefit of clergy was forbidden for those who murdered in a hallowed place, on the king's highway, or in the course of a burglary.[49] This act soon lapsed, but new regulations were put in place by the statute 23 Henry VIII c. 1, which forbade the benefit to all murderers (unless they were in the higher ecclesiastical orders) and their accessories. Murderers were again excluded by a celebrated act concerned with the criminal law at the beginning of the subsequent reign (1 Edward VI c. 12). This was also the situation under the two Tudor queens.

Not until the trial jury had convicted and judgment had been pronounced did there come the last stage in the investigation of a murder. This occurred at the gallows as the murderer was about to be hanged. The condemned person recognized that he, or she, was expected to make a confession of guilt. This was doubtless prompted by the officials in attendance, the cries of the observing crowd, an acceptance that it was traditional and the desire to clear a conscience. Such confessions were sometimes mere reiterations of what had been admitted in court; but on other occasions they were in absolute contra-diction of earlier denials of involvement in the crime and might explain aspects of the murder hitherto unsolved. It must have been primarily the possibility of further revelations that drew so many people, a fair percentage of them of some substance, to the scene of the execution. The general tenor of gallows speeches in the later sixteenth century, whether or not the speakers overtly admitted to the crime of which they had been convicted, was that they deserved their fate because of their sinful lives. Their crime had been exposed and they had been accused and convicted because God was disgusted by the nature of their everyday earthly existence, their lives as a whole, as much as by their recent felony. One reason condemned traitors frequently admitted they deserved to die seems to have been in order to obtain some benefit for the wives and families they were leaving behind: some of their goods, even some of their lands, might escape forfeiture to the Crown. Whether condemned murderers were able to obtain similar treatment is not clear, but confession and repentance may have helped to reduce community hostility towards their bereft families.[50] A desire to do everything to ensure that their corpses were not hanged up later in chains to decompose may also have contributed in producing last-minute confessions. Some of those convicted may have hoped, by confessing a little earlier, to escape the even nastier fate of being hanged alive in chains. William Harrison, writing in the 1580s, implies that at that time such was a common punishment for murderers, although, he adds by way of qualification, some were 'strangled with a rope' first 'upon compassion'.[51] The severity of hanging murderers alive in chains would doubtless have been approved by the chief inspirer of the strong Protestants of Elizabeth's reign, John Calvin, who specifically defended such distinctive and extremely rigorous penalties as were inflicted for the crime in various parts of the European Continent.[52]

Chapter 2

WRITING ABOUT MURDER: FROM THE LATE MEDIEVAL PERIOD TO THE REIGN OF ELIZABETH I

This book examines four cases in which juries convicted persons accused of murder in the mid-Tudor period. The first, in chronological order, occurred in 1538, the fourth in 1573. The reason for their selection is a simple one. While there were other murders felt worthy of comment by contemporaries, these are the cases about which the greatest amount of detail can be gleaned by modern historians. If we exclude the Richard Hun case (1514), this is true for the whole century, and, indeed, for earlier centuries. They are, in fact, the first English murder stories that would be recognised as such by the modern reader. Women have a role to play in each; it is only a modest part in one of the cases, but a crucial role in the other three. Three of the crimes can be called domestic ones. One has a village setting, two concern the upper middle class, while the fourth is best categorised as a murder that occurred in an upper-class feud of the old sort – that is to say, over property rights. Yet before we come to these four detailed studies it is important to take notice of the general context of murder in the Tudor period and give some consideration to those other instances of the crime that received notoriety in their day and were duly reported, but that have left relatively little mark in the records. We must also consider the nature and history of murder reporting from the rudimentary beginnings in the medieval period to the *floruit* of Elizabeth's reign. This necessitates, *inter alia*, discovering what elements a murder had to possess to make it 'newsworthy' and attractive to the reporters and their readership, and what it was that caused a limited number of these crimes to be of exceptional interest.

An alternative title for this chapter, and indeed for the book, might be 'The Origins of the Historical English Murder Story', for it is not the slayings as recorded in legal rolls or files that provide the tales but reports set down in a variety of ways by non-legal writers within a relatively short time after the crimes' occurrence for persons who might be interested in reading about them. That is not to say we should not use legal and administrative records where, occasionally, they can supplement such information, but they are very definitely a minor source. Little information about what may be called the social background of individual murders is to be found in the records of the courts before the seventeenth century. As we have seen, indictments and the ancient accusatory process known as appeal provide us with the names of the accused and victims, the location and date of the crime, those who were accessories, and often the verdict and the judgment (sentence).[1] Yet the cause of the slaying, the details of its planning and execution, the relationship of victim and accused, their reputations and social connections, are nearly always lacking. As has been noted above, coroners' inquests, which often provide the initial legal record in the case, offer little more, although, if the testimony of witnesses and neighbours, which was certainly taken in some cases, had survived, our knowledge would be much more substantial. What makes the notorious death of Richard Hun so intriguing is the setting-down of just such evidence.[2] Attempts to reconstruct the details of particular late-medieval murders, such as the slaying of Sir William Cantilupe in Lincolnshire in 1375, or the death of Edmund Clippesby in Norfolk in 1392, although exhaustively conducted, have met with only marginal success because the sources are almost entirely terse statements in legal and administrative records.[3]

It might be thought that the extensive English chronicles of the fourteenth and fifteenth centuries would offer a fair amount of detail about individual murders, but this is not so. The chronicles, which were compiled by men of clerical status – that is to say, they were either monks or secular clerks – devote most of their space to political events, largely the doings of kings and of the Church, and wars both foreign and civil. The sections allotted to what may be called 'low history' are slim. Recurring within them are references to human misfortunes: bad weather, plagues and diseases figure prominently. Crime is mentioned but rarely and murder hardly at all. Henry Knighton, for example, mentions only a single murder case, albeit a colourful one (a local woman who slew her husband and was burned at the stake). Thomas

Walsingham mentions no individual crimes of the lower classes, although he does devote a little space to murder done or caused by the nobility.[4]

In contrast with the fourteenth century, many of the chronicles of the fifteenth were the work of London laymen, vernacular writers whose origins were in the commercial or merchant classes. As might be expected, they were especially interested in events in their own city and their own stratum of society. They provide an assiduous noting of notorious crimes, specifically treason, heresy and murder; but instances of the first two of these offences greatly outnumber those of the third. Noticeable, and relevant to other parts of this book, is the attention London chroniclers gave to cases where the offenders in various types of crime were female, which was symptomatic of their interest in troublesome women (particularly whores and bawds) in general. William Gregory, for example, tells of a woman burned for slaying her husband, and of a Breton who had killed a rich woman being stoned to death by women of the locality, and explains how whores are put in the pillory. Similarly the *Brut* tells of women burned for murdering their husbands (1421 and 1438), and of a man murdering members of his household including his pregnant wife, and, like Gregory and another London chronicler, provides a fair amount of detail about the plan of Eleanor Cobham, Duchess of Gloucester, to kill the king by means of witchcraft.[5]

None of the fifteenth-century London chronicles is of any great length; indeed, most are small in volume and terse in comment. Their staple fare, apart from great happenings like wars, the deeds of kings and natural disasters, were what we would call curiosities, local events that titillated the interest of the citizenry, such as the birth of human or animal freaks, visits of royalty, performances of acrobats, civic spectacles and tournaments. There was also the drama of the pillory and the gallows, but only when those who suffered were either infamous or unlikely criminals, or their offence was both heinous and uncommon. That compilers were ready to devote a few lines to local murder is revealing. It proves the emotional impact of that crime on the community and, perhaps, a growing sensitivity to violence that was sudden and fatal. What the chroniclers of the fifteenth century, like those of the fourteenth, fail to provide are references to the trial of murderers or, indeed, to any part of the legal process against them, unless we count as such their public execution.[6]

The pre-eminent chroniclers of the later sixteenth century, Holinshed and Stow, were the literary descendants of the fifteenth-century London historians, although they differed from their predecessors in the much greater amount of detail they provided. For their coverage of the earlier sixteenth century they relied a good deal on the *magnum opus* of Edward Hall, *The Union of the Two Noble and Illustre Famelies of Lancastre and Yorke* (1548). However, whereas Holinshed and Stow combine wars and the doings of monarchs and nobles with events of social importance, Hall, writing a generation earlier, is somewhat different. His interest, as the title of his book shows, was the English Crown, its wearers and its descent, together with royal spectacles and wars in which the monarchs participated. The detail here is impressive; the work has provided material for generations of political historians. While there is occasional reference to natural disasters and disease, there is no mention of murder among the non-administrative classes, the politically significant Hun case apart, until Hall reaches the twenty-fifth year of Henry VIII's reign.

At about this point Hall is believed to have ended his personal authorship of *The Union*, the remainder being edited from his notes, probably by Richard Grafton. Thenceforward short commentaries appear in the work on a number of murders of lesser folk. In 25 Henry VIII, it is noted, a London whore and her husband, one Wolfe, enticed two merchants to a boat on the Thames, murdered them and then robbed their chambers. Later the culprits were tried, convicted and executed. The executions were notorious, because the wife's body, rather than being cut down and buried, was left to hang on the gallows, with the result, states the chronicle, that 'beastly and filthy wretches . . . most shamefully abused her being dead'.[7] Further on, the compiler records the slaying of Robert Packyngton, a wealthy and very religious London mercer, in 1536 or 1537. He was mysteriously killed by a shot from a gun while going to the mercers' chapel. The writer believed his death was murder and that he was 'mooste lyke' killed by a member of the clergy, whose 'covetousnes and crueltie' Packyngton had 'talked somewhat against'. Thus he was slain for the same reason, in the popular mind at least, as Hun. Here the elements that attracted the chronicler seem to have been a belief in a conspiracy by the clergy, a relatively novel method of killing, and the fact that the victim was a prominent member of the London merchant class. Less clear are the reasons for the inclusion of the writer's next murder. He tells us that Roger Cholmeley, a member of the squirarchy, was killed 'of malice prepensed' by three of the prince's servants, who were hanged in March 1538 on the south side of St Paul's. They died wearing their livery, suggesting it was the royal connection that attracted attention. Details of the crime are lacking. The only other murder case to which the writer refers before the chronicle ends is the more celebrated incident involving Thomas Fiennes, Lord Dacre of the South, and his associates, which occurred in 1541. Although well supplied with information about the resulting executions, he is able to tell us only that the crime 'was a murder of a simple manne, and an unlawful assemblie made in Sussex'.[8]

From his treatment of these few murder cases we are provided with some clues as to what attracted Hall's or Grafton's attention to them and justified their inclusion in the work. We notice immediately that the crimes were committed in or close to London, and that three of the victims were of the merchant class. More importantly, the murders were what the twentieth and twenty-first centuries would rate as definitely 'newsworthy', because of who the victims or perpetrators were, the uncommon method of the slaying or a novel scene at the gallows or at the trial. Thus the non-London murder committed by Lord Dacre and his confederates while hunting in Sussex had a culprit of noble rank whose trial was before the Lord High Steward at Westminster. Furthermore, despite his peerage, he was hanged at Tyburn ('strangled as common murderers are') rather than being allowed the more noble end of being beheaded. The London connection was through three gentlemen, who were Dacre's associates in crime, being hanged at St Thomas Waterings. In regard to these four post-1534 murders the date of the publication of Hall's chronicle, 1548, is significant. The book appeared at the time of a Protestant regime, one that seems to have provoked a greater interest in the crime of murder and its punishment, and thus was probably responsible for the inclusion of the four cases just noted. Whether he was responsible for providing the details of these particular murders or not, Richard Grafton made a point of including them in his own *Chronicle* two decades later, and in similar words. Like Hall, Grafton was interested chiefly in the deeds of important men and women, in high politics, rebellions, wars and royal events. In general he provides only a modest amount about events affecting the lives of lesser people.[9]

References to murder in John Stow's *Annales* for the Tudor period prior to the death of Henry VIII are similarly few. They are only slightly different from those provided by Hall's chronicle and Grafton's work of 1569. Stow gives brief reports of the Wolfe and Dacre cases as well as of the murders in 1530 of Dr Miles and 'a maid' of 'Master Knevet', the last two crimes not appearing

in *The Union* or Grafton's *Chronicle*. Stow's interest in the crime and fate of
Lord Dacre is generally sympathetic. He calls the deed a 'transgression' and
tells how Dacre was expected to be pardoned until the last minute. He notes
that the nobleman was only 24 years old and was 'a right towardly gentleman'. Subsequent to the Dacre case Stow records no murders in his text until
that of Thomas Ardern in 1551 and then those committed on Lord
Stourton's orders in 1557. Stow's inclination in regard to murder in the pre-
Elizabethan Tudor period appears to have been conservative. There are only a
few words on the death of Richard Hun, no mention (unlike in Hall and
Holinshed) of the accusation against Lord Ogle (1520), and little on the
Ardern and Stourton cases. The impression given is that Stow recorded those
murders he did because, at the time he wrote, such events were expected by
his readership. He does not seem to have been particularly interested in such
crimes himself or to have gone out of his way to gather information about
them.[10]

In comparison with Hall's opus and with Stow in the chronicle he
authored by himself, the compilers of Holinshed's *Chronicles* (Holinshed
himself in the first edition and a syndicate, which included Stow, in the
second) show superior legal understanding as well as a greater interest in the
crime of murder. The compilers of the second edition, propelled doubtless by
the demands of the expected readership, were ready to insert a considerable
amount of material relating to murder that did not appear in the first. In
regard to the law of murder, this version of the *Chronicles* expands what Hall
tells us when it notes that under Henry VII it was decided that murderers
who on arraignment obtained benefit of clergy were to be branded with an
'M' on the brawn of the left hand, and were to be executed should they so
offend again. It also refers to the law of 1504, which ordered that murderers
obtaining their clergy were to be held in the bishop's custody. The authors
were noticeably interested in curiosities of the criminal law, even those of the
medieval period, especially if they concerned London or Kent. Thus we are
provided with some detail about the 1431 murder by a Breton of a London
widow. We are told that she had 'maintained him by alms' and in her own
house; that, having killed her, the Breton fled to sanctuary and then abjured
the realm, only to be stoned to death by local women as he made his way
under guard past Aldgate to the port of embarkation.[11]

The first edition of the *Chronicles* has little to say about the notable murders
of the first thirty years of Henry VIII's reign. The second edition, which

follows Hall/Grafton closely, has more. However, when it mentions the murders by the Wolfes, it omits to say that the corpse of the wife was abused while hanging on the gallows, as reported in *The Union*. Also, this edition tells us that a felon tried at Banbury a fair time after the murder of Robert Packyngton confessed to being the killer. The first discrepancy suggests the readership and sensitivities had altered between 1548 and 1587, while the second demonstrates the compilers' readiness to seek out information about crimes that interested them.[12]

From 1540 onwards the second edition of Holinshed becomes the prime chronicle source for notable murders, in depth if not in number. It reports that in September of that year a foreigner, James Rination, who had killed his master, a Florentine, over a harlot, was hanged in Moorfield.[13] Noteworthy is the compilers' interest in homicide by 'strangers' (that is, foreigners) living in England. When this edition of the *Chronicles* deals with its next murder, that committed by Lord Dacre of the South and his associates, it is able to rely on Holinshed's earlier success in collecting a good number of details. Holinshed shows that the intent of the culprits was to hunt in the park of a Sussex esquire, Nicholas Pelham, at Laughton in that county, and he provides the names of five gentlemen and two yeomen in the party. They set out on the night of 30 April 1541 in two parties from Dacre's house at Hurstmonceux. At 'Pikehay' they encountered John and James Busbrig and Richard Summer and fell to quarrelling. This led to an affray in which John Busbrig received such hurt that he died two days later. This information Holinshed seems to have acquired from the actual indictments to which the intruders had to respond in court. Certainly the form of words is very like that in the records. Indeed, the only way Holinshed differs noticeably from the indictments is in his failure to list the full number of Dacre's supporters and to notice a crucial phrase that the Crown's lawyers had inserted into the charges, which was that the offenders, before setting out on the enterprise, had sworn 'to stand against all lieges of the king' and kill any who might oppose them. Thus, by finding a prior homicidal intent, the Crown made murder out of what otherwise would have been considered as killing by 'chance medley' (that is, in hot blood), which was mere manslaughter and readily pardonable for the wealthy. Holinshed also fails to report that at his trial in the Court of the Lord High Steward Dacre confessed his culpability immediately by pleading guilty. Yet, overall, Holinshed's coverage of the crime is impressive for its accuracy. So also is his detail about what happened after the trial – the delay of Dacre's execution, the expectation of a pardon from the king, and the lamentation at the death of so young a nobleman.[14]

It is only in the second edition of the *Chronicles* that we find mention of a murder that occurred in 1550. On the night of 19 January in that year were murdered near Newgate two captains, both foreigners, Peter Gambo and one Filicirga, who had fought for the English at Boulogne. The chief culprit was said to be Charles Gavaro, a Fleming, who had hurried from Berwick to accomplish the deed. After conviction he was taken with three confederates by cart to Smithfield to be hanged. On the way he had his right hand struck off on the cart wheel. At the gallows he was exhorted to confess his crime, reconcile himself to God by repentance, and ask for divine forgiveness; but he 'desperately' answered that he would never repent the deed. Clearly it was the cutting-off of the hand and his curt refusal to 'disburden' his conscience that caught the compilers' attention, although doubtless the accused's foreign nationality may have helped. Repentance, a novel concern at this point in time, was to become an important matter for clergy attending executions in the second half of the sixteenth century, and indeed for those who wrote about the fate of felons and traitors at that time and their readership. The *Chronicles* fails to tell us that the victim was slain by a dagger stroke and that the perpetrator was *recte* Charles de Guevara. Nor does it report that Gavaro pleaded guilty but the three accessories not guilty. Although interested in the legal aspects of the criminal cases they report, the compilers had a good journalistic sense of when they should not burden their readers with such detail.[15]

Further on the *Chronicles*, in both editions, launches, not without an apology, into a long account of the murder of Thomas Ardern at Faversham, Kent, in 1551. The original writer, Holinshed, admitted the novelty of his treatment. He says, 'it may seem to be but a private matter and therefore as it were impertinent to this historie', but he has thought it good 'to set it foorth somewhat at large' on account of 'the horriblenesse thereof'. He was also motivated by his acquisition of a detailed account of the crime, one that resulted in the burning of the chief culprit, the victim's wife Alice, and the death on the gallows of several fellow conspirators. As we have seen, this was by no means the first case of husband-murder to be reported in a chronicle, for there was one reported by Henry Knighton and three mentioned by London chroniclers as having occurred between 1420 and 1443. The Ardern case is, however, the first such murder case to be described in any depth;

indeed, if we exclude the Hun case, it is the first murder of any type to be so reported. It is also the first domestic English murder story.[16]

It seems that some contemporary believed the Ardern murder and the fate of the murderers deserved to be recorded with care, and his efforts provided the information that eventually came into Holinshed's hands. Yet how was it that a contemporary felt the need to make such a record when similar but earlier Tudor murders had not been so treated? The answer may lie in Edwardian religious politics. The swing to Protestantism was rooted in the study of the Bible in general and the Old Testament in particular, which tended to promote conservative socio-legal attitudes. The effect of this we can detect in Edwardian criminal law. Thus the statute 1 Edward VI c. 3 inserted the word (and condition of) 'slavery' into legal terminology from which it had lapsed in the eleventh century. It also featured the use of iron collars, of iron rings around arms and legs, and the advocation of 'beating', none of which had ever appeared in earlier statutes, not even in the draconian criminal-law legislation of Henry VIII. Another biblical influence can perhaps be found in the increasingly common requirement that criminal accusations should be supported at indictment and/or arraignment by the testimony of two witnesses; in at least one category of offence witnesses actually had the power to convict. There was also the reintroduction of the death penalty for buggery, made a felony once more under the act 2/3 Edward VI c. 29. There are, furthermore, indications of a particularly high conviction rate of felons in general in Edward VI's reign.[17]

One feature of the Ardern case that must have attracted the chronicle compiler and his readership in the 1570s was the outcome. The principal murderers all confessed their guilt, thereby affording readers of the account the comforting thought that God would see to it that 'murder will out'. Another element that helped to ensure that a report of the case appeared in print must have been the very nature of the crime: it was not simply murder, it was husband-murder. Furthermore, the culprit was a handsome, well-connected gentlewoman, and the victim a wealthy member of the merchant class with business interests and a residence in London, details that would make the crime of consuming interest to the commercial class of the Tudor capital. Additionally, since as early as the 1530s there had been considerable debate in printed works on the merits and frailties of womanhood, which, for those who read books, or heard them read, may have stimulated their concern over Alice Ardern's motives. No substantial account of the case appeared in print before Holinshed's, although Machyn and Grafton, writing earlier in Elizabeth's reign, each give it a passing mention.[18] Only, it seems, when there were both a Protestant climate and other infamous instances of women involved in murder to excite debate did the time seem right for an extended treatment of the murder of 1551. When Holinshed was compiling his *Chronicles*, the homicidal follies of Mary, Queen of Scots, and Catherine de' Medici, and, in London, of Ann Saunders and her partner Ann Drury, must have still been fresh in the popular memory.

In the *Chronicles* subsequent to the Ardern case and before the murder of George Saunders – that is, in the period 1551–73 – there are reports of four murders, two described very briefly and two in a slightly more extensive manner. We are told that in December 1556 a Frenchman, Gregory Carpenter, when being arraigned for counterfeiting keys to Newgate jail with intent to free the prisoners there and to kill the keeper, stabbed a fellow inmate who had given evidence against him. For this he was immediately taken from the courtroom and the offending hand cut off before he was hanged on a gibbet especially set up for the purpose.[19] The compilers' interest appears once again to lie in the striking-off of the hand and in the fact that the perpetrator was a foreigner. A more extended treatment is accorded to the murders committed on the orders of Charles, Lord Stourton, in 1557. We know from other sources that the case was, as Holinshed states, 'a veryie shamefull and wretched murther'; but, probably because it had occurred in Somerset, he lacked details. He accurately names the victims as 'Hargill', father and son, and how and where the couple were slain, but tells us nothing more about the crime. He knows more about the trials, which were at Westminster, and the executions. How Stourton was taken pinioned, legs bound under his horse's belly, from the Tower to Salisbury, catches his attention, as does the interest shown by Queen Mary, and her command that Stourton was to be used according to justice, meaning there would be no pardon. Stow, as usual briefer on such matters in his own chronicle than in the second edition of the *Chronicles*, confirms the information that Stourton had the victims buried 15ft deep in his own house, and a third chronicler, Wriothesley, is able to tell us that the Hartgills were struck down with clubs and then had their throats cut.[20] The news value of these murders is obvious, yet none of these chroniclers was able to give the local background (in Somerset and Wiltshire) to the feud that caused them. Holinshed and Stow appear to have been slightly reluctant to give emphasis to a case resulting in that very rare event, the execution of a nobleman for felony. The narrow geographic focus of the chroniclers in murder cases is reflected in their failure to mention the celebrated murder at this time of Lewis and Edmund West, the sons of Sir William West of Darley Abbey, Derbyshire, by the sons of Lord Darcy, near Rotherham.[21]

After the Stourton case, neither edition of the *Chronicles* reports a murder until the year 1571 is reached. In that July, we are told very briefly, Rebecca Chamber of Harrietsham, Kent, poisoned her husband Thomas, was convicted at Maidstone assizes and was burned. In July 1576, it is noted, there occurred a similar case, which was also in Kent. A woman, whose name is not supplied, was burned at Tonbridge, also for poisoning her husband; but in this case there was an accessory, one Oxleie, who was hanged at Maidstone.[22] Between these two cases Holinshed records two murders in greater detail than any others he provides, the slaying of Thomas Ardern excepted. The accounts of these crimes suggest both that he was catering for a growing interest in murder and that he was happy to benefit from the ready supply of information available about recent crimes of that type. In the first account, which runs to about 600 words, he tells of the killing, in the spring of 1572, of a London merchant, Arthur Hall, by Martin Bullocke. Bullocke had Hall inspect some plate in his possession with a view to purchase. Hall noticed that the plate had someone else's mark on it and said so. Bullocke agreed but said the person had appointed him to make the sale. Then, as Hall was weighing the plate, Bullocke came up behind him and struck him twice on the head with a thick washing beetle. He took Hall's dagger from him, stabbed him and cut his throat. He tried to put the body into a Danzig chest, but the chest was not long enough. So he tried to drag the corpse down winding stairs to the cellar, but failed, 'wherefore he cut off his legs with an hatchet and in the end trussed him with straw in a drie vat'. Saying it contained his clothes and books, he had the vat taken down to the Thames and shipped to Rye in Sussex. However, suspicion arose against Bullocke and he was examined by Alderman Branch, a sheriff of London; apparently there was no strong evidence against him, for he was released on the surety of Robert Gee, a cloth-worker. Taking advantage of his freedom, Bullocke went to Westminster and thence by boat to Wokingham, but then returned to London and lodged in Holborn. When it became known that Bullocke had left London, Gee was committed to jail but was allowed to send men to look for the fugitive. Gee also sent one of his servants to Rye, where he found and opened the vat and discovered Hall's mangled corpse. 'At the verie same time', Bullocke was arrested in Holborn, where he had been found. Holinshed fails to tell us if Bullocke confessed to the murder, and says nothing about the trial. He simply notes that on 24 May 1572 Bullocke was hanged for murder and robbery on a gibbet, in London, 'by the well with two buckets in Bishopsgate Street'. 'The truth of the matter', adds Holinshed, had come to light 'by the good providence of God, the revealer of such evill facts'.[23] This seems to be the first reference to God's providence uncovering murder in Tudor chronicles. Holinshed's interest in the case and his access to information again seem to derive from the London commercial milieu. The dismembering of the body and the providential return of Bullocke to London were probably additional reasons for his including the case.

Holinshed's next murder is that of George Saunders in March 1573. The crime had several elements in common with the slaying of Thomas Ardern in 1551. Both were husband-murder, and the victims were wealthy and did much business in London. They were both handsome but in all likelihood considerably older than their wives, who were also good-looking. In both cases the wife used a male acquaintance, who hoped one day to be her husband, as her instrument, and servants were members of the conspiracies to murder. In both instances military men were designated as the killers and there were several attempts before the successful one.[24] There the similarity ends, for, whereas Alice Ardern was the tactician in the plot to kill her husband and a participant in his death, Ann Saunders kept her distance from the murder, left the planning to her friend Ann Drury and professed total ignorance of the conspiracy until just before her execution. Whereas there are recorded no last farewells of the Ardern conspirators, great play is made in Elizabethan writing of efforts made to bring Ann Saunders to a state of repentance.

This is not to be found in the *Chronicles* nor in Stow. From the 1570s, murders of the right sort were of such general interest that they were recorded in cheap pamphlets, the Saunders case being so served, it has been suggested, by the strong Protestant Arthur Golding. Because of Ann Saunders's refusal to acknowledge her guilt and the refusal of her lover, the actual murderer, to implicate her, the pamphleteer (and also the author of a play about the murder, which appears to be historically accurate) decided to include some mention of the actual trial of the culprits.[25] This was a novelty.

Here we have references to indictments (even to a precise and accurate mention of accessories before and after the fact), to witnesses, evidence, prosecuting counsel, and judicial interrogation of the accused. Such elements were only rarely to be found in other non-legal literature of the sixteenth century which dealt with crime. The Saunders case was also notable for providing us with two of the earliest recorded 'last speeches' of persons about to be executed for murder. Ann Drury's was atypical in that she did not apparently mention her role in the murder for which she was being executed but rather denied other offences of which she was suspected at large. Ann Saunders, whose last words were many, admitted she had had 'a good husband', 'manie children' and had lived in wealth, but had been corrupted by the devil, who had kindled lust within her. She asked for the forgiveness of her children, kinfolk and friends, and ended with a prayer emphasising her repentance.[26]

Published in the same year that George Saunders was slain was a pamphlet, brief but of some literary merit, concerned not with husband-murder but with wife-murder. The assailant was John Kynnestar, a shearman of the city of Bristol. The crime was apparently unknown to Holinshed and Stow. The author of the account must have been a constable or member of the Bristol watch. He tells us how, in the night, a woman had been thrown out of a house window and lay dead on the ground. The writer seems to have risen from his bed when the cry went up, and, acting on the common belief that the death was the doing of the woman's husband, John Kynnestar, had gone to his house and asked where his wife was. 'I cannot tell,' was all Kynnestar would say. The writer took him by the arm to show him his wife's body; he said he did not know her. Kynnestar must have given the impression of being disturbed in his mind, or had a reputation for being so, for a bystander asked him if he was 'distracted' when he attacked her, and added that he should have opened up his mind to God. The writer then took Kynnestar to the sheriff and subsequently, on the latter's orders, to prison. On the way he asked his prisoner why he had killed his wife; surely 'the devil was great in thee', he said. Kynnestar did not prevaricate: 'she is now rewarded for her paine that she hath doen to me'.[27] When asked in what manner he had killed her, Kynnestar said that he and his wife had been merry, and without any quarrelling, the previous night, but as he slept a thought came into his head that enraged him, and he felt compelled to kill her. He went down into the hall of his house and got a knife. He went back upstairs where his wife was still abed and stabbed her to the heart twenty-five times. She started out of bed and begged him not to strike again. She asked for God's forgiveness on him and then fell dead. He told the writer that, had he been able to find a candle, he would have called in a neighbour but, being unsuccessful, he got back into bed. He felt no sorrow, but sleep would not come, so he arose again and 'out at a windowe I her cast' so people would see.[28]

When he was put on trial at the sessions Kynnestar pleaded guilty and was sentenced to be hanged. There is no suggestion in the pamphlet that the court thought him insane. The writer tells us that a preacher exhorted him to repent so God would receive his soul. The pamphlet concludes in a manner quite different from others of the genre. There is an 'admonition' that recognises conjugal relations are frequently under stress. Each man should take heed to behave himself in living with his wife, it states. If she 'does abuse', admonish her, and if that fails, 'separate thyself from her'; for in that case it is better to live alone. This remarkably pointed piece of advice concludes with the writer advocating self-examination, and reminding men that they have a duty to 'maintain' – that is, to provide moral and material support for their wives and families if harmony is to prevail. This advice is the more striking because it was offered in an age that is typically cast as strongly patriarchal, and, indeed, the pamphlet is redolent with Protestant attitudes and sentiments. The devil and his evil work figure quite prominently: Satan is always on the prowl 'sekyng who he maie devour'. Emphasis is placed on the need for all men to control their lives: 'take good heede how thei doe leade their life'.[29]

Despite the publication of pamphlets dealing with the Saunders and Kynnestar cases, the main source for the popular history of murders of the later 1570s is Stow, both in his own *Annales* and as editor-in-chief of the second edition of the Holinshed–Reyner Wolfe opus. He begins his editorship of the latter by recording a case of fratricide in Worcester in November 1576. Motivated simply by greed for the victim's goods, one brother brained the other with an axe and buried him under the hearth. As might be expected, it was the 'unnaturall' nature of the deed that caused it to be remembered and the killer referred to as 'another Caine'. That the information about the murder came from as far away as Worcester is worthy of note. In short order Stow then refers to an Irishman who murdered a man in a Stepney garden and was hanged in chains (February 1579), the murder of Serjeant Grace by

Francis Glover, whom he had arrested (March 1580), and the murder of a widow, Mistress Skinner, by Richard Dod (also March 1580). Stow's interest in the last two cases was stimulated in part by the fact that the gibbet on which Glover was hanged was also employed, after removal to another location, for Dod. The last murder in this volume is the slaying by Philip Prise of a sheriff's serjeant who had just arrested him (June 1582). This case, like the one involving Serjeant Grace, shows that murders were of note when the victim was a law officer; but the Prise case had an additional element of 'newsworthiness'. At the gallows Prise was very emotive. He was 'tearful', venting 'greevous grones', which caused all the spectators to have 'wet eies': an uncommon situation, a memorable execution and thus a celebrated murder case.[30] Then, as now, reporters knew the value of principal characters who were emotionally aroused.

There seem to have been set down no detailed accounts of individual murders in the 1570s after the Saunders case, and there was certainly no piece of writing whose stated purpose was to collect such cases together. This deficiency, and opportunity for profit, was noticed by the young Anthony Munday, who sought to remedy it through his pamphlet *A view of sundry examples* (1581). This shoddy piece of writing provides brief notes on five suicides, one infanticide, a slaying that was called misadventure, and thirteen murders, all of which crimes had occurred during the previous eight years. The murders included two matricides, one fratricide (the Worcester case), a case where the victim was the assailant's brother-in-law, one where the murdered man was an officer of the law (the Grace case) and another where a mother 'brayned' her two children.[31] Each of these deaths was described in the vaguest of terms but the circumstances of another murder, that of Abel Bourn, a London hosier, were provided *in extenso*. Interestingly, this account reveals that at the time Munday was writing the chief suspect had recently been arrested but not yet put on trial. This may well have been the event that prompted Munday to take up his pen. Whether he hoped to influence the course of justice is not clear.

Where Munday differs markedly from Holinshed and Stow in his treatment of violent death is in his moralising. The temptations of the devil, he tells us, are what lead men astray. Illicit sex gets great emphasis: 'what wicked wretches are wee which abuse our bodies with voluptuous pleasures, with carnal delights and wicked inventions, and with sin out of measure.' Then, in what was to be a standard refrain in pamphlets on crime by Protestant writers, he tells his audience: 'yet can wee not hide our sinne but God seeth it, and no wilful murther will he suffer unrevealed, though we collour it for a time, though we think it cleane out of remembrance . . . yet wil hee cause the very fowles of the aire to bewray it; our owne consciences shall cause us to open it, our lookes wil bewray us, our deeds wil deceive us, so that wee shall need no more evidences then our owne selves.'[32]

Yet in the chronicle tradition Munday provides alongside his litany of violent deaths the usual array of curious facts, which were doubtless, for a short while, the basis of London small talk and street gossip. These sections are excellent examples of the sort of information with which tales of murder had to compete in order to attract popular attention. Like many contemporaries, Munday was much impressed by 'monstrous' births – children and animals born with severe deformities; so much so, in fact, that he was ready to take his examples from continental Europe as well as from England. He also demonstrates a wide-ranging interest in recent seismological disturbances and extreme weather conditions, which he regards as 'a token of the indignation of our God against our wicked living'. 'Let us remember,' he says in conclusion, 'three of the fairest Cities in Asia sunk for sinne'.[33] Munday's essay shows that in 1581 a religious message was becoming the expected companion of any description of newsworthy murder. He was following, in a primitive and slightly less Protestant fashion, Golding's pamphlet on the murder of George Saunders.[34]

One section of Munday's pamphlet, the death of Abel Bourn, provides us with something that is virtually novel in the history of reporting murder. It is his use of the depositions of suspects and witnesses before the coroner. Although these do not identify the killer conclusively, they help our understanding of the Tudor investigative process in murder cases. Words uttered by Bourn's ex-mistress helped to make her a prime suspect; a woman who heard that there was going to be a fight and saw Bourn going by armed with sword and dagger had her home searched and was taken to view the corpse; her 'wench' was also brought before the coroner and gave information that the rushes in their house had just been removed and fresh ones put down. The chief suspect, it seems, was a serving man, claiming to be a falconer, who refused to say where he was on the day of the murder and the subsequent night. To questions put to him he answered 'very evil favouredly' and was sent back to prison. The work of detection, if primitive, was undoubtedly sensible. The coroner took the trouble to obtain testimony from the victim's recently cast-off mistress, from a friend, from a neighbour and from a witness to his fear of assassination. Such depositions, as we have observed, even if at second hand, are very rare from the sixteenth century.[35] Yet we cannot credit Munday with deliberately casting light on this aspect of the criminal law. He did so probably because this inquest material was readily available about an interesting case that had still to come to trial. He recognised a publishing opportunity.

A popular account of a particular murder by a writer of strong Protestant inclination appeared in print in the same year as Munday's *A view of sundry examples*. Like the latter it was not a pamphlet in what may be called the main tradition of such writing. The author's intention, apparently, was to show Catholics in a bad light, and for this purpose he used the murder of Richard Hobson by William Sherwood, both of whom were Catholic prisoners in the Queen's Bench jail at the time. The moral that the author drew from this crime was that the papists were 'like madde Dogges' wishing to 'delight their eies with beholding our channelles running and reking with the warm blood of Protestaintes', but, failing this, ready to 'washe their handes in the blood of their own brethren'. The murder further demonstrated, so the pamphlet writer argued, that Catholics were always a danger to those not of their faith. They were unable to master their passions and were even ready to kill their own: therefore 'what shall we looke for at theyr handes'; 'they will devowre poore Protestauntes as Beastes eate grasse'; 'they are making of the halters to hang us'; 'they are whetting of their knives to cutte our throats'; 'they will byte us, nay they will bayte us to death'.[36]

The religious fervour that the murder engendered in the author emerges again in the last section of the pamphlet, where Sherwood's execution and its preliminaries are described. The night before, and the morning of, the hanging he drove away by his 'scoffes' those who 'exhorted' him. At the gallows he asked for the prayers of any Catholics present, but wanted none from Protestants. When a preacher told him to put his hopes in the mercy of Christ, he cried out: 'Away with the Woolfe, he perverteth the truth and troubleth me.' Efforts were made (we are not told by whom) to get Sherwood to confess to the murder, but he persisted in his denial 'contrary to all evidence'. Only when there appeared to be no hope of a confession or recantation did the sheriff order the hangman to proceed with the execution.[37] The author of the Sherwood pamphlet was thus the first describer of murder since Golding with a serious religious interest. Yet, in essence, the piece is a political tract and as such free of spiritual and philosophical propaganda on behalf of the Protestant religion.

A pamphlet about murder published two years later, in 1583, was, in contrast, definitely in the Golding tradition. The author gives details of two murders, both of which occurred in Worcestershire.[38] The first, which was committed in Evesham, was a straightforward tale of the treacherous slaying by one young businessman of another. Thomas Smith, a good-looking son of a leading townsman, because he envied the wealth and commercial success of Robert Greenoll, invited him to his house for an evening's conviviality. When the opportunity offered itself, Smith killed Greenoll by two blows to the head with an iron pestle and buried his body in the cellar. Smith's undoing was, first, in transporting some of the victim's goods to his own house that same night, and being observed by the town watch; secondly, in leaving a piece of earth out of place in the cellar after burying Greenoll.[39]

The second murder occurred at Cotheridge, just west of Worcester. The wife of a respected husbandman, Thomas Beast, fell in love with their servant, Christopher Tomson. Frequently, says the pamphlet, 'they would carnally acquaint themselves together till lust had gotten so much power of the woman' that 'she began altogether to loathe and dislike her husband, and prefer the fleshly dealings of her new companion'. Neighbours warned Thomas Beast, who was well reputed 'both for his housekeeping and his Godly and honest behaviour', of his wife's infatuation with 'her lusty Yonker'. He ordered Tomson to leave, but his wife was able to change his mind. So great was the wife's desire for Tomson 'as she must needs seeke and practise the death of her husband'. She asked her lover to prove his love for her by killing him. At first Tomson refused, but his reluctance lessened when she assured him that through her friends and her money she would ensure that he did not go to the gallows.[40] She provided him with a forest bill, which she herself had sharpened, and instructed him to make sure her husband died immediately and was thus unable to name his assailant. Tomson sought out Beast in the fields, told him he was quitting his employ and asked for his wages. As Beast turned to open his purse, the servant killed him with one stroke. He then fled, but was soon captured and revealed how his mistress was the cause of the deed. Both were sent to Worcester jail. There their infatuation flourished rather than diminished: 'very often she would solicite her sweet Christopher with mony handkerchers, nosegays, and such like amorous and loving tokens, and he besotted in his naughtie affection would shape all his conditions to please her.' At the Worcestershire assizes held at Evesham, Tomson and Mrs Beast were convicted. He was hanged (and his body later hung up in chains) and she was burned 'for an example to all lighte and lascivious women'. At a later Worcestershire assizes, also held at Evesham, Thomas Smith was adjudged to hang, although through the intercession of wealthy friends he was spared being hung in chains.[41]

It is the introduction to these two tales that delivers a strongly Protestant message. The author, who uniquely among Tudor pamphleteers claims to have visited and interviewed a murderer (Smith) in jail, emphasises that the age is a most sinful one: 'daylie doo fresh enormities spring up.' These 'sinnes of the earth hath fumed up into the nostrils of the Almightie', so that he feels it necessary to strike the 'stiff necked Pharao with the rodde of his furie' to call us back from 'the flesh pots of Aegypt and from our owne filthie and odious vomit'. Human inclination towards sin is given impetus by the devil: in the first case, for example, by his fuelling of Smith's envy of Greenoll and then giving him the opportunity for mischief. The account of the second murder finishes with the writer calling Mrs Beast a devil rather than a woman, one with a devilish desire to kill her husband through her lust for Christopher. Also worthy of note is the author's admonition, at the point in the narrative where he is about to provide details of Mr Beast's death, to 'chaste and grave matrones' in his audience that they should stop their ears, as they might find it odious to be told about 'a gracelesse strumpet' who had dishonoured her 'noble sexe'.[42] The portrayal of Mrs Beast as the prime conspirator in the murder of her husband, and the actual murder stroke by the servant for whom she lusted, offers a good example of what has been called the 'inversion' factor, namely the overthrow of the head of the family by his social inferiors. This is a theme that recurs periodically in murder accounts of the next half-century.[43]

The account of the murder of Thomas Beast has much in common with the reporting, by means of chronicle, pamphlet or theatrical presentation, of several murders that occurred around 1590. Stow mentions a 'wench' burned in March 1590 for poisoning her mistress and another woman, and two women burned (June and September 1592) for poisoning their husbands.[44] The first of these husband-murderers (the crime occurred in January 1590) was exotic enough in its details to give rise to a pamphlet entitled *The trueth of the most wicked and secret murthering of John Brewen, Goldsmith of London, committed by his owne wife through the provocation of John Parker whom she Loved*. In this account Anne Welles, a 'proper young woman' of London of 'comely personage', had two suitors, both goldsmiths, John Brewen and John Parker. The latter was 'better beloved yet least deserved it'. Brewen, recognising his suit would not be crowned with success (despite the support of Anne's friends and kinfolk), asked for the return of the things he had given Anne 'upon a promise betweene them'. She refused and so he had her arrested. She was so dismayed by this that she said she would marry him if he withdrew from his action. We may suspect that she was also motivated by the behaviour of her lover, Parker, who 'had lien with her and gotten her with child', but who refused to marry her. Parker was aggrieved by her compact with Brewen and 'continually urged her to make him away'. She eventually agreed to poison her new spouse, and Parker, for his part, agreed to marry her when the deed was done.[45]

We are provided with some intriguing insights into marital relations between Welles and Brewen. She had been married to him for only three days 'when she put in practise to poison him'. Although Brewen 'loved her tenderly, yet she had conceived such deadly hatred against him that she lay not with him after the first night of the marriage'; 'and to excuse her from his bed she sayd she had vowed never to lie by him more till he had gotten her a better house'. She also insisted on keeping her maiden name. The poison to be used, which was obtained by Parker, was reputed to kill without any swelling of the body or other outward signs. Anne took it to her husband's house 'with a mery plesaunt countenance and very kindly asked her husband how he did, giving him the good morrow in the most courteous manner'. She asked him if he would like some sugar sops. He answered that he would and said how kind she was. 'Alas husband,' she replied, 'if I could not find it in my heart to doe so small a matter for you (especially being so lately married) you might iustly iudge me unkinde'. Brewen, after one portion had been spilled, ate the poisoned sugar sops, vomited violently and went to bed. Despite his pleadings, his wife went back to her own lodgings and refused requests to return as Brewen continued to vomit 'til his entrailes were all shrunke and broken within him'. When Anne returned next morning, Brewen reproached her for not staying overnight, to which she answered that surely he would not have her break her oath not to live with him until he got another house. Soon Brewen died of the poison; but no suspicion fell on Anne, her difficult relationship with her husband being attributed to the foolishness of youth. When the child she had by Parker was born, it was assumed to be her late husband's.[46]

The remainder of the account up to the discovery that Brewen's death had been murder concerns the deteriorating relationship between the two conspirators, and it is very graphic. After her husband had died, the 'lusty' Parker was a 'continuall resorter' to the house of Anne, 'whose welcome was answerable to his desier'. Although he was not married to her, she became totally subject to him; such 'slaverie and subiection did he bring her that she must runne or goe wheresoever he pleased to appoint her, held he up but his finger at any time'. Should she deny him money 'or whatsoever else he listed to request', he became violent. He would 'haule and pull her as was pittie to behold: yea, and threaten to stabbe and thrust her through with his dagger did she not as he would have her in all things'. Whatever she did for him failed to please him. So it was for two years following her husband's death. The sexual relationship, however, continued, for 'at length he got her with child againe'. To save her reputation Anne tried to conceal her pregnancy from the world as long as possible, while at the same time begging Parker to marry her. He was unmoved by her plea and retorted viciously that he would be foolish 'to wed such strumpet as thyself' and then 'reviled her most shamefully'. She answered that she had been a strumpet only to him; she had given him all her love and received precious little in return. Parker said she wanted to marry him in order to poison him as she had Brewen: 'I meane to keepe me as long out of thy fingers as I can.' 'Why thou arrant beast,' replied Anne, 'what did I then which thou didst not provoke me to doo? . . . thou gavest me the poison and after thy direction I did minister it unto him . . . it was for thy sake I did so cursed a deede.'[47]

These arguments, made 'in vehemence of spirit', were the pair's undoing. They were overheard and reported to the magistrates. Anne was taken before Alderman Haward to be examined and Parker before Justice Young. Neither would confess anything until Anne was made to believe that Parker had confessed the crime, which caused her to do the same. Whether in fact Parker had admitted their guilt is not clear; the implication is that the examiners acted duplicitously. The trial of the pair was delayed until Anne's child had been born, then they were both arraigned and convicted at Newgate sessions. The judgments were that Anne should be burned at Smithfield and that Parker should be hanged there before her eyes. This was done on Wednesday, 28 June 1592, two and a half years after the misdeed. The account was written during the subsequent week.[48]

With only the briefest of homilies, to the effect that God will see to it that murder is revealed, the account ends. Apart from this epilogue and the prating introduction, both in accord with the temper of the times, the pamphlet retains our interest throughout. The style is not only lucid but concisely elegant. There is no reiteration or spurious lamentation. The vocabulary and syntax are much superior to most writing of the genre. The account of the relationships between Welles and her two lovers, remarkable though they were, is convincing; the altercations between Anne and Parker particularly so. The author's name, which appears at the end of the piece, is Thomas Kyd, the playwright. He produced the account probably at the request of his brother, whose name also appears on it, though as publisher. While Thomas Kyd's authorship accounts for the dramatic and literary quality of the piece, it also gives rise to concern as to the veracity of the details, particularly the direct speech, of which there is a greater amount, relatively, than in any other sixteenth-century murder account. Might not Kyd, a writer of tragedies replete with violent death, have fabricated or at least enhanced the dialogue, dialogue that, because of the rarity of direct speech by females of this period concerning their emotional relationships, is of particular importance to historians? This question cannot be answered with any certainty, but it is quite likely that Kyd, who wrote soon after the executions, got his information from the examinations of the witnesses who had overheard the recriminations of Welles and Parker (or even from the witnesses themselves) and thus his report is soundly based.[49]

More in the mainstream of murder reporting in the late Elizabethan period were two notorious instances that occurred late in 1590 and early in 1591 in Kent and Devon respectively. These cases are to be found in a pamphlet entitled *Sundrye strange and inhumaine murthers lately committed*. The writer quotes from Plutarch, Erasmus and the book of Genesis in his condemnation of murder. He argues that even vegetation and animals can cause the guilty party to be revealed. Rehearsing a now-familiar theme, he tells us, 'God seldome or never leaveth murder unpunished', adding a rider not found elsewhere to this point, namely, 'nor will the worke of murther goe forth of the murtherer's weapon'. His observations lack, however, the heavy emphasis of strong Protestant commitment.[50] The first case reported concerns a widower, Nicholas Lincoln of Warborne, Kent, about 50 years of age, who sought the hand in marriage of a fairly wealthy local widow. She refused him because he had four children 'of his great charge'. 'Whereat, as it seemeth, the devil entered so farre into his minde that he cast many wayes in his thought how to make them awaie.' He approached the labouring man 'that wrought with him in his house', explained his predicament, and eventually got his agreement to murder the children (three boys and a girl) in return for forty shillings and a cow. The father promised his hireling that after the murders he would not 'pursue him', but if compelled to do so he would 'let fall his sute rather than to take his oath to saie he was the murtherer'. This meant that Lincoln promised he would not testify to his servant's guilt at the coroner's inquest or the actual trial, if there was such.[51]

The murder was planned with some care, the design being to ensure that Lincoln himself would not be suspected. Thus one Saturday in December 1590, after breakfast, Lincoln set off for market at Ashford, four miles distant, with his eldest son (aged 15) and the labouring man. The latter soon turned back, returned to the house, and killed the three children there by 'knocking them on the heads with a hatchet and cutting all their throats'. To give himself an alibi, the father, when he reached the market, bought three pairs of shoes. As he returned home he sent his eldest son on ahead. The boy, finding the house door barred, looked in the window but could see none of his siblings stirring. Then Lincoln arrived. He made no effort to enter the house but instead went to a neighbour's to ask for someone to return with him to 'see what had happened'. Thus he was able to enter his house with a 'companie' who were 'eie witnesses' of the 'tragicall spectacle'. These were amazed that Lincoln was so unmoved that he 'made no signe of sorrowe' for his children's deaths, and made no effort to pursue the murderer. The latter was assumed to be the labouring man, since he had been seen about the house while the father and eldest son were at the market. However, Lincoln commended him as 'a verie honest fellow', and astoundingly intimated his eldest son must be the culprit.[52]

Initially Lincoln would not see to the burying of the dead children 'nor that the coroner should view them'. He attended to the burials only three days later, after a 'gentlewoman' had reproved him; he dug a hole 2ft deep in the house for a grave, which filled with water and turned the bodies white. Five days later the coroner came and had the bodies taken up. In the meantime the labouring man had been arrested. He was brought before the corpses and the wounds began to bleed afresh. The coroner ordered him 'to looke upon the children'. He did so and called them by their names. Whereupon the bodies, which had appeared to be white, 'sodainly received their former 'coulour of bloude and had such a lively countenance flushing in theyr faces as if they had beene living creatures lying asleepe'. This 'wonderfull miracle' caused the murderer to admit his guilt and also point to Lincoln as the principal planner of the murders. As a result, Lincoln and his assistant were put on trial at the Kent assizes in February 1591, and both were convicted, although the former denied his guilt and continued to do so until he was about to be hanged. Then he confessed, his conscience, according to the writer, being 'overcharged' with the crime and not allowing it to be concealed any longer. The moral of his account, says the author in conclusion, is that, even if there is no one to accuse a murderer, merely suspicion against him, the corpse will 'give evidence against him'.[53]

The case was a bizarre one and by the standards of any century well worth reporting. The readiness of the father to achieve the deaths of at least three of his children, all apparently begotten by himself, merely for financial advantage; his careful construction of an alibi; his precautions not to be at the scene of the crime until the moment when the corpses were discovered; his intention to divert suspicion onto his eldest son: all suggest the ultimate in villainy. These elements were bound to attract the attention of a reporter and guarantee a substantial audience even if, as was becoming a desideratum by this time, a female playing a major role in the case was lacking.[54]

Another murder recorded in the pamphlet is very different. This, entitled *A true discourse of a cruel and inhumaine murder committed upon M. Padge of Plymouth*, makes Mrs Page, the principal planner of the murder, the chief character in a tale that is reminiscent of the slaying of Thomas Ardern. She was the daughter of a Tavistock (Devon) merchant who, it appears, made over his business to a young man named George Strangwich and retired. It was generally expected she would marry Strangwich, but her parents were determined she should marry a widower, Mr Page of Plymouth, 'one of the cheefest inhabitants of that towne'. They had their way, 'notwithstanding that she had protested never to love the man with her hart nor never to remove her affection settled upon the saide Strangwidge and he to her. . .'. The marriage took place, but very soon Page and her lover practised 'day and night' how to kill her husband. During the next twelve months she attempted several times to poison him, but, although 'he was compelled to vomit blood and much corruption', he survived. More direct methods were called for. Since Mrs Page and Strangwich had available to them 'a great store' of money, they were able to enlist the services of one of her male servants and another man for the purpose of murder. These hirelings were to be rewarded well: the first, Priddis, was to receive an unspecified down payment and no less than another £140 later on; the second, Stone, was also promised 'a great sum'.[55]

The deed was done on 11 February 1591 at a time when Mrs Page, who had chosen the day, 'lay not then with her husband' but in her own room, because of the premature birth of a child. The writer notes that she had sworn she would never bear a child by Page 'that should prosper' and in fact was responsible for the deaths of two of her children. At 10 p.m., when Mr Page was in bed but not asleep, Priddis let Stone into the house, and they made their way to Page's bedroom. Priddis leapt upon him, but Page managed to get to his feet before Stone tripped him and the pair of assailants throttled him with his own kerchief. Then they broke his neck and put him back in bed as though he had died naturally. Priddis informed Mrs Page the misdeed was done, and she, after an hour had elapsed, called out for a servant to look into her husband's room, since 'me thinkes I heare him grone'. The maid who answered the call was sent into the room while Mrs Page stood at the door. When the husband's body was found to be cold and stiff, the wife cried out that Page was dead. She sent Priddis to summon her father and also a sister of her husband, who was told to come immediately if she wanted to see her brother alive, since he was taken with the disease known as 'the Pull'. There was no suspicion that Page had died through foul play until his sister, Mrs Harriss, 'spied blood about his bosome', the result of his clawing at his neck as he strove to prevent strangulation. Then his neck was found to be broken, and skin had been scraped off both knees as he struggled to preserve his life.[56]

Recognising from these signs that her brother had been murdered, Mrs Harriss went to the mayor 'and the worshipfull of the towne' and asked them to come and see the body. They came immediately, and 'by searching him' concluded he had been murdered that very night. The mayor committed Priddis to jail, although why he was suspected we are not told. Sometime later he was examined. To his interrogators he answered that Stone was the chief culprit. So Stone, who had got married on the day after the murder, was taken from his celebrations. Although the writer does not say so explicitly, the examinations of Priddis and Stone must have revealed that Mrs Page was the person who planned the murder. She was examined by the mayor and other magistrates of Plymouth, and also by Sir Francis Drake. Apparently she did not deny the accusations against her but boldly retorted she would 'rather dye with Strangwidge than live with Padge'. Her lover, who had been away in London and was depressed at having agreed to the murder, arrived in Plymouth as Mrs Page was being examined. He was taken before the justices of the peace, where he admitted to all that Mrs Page had, but he also offered to prove he had written to her begging her not to execute the murder. Since Mr Page had been slain before the letter arrived, this excuse was not accepted, and Strangwich was arraigned with his confederates at the Lenten assizes. There all four were convicted, sentenced to death and executed.[57]

At this point, without any details of the executions or of preceding gallows speeches, the account of the crime ends. There follow, however, descriptions of two strange omens that occurred at the time, and the writer concludes his piece with a homily that turns from being the moral lessons to be learnt from his 'examples' to a seemingly patriotic prayer. 'Eternal God,' it runs, 'preserve this little Iland, blesse the Queenes Maiestie and her honorable counsell'. Queen Elizabeth is called 'our Moyses' and the writer expresses the wish that she may 'long live to hold up the Tables of the Law', and her subjects seek continually to please her 'in such due sort as she may have no iust cause to throw them down'. The pamphlet was written between the end of February and mid-July 1591. It was a time when there was an unsuccessful legal challenge to the authority of the Court of High Commission, and the common law judges confirmed the queen's title as Supreme Governor of the Church. It was also the year the government sought, unsuccessfully as it transpired, to convict Thomas Cartwright and several other Puritan leaders in the Court of Star Chamber for their meetings and conferences. Thus issues such as the legality of the ex-officio oath and Puritan voluntary meetings were to the forefront at the time and were probably the cause of the writer's subtle plea for 'due process of law'.[58]

In his two accounts the author of *Sundrye strange and inhumaine murthers* is only moderate in his religious emphasis; he was probably a layman. Where gender is concerned, he shows no particular animosity against women. Indeed, he appears to place the blame for Mrs Page's evil-doing on the marriage into which she had been forced. In contrast, he finds absolutely no redeeming features in the excessively cruel behaviour of Lincoln. He follows convention in stressing that murder 'will out'. He emphasises that Lincoln's children's corpses caused the murderer to confess. However, he is also keen to show, in forensic fashion, that, if examined carefully, the body of the victim will provide crucial evidence. He was clearly much impressed by the careful construction of alibis by the two chief planners of the murders. The readiness of servants, if rewarded financially, to do the actual slaying is strongly emphasised in both cases; it must have alarmed many pamphlet readers and increased sales.

Within a year of the slaying of Page of Plymouth there occurred another celebrated murder, in no way domestic, which also gave rise to pamphlet literature. The victim was a nobleman, John, Lord Bourke (or Bourgh) of Castleconnell, County Limerick, Ireland, and the author of one pamphlet was W.R., one of his servants. The deed was done in Wandsworth Fields, Surrey, by Arnold Cosby, with whom Lord Bourke was intending to fight a duel. Stow tells us the pair had quarrelled and fought a duel at Greenwich twelve months earlier but then 'were made friendes'. Cosby, a professional soldier and likewise an Irishman, 'wanderd', we are told by the pamphlet writer, 'in the courte, amongst the princelike traine of her Maiesties followers'; he was a man 'of proude conceipte, born of mischeefe', indeed 'predestinated to destroie'. Why he had quarrelled with Lord Bourke on this occasion is mentioned only vaguely: he had become too familiar and even 'contemptuous' of him. The quarrel led to Cosby challenging Bourke to a duel by letter, one that was scornful and made 'odious comparisons'. This moved the nobleman, who was of 'milde and curteous demenour', to take up the challenge. Because Cosby was a soldier 'and in that respecte a gentleman', he did not consider a duel with him to be 'much preiudicall to his honour'. Through the 'chastisement of his sword', he would teach him his duty and better manners.

Cosby, who believed the nobleman would decline his challenge, 'began now to quaile' at the thought of the duel. Desperately 'he entred into counsel with the curssed ruler of darknesse' as to how he might 'worke mischiefe and yet defende his owne credite from blot of infamie'; he was planning murder. Neither man told anyone of the duel they had arranged. The day was dark and wet as first Cosby and then Bourke arrived at the place appointed. Cosby insisted on measuring the rapiers to be used but then, remarkably, suggested there was no need to fight the duel. They should break off a rapier point, scar their faces with it, and return to London claiming they had fought. When Bourke scorned this subterfuge, Cosby told him he should take off his spurs so they would be no hindrance in the coming duel. Bourke started to do so using his right hand while he held his rapier in his left. Whereupon Cosby, 'with all the violence his coadiutor, the devil, could lend him', ran his rapier twelve inches into Bourke's chest. Then, with his dagger, he stabbed the nobleman no fewer than twenty-three times so that he would never be able to reveal anything about the murder or murderer.[59]

Cosby then rode off, but his horse went lame. Amazingly, Lord Bourke for a short while survived his many wounds. He was discovered by John Powell, Yeoman of the Bottles in the queen's household, and carried to a house in Wandsworth. There, before he died, Bourke was able to recount the treacherous attack to the Earls of Essex and Ormond. Powell meanwhile pursued Cosby until he took refuge in a thick wood. When night came, Cosby resumed his flight but the first house he passed was the very one where lay the now 'breathlesse bodie' of Bourke. As Cosby went by, we are told, its wounds began to bleed once more, causing those in the house, believing the killer must be near at hand, to renew the search. As a result, Cosby was arrested at 'Newington'. All these occurrences leading to Cosby's capture were attributed, in strong Protestant style, to the providence of God. On capture, Cosby was imprisoned in Newgate and then arraigned for murder at Southwark sessions house. At this point, with a short paragraph warning noblemen against sycophants of inferior status, the writer closes his account.

A second pamphlet writer who describes the murder of Lord Bourke covers relevant events both before and after the deed in about the same amount of detail as W.R., but in a different format and from a slightly different angle. This is because the pamphlet is concerned essentially, if imprecisely, with Cosby's trial. The title is *The Arraignment, Examination, Confession and Iudgement of Arnold Cosbye*, and thus the pamphlet, in providing us with details of a murder trial, is a valuable rarity, even if it does not include pre-trial examinations/depositions. The writer notes that the crime was committed within the verge of Queen Elizabeth's Court and that the trial was held at a sessions at Southwark. The presence of the Knight Marshal and the Lord Chamberlain as justices suggests that this was the Court of the Household. John Popham, the Attorney-General, prosecuted the case for the Crown. Intriguingly, Cosby, who at an examination earlier on had confessed to the crime, pleaded not guilty when called to the bar. Therefore a jury, a 'substantial' one, was sworn to hear evidence offered by Popham. This included an account of the cause of the quarrel, including the reading of a letter that Cosby had sent to Bourke containing 'very indiscreate tearmes', the displaying of Cosby's bloodstained sword, testimony by the finder of the dying

Bourke to the effect that the nobleman had named Cosby as his assailant, testimony by another soldier, a captain like Cosby, of the latter's general cowardice, the reading of Cosby's confession and a statement by him that he did not intend hurt to the nobleman.[60]

When the jury retired to consider its verdict, the Lord Chamberlain addressed Cosby at some length on the matter of his failure to flee from the scene of the crime: God, he asserted, had taken away the murderer's ability to do so. When the jury had returned a verdict of guilty, and before judgment was given, Cosby asked that he be 'shotte to death with bullets' rather than hanged. This the bench refused, but a second request, that his execution be delayed for a day or so that he might have a preacher 'to comfort him to Godward', was granted. In pronouncing the judgment of the court, which was that Cosby should be hanged in the place where the murder had been committed and then later his body hanged in chains, the Attorney-General, in Protestant fashion, advised Cosby to think of the afterlife and to ask for God's mercy, for had not God said that no sin was unpardonable? The court then broke up and the condemned man, 'Captain Cosbye, Irishman', 'apparelled in a yellow fustian dublet', was taken off to the Marshalsea jail. The pamphlet goes no further.[61]

While these authors say nothing about Cosby's behaviour at the gallows, a third pamphlet, also written close to the event, satisfies our curiosity. It also offers us verses supposedly written by Cosby during his imprisonment. This pamphlet was very probably written by one of the 'learned preachers' who visited Cosby in the Marshalsea prison after judgment. Certainly the vocabulary is strongly Protestant: indeed, it is a classical example of the genre. These visitors, we are told, emphasised to Cosby that he could obtain remission of his sins and enter heaven only through faith in Jesus Christ and telling God of his repentance. Cosby obliged handsomely with a 'godly confession' accompanied by 'bitter teares', and lamentations on his 'follie and fall' caused by his pride. As he awaited execution he spent time meditating on a copy of the New Testament. At 9 a.m. on 27 January 1592 he was taken by cart from the Marshalsea jail to Wandsworth town's end, where a gibbet had been set up on a hill. There to see the hanging was the Earl of Ormond with 'manie knightes, captaines and gentlemen'. To provide final spiritual comfort there was present the Bishop of Bristol. The Bishop persuaded Cosby to confess his crime to the crowd and then prayed with him. To clear his conscience Cosby also admitted at this point to several other heinous crimes.

Still calling on God to forgive him, 'even to his last gaspe', he was turned off the ladder (that is, he was then hanged). After death he was hanged up in chains as specified in his judgment. This pamphlet concludes with what is claimed to be Cosby's last farewell to 'the vaine world', written in verse in the first person when he was in the Marshalsea prison awaiting execution. Unlike most pieces of this sort, it is well composed, by someone possessing definite poetic skills and a knowledge of the Elizabethan martial class. In it Cosby seeks pardon not only from God ('great commander of this glorious round') but from his friends, military associates, kinsfolk, country and queen, all of whom he has shamed. There is also an interesting (and historically early) reference to misspent youth.[62]

If we consider why the murder of Bourke resulted in three popular pamphlets, a fair number of reasons suggest themselves. The murder of a peer was a rare thing, and the sensational nature of the event, if lessened because of his Irish title, was at the same time enhanced by the fact that the killer was an intimate. That Cosby was known for his loutish behaviour around the royal Court would have been welcome as confirming popular prejudice against both professional soldiers on the loose and overbearing courtiers. For the gentleman reader, the account would have brought home the dangers of participating in a duel without having a second present. The fact that Lord Bourke was ready to duel with a man of much lower rank and not refuse on the grounds that it was prejudicial to his honour would have made him a popular martyr. For the writers, the hand of God in revealing the murderer and Cosby's good Protestant end were important, and probably so for the readership. Equally vital for the 'newsworthiness' of the murder was probably the simple fact that it occurred on the outskirts of London, the city where most readers dwelt. Lastly, Cosby was the perfect villain: Irish, two-faced, a braggart but a coward, and, best of all from the writers'viewpoints, a wonderful emoter in prison and at the gallows.

The murders reported at any length by pamphleteers in the middle years of the 1590s had in common the fact that they occurred outside London. Two of the most distant, reported in a pamphlet of 1595, were committed in Lincolnshire, one not far from Grantham and the other at Bourne. *A world of wonder. A masse of murthers. A covie of cosonages* is the title of this rambling piece. It tells us that a traveller, stopping for the night at an inn at Caythorpe, mentioned to the innkeeper's wife, whose husband was away on business, that he was carrying a large amount of money with him and that he wanted a room that was secure. She obliged him and said that furthermore she would not allow any 'suspicious' person to stay there that night. The traveller, who is never named, put his money under the bedhead and made sure the door of his room was locked before he went to sleep. When her servants were asleep, the innkeeper's wife, 'incensed by the divell', opened the door by means of an instrument. She took the traveller's knife from its sheath, laid her hand over his mouth and cut his throat. Then 'shee fastned the mans hand to the knife which she left sticking in his throate and so departed'. Only when the next day was 'drawing well on' did she send a maid to see why the traveller had not left his room. When told of the man's death, she 'counterfeited swooning'. On what followed, the pamphlet is brief: 'A quest is panneld, verdict given that he himself was guilty of his own death', and thus he was buried out of Christian ground.

That the death was really murder came to light only three or four months later when the wife gave the smock she had been wearing as she committed the crime to a poor woman so that she might remove the bloodstains. As she washed, the woman found the stains became increasingly 'fresher', which she mentioned to the local constable. He examined the wife. Concludes the writer tersely, 'after some examinations (she) confessed the matter and had the law at Lincolne and was executed for the same'.

The second murder that this pamphlet writer recounts in detail concerns an unthrifty country mercer who wanted his wife to sell 'a prettie piece of land' that was her own. Thinking of possible widowhood, she refused. The husband told his woe to his two brothers, one of whom, a butcher, advised 'dealing extremely' with her. They agreed to kill her and told a maid, who knew of their plans, that she would die too if she betrayed them. With the maid holding the candle, the butcher 'after his butcherlike trade' quickly dispatched the wife. All we are told about the aftermath is that the maid revealed the crime to others and the miscreants were apprehended 'and had the law accordingly'.[63]

These two crimes are not the only murders mentioned in the pamphlet – it purports to provide a good selection – but the other cases, which are from as early as the mid-fifteenth century, are treated very scantily. Among them are the deaths of Thomas Ardern of Faversham (thirty-two words) and of George Saunders (twenty-seven words). Exceptional because of their relative length are the treatments of the slaying of Arthur Hall by Martin Bullocke (220 words) and of an infanticide committed in Whitechapel parish near London in 1584 (470 words). The pamphlet has its fair share of moral admonition – 'what fond affections and most wicked and abominable practices we are lead to for want of grace' – and there are several references to the 'divell'. Yet one of the writer's main didactic purposes appears to be to warn employers against 'over hard usages of their apprentices and servants' either through too much generosity or too little, causing 'whoredome', dicing, lewdness, rioting, the embezzlement of their master's goods and theft in order to buy victuals. This admonition is tied to the crime of murder only loosely, and to the examples he has provided hardly at all. Very noticeable is the author's lack of interest in the gallows scene and in whether there was repentance and harrowing last words. The writer does, however, express his approval that the murderer of a chandler is still hanging on a London gallows and this is 'a terrour to the wicked and reprobate'. As to the causes of murder in general he indicates that he believes the desire to acquire the wealth of others is paramount. He offers also one other reason, one that is unique. This is killing 'upon harbrannes', by which he seems to mean murder with no obvious cause in that the slaying was by totally reckless or deranged persons. The pamphlet is really a medley of criminal activities that have recently come to the writer's notice. It has as its main purpose simply the intent to warn the reader, through titillating examples, to be on his or her guard. Perhaps we should connect *A world of wonder* with an increasing fear of lawlessness generated by riots in the city of London at about the time of its publication. Probably the most arresting feature of the murder section of the pamphlet is the efficient and professional way in which the Caythorpe innkeeper's wife slays her victim unassisted. Finding and using the traveller's own knife, putting her hand over his mouth to ensure others at the inn were not awakened, cutting his throat and then putting the knife into his hand – all this suggests a cool head and a strong and steady hand. The slaying is unique in that in all other sixteenth-century murders appearing in pamphlets or chronicles, where women were responsible, they either used poison or had men do the initial deed for them.

In contrast with *A world of wonder*, another pamphlet of 1595 is devoted entirely to the crime of murder. It is not a particularly dramatic piece of writing despite its prolix title – namely, *Two notorious murders. One committed by a tanner on his wives sonne nere Hornchurch in Essex. The other on a grazier near Ailsburie in Buckinghamshire. With these is intermixt another murderous intending fellonie at Rislip in Middlesex. All done this last month.* The two murders in this piece seem, on inspection, to lack the features that would have made for an intriguing murder story at this late stage of the sixteenth century. In the Hornchurch case a stepfather, in alliance with his stepdaughter's husband, planned the murder of his stepson, who was about to receive an inheritance. Both were prepared to commit the deed, but the opportunity came to the stepfather, who brained his stepson with a stake taken from a stile. The body was discovered by a greyhound. It was decomposing, and the sight is described with some relish by the writer: 'wormes cralled in his mouth, nose, eares, and his whole body was putrified.' When it comes to how the murderer was detected the author is vague in the extreme: the stepfather had been absent from his home on the evening of the deed, he had spoken some suspicious words, 'but cheefely God's will made Wright [i.e. the stepfather] to be suspected'. At first 'he sought to face it out, yet before a Justice he confessed it presently', and was hanged at Romford. His ally, his stepdaughter's husband, was still awaiting trial at Chelmsford, we are told, when the account was being written. One feature of the case that attracted the writer is revealed in the final words of the account, which describe the stepfather's 'lamentation', presumably made at the gallows. In this all stepfathers and the widows who wedded them are advised to 'remember the children . . . committed to their patronage' and to care for them 'as derely as their naturall children'.[64]

The grazier who figures in the second murder in the pamphlet was William Randolph of Cardiff. He was returning to Wales from London carrying a sum of £300 when he was killed at Aylesbury by the pistol shots of two confederates of an envious Essex grazier, Dernley. The murderers mangled the body with more wounds and deposited it in a thicket, where it was found two days later. The crime was notable for the wide-ranging hue and cry that followed: 'to London, toward Wales, and every way'. The hunt for the murderers must have been assisted by descriptions of the pair given by an inhabitant of Aylesbury, who had ridden in their company for a while and, indeed, had voiced his suspicions about them to Randolph. One suspect was captured in Wales and the other at his home in London. Both eventually confessed to the crime and accused Dernley as the instigator; 'they are all gone to suffer deserved death', adds the writer laconically.[65]

The writer shows Protestant inclinations at several places in his account. He notes that it is a time when 'iniquitie rageth'; and the 'scripture' and 'the devill' make appearances, as does 'the hell of conscience'. The details about the decomposition of the corpse in the Hornchurch case are quite Lollardian. There is, however, some novelty. The writer shows interest in the Aylesbury murderers' background: how it was they came of honest parents and were 'faire conditioned' without evil reputation, yet Dernley knew them as killers for hire.[66] But the real innovation was the writer's lamentation over the misery murder caused for the parents, wives, children and followers of the victim. This concern, together with his earlier warning to step-parents, shows a sensitivity rarely apparent in the earlier history of murder. The inclination of the writer to sympathise with children in particular is also demonstrated in a third section of the pamphlet, which describes an attempt at murder that failed, where the victim, a boy aged 10, is lauded for his 'constancie' in accusing his attacker after recovering from his wounds, and giving evidence in court.[67]

This appreciation of how a criminal might be convicted out of the mouth of a child occurs also in another report of the same year, one concerned with a wife-murder in Sussex. It tells how Ralph Meaphon, Meophon or Mepham, a miner who worked near Mayfield, left his job at 5 p.m. on a dark evening and went home. There 'he fel to rayling and chiding his wife' and eventually drew his knife and cut her throat. Then, 'leaving her weltering in her owne goare', he returned to his mining 'without making any semblance of sorrow'. He left at home his little son, scarcely 5 years old, who had witnessed the murder. Whether deliberately or not, Meaphon left a candle or fire burning when he departed, which caused the house to catch fire. Neighbours rescued the child. The body of Meaphon's wife, which was discovered in the debris, was viewed by the constable of Mayfield, who, not knowing how to find the murderer, sent for the coroner. The latter examined a woman who had given the fire alarm, but she could throw no light on the murder, so then the child was questioned. In response the boy, 'without any blushing feare (as commonly is seen in Children)', told how his father had returned when his mother was abed 'and first used some churlish speech unto hir' and then 'drew out his knife, cut hir throate and so left hir'. He was able to describe the knife, but when asked why it was his father committed the deed 'hee coulde not say any thing'. The father was sent for and examined. He denied committing the crime and claimed to have been at work all day. The coroner asked him to show his knife. It matched the boy's description, but Meaphon claimed it was a knife he had borrowed. The son affirmed it was his father's own. When Meaphon's fellow workmen were examined they said he had been absent from work between 5 p.m. and 9 p.m. on the day in question. Meaphon continued to deny his guilt but was committed to Lewes jail and then, months later, arraigned at East Grinstead assizes. His son was present at the trial and gave evidence 'with a voice lawdable which was in the child admired'. Meaphon was found guilty and sentenced to death. He had denied his guilt before and at the trial. Whether he confessed to the murder at the gallows we are not told.[68]

The lessons to be learnt from this episode the writer keeps to a minimum. In essence they are that murder will always be revealed and the culprit punished for his sin. He hopes the tale 'may move us to repentance and give us grace to eschew the like, Amen'. As to the motivation behind the killing, if we reject the very unlikely supposition that Meaphon slew his wife because he had suddenly gone insane, or the somewhat less unlikely theory that, while brooding, at work, on the animosity between them, he suddenly decided to silence her for ever, we are left with the possibility that he heard from his fellow workers something scandalous about his wife's behaviour and decided to confront her about it immediately, the confrontation leading to violence and her death. The most likely cause for this violence would probably be tales or rumours of his wife's sexual infidelity. This might account for his setting fire to the house (if indeed it was a deliberate act) and thus killing the son whose paternity was now in doubt.

The final years of the Elizabethan period saw the committing of a few murders of a quite sensational sort. One was the killing, in 1597 or 1598, of his wife by Henry Robson, a fisherman of Rye (Sussex). A pamphlet tells us that he was respected by his neighbours, but he was inclined to spend lavishly. He got himself into debt, and then the suits of his creditors landed him in jail, where he was likely to remain for a good while. His wife, who was well liked in the locality, did her best to 'relieve' his misery, presumably by frequent visits and the sending of food. Why Robson took it into his head to kill his attentive wife we are not told directly, merely that he believed he would never get out of jail while she was alive. This suggests he would inherit wealth of some sort on her death and thus be able to pay off his creditors. He explained his situation to a fellow prisoner surnamed Glasier, who replied that, if his own wife stood between him and his freedom, he would certainly kill her. He offered to show Robson how this could be accomplished without incurring suspicion. Glasier was soon released and with Robson's reminder of this conversation in his ears he went to a mercer in Rye, bought a pennyworth of ratsbane (arsenic), and passed it secretly to the prisoner on a visit to the jail. He also instructed him on how to use it.[69]

This, according to the title of the pamphlet, was 'in the strangest manner that ever hitherto hath been heard of', and, indeed, the author was hardly exaggerating. Robson was to mix the ratsbane with 'glass small beaten and wrapt in the skinne of a shoulder of mutton to the quantity of a hasle nut or lesse'. Then, when his wife came next 'to lie with him', conjugal copulation being frequently allowed in Tudor prisons, 'he should convey it into her privy parts', which would ensure her death. When his wife next visited him a week later, he greeted her 'with a dissembling shew of friendship'. When at night she was about to depart, he persuaded her to stay until morning, 'which was the dearest nights pleasure that ever woman had: for in the night', continues the account delicately, 'hee put in practise his former imaginations'. The wife, at home, began to feel herself 'grieved'; her body swelled as the poison 'began to eat into her veins'. She took to her bed, and the physicians who had been summoned agreed she had been poisoned. They purged her but to no effect and soon she died. They were suspicious enough, however, to obtain a licence for her to be 'ripped'; and 'in everie vaine both glass and ratsbane' they found. The physicians were puzzled, being sure these substances could not have come from food or drink.[70]

Therefore the shops in Rye were visited to discover who had recently purchased ratsbane, and one merchant reported that Glasier had bought a pennyworth a fortnight earlier. He was then searched for, but managed to flee the locality. However, someone remembered he had been in jail with the victim's husband, Henry Robson. On checking, they learned that Robson's wife had slept with her husband in the jail less than a week before. 'This all being put together they began to conjecture of the matter.' The Mayor, jurats, and Recorder of Rye ordered Robson brought before them. The Recorder, Master Boulton, informed him, quite untruthfully, that Glasier had told them he had bought ratsbane on Robson's behalf and that they wished to know the reason for the purchase, particularly as he had been 'manifestly accused' of his wife's death. This last must have been the common gossip around the town. When Robson protested his ignorance of the poison and the crime, the Recorder told him that Glasier would be brought to testify to the contrary. At this Robson admitted to having had ratsbane in his possession but claimed it was to kill the rats in the jail. When this explanation was derided, he then said that he had bought the poison because he believed it would break open any lock. The Recorder told him he was lying and that in fact he had mixed ratsbane and glass to poison his wife. If he hoped for 'any favour at our hands', said the recorder, he had best confess how the poison was administered and who advised him to do so. Robson, who seems to have been surprised that the magistrates had discovered the poison and its nature, and believing therefore that Glasier had been arrested and had revealed all, admitted his guilt and revealed how the poison had been administered.[71] He was remitted to jail, tried at the sessions day, convicted and hanged. The account ends with a Protestant prayer about refusing Satan's temptations and avoiding his snares, but this is the only hint of religious propaganda in the piece; there is no reference to repentance by Robson, nor any gallows scene.

The essential newsworthiness of this murder is undeniable. Such a death would be a hot topic of conversation in any century. Also noteworthy was the efficiency of the investigation by the authorities. The account in this respect is notable for what it tells us, at some length, about the examination of the suspect. The magistrate in charge, the Town Recorder, is shown using a ruse employed by criminal-law interrogators over many centuries. This was to pretend, quite falsely, already to possess good knowledge from another source of how the crime had been committed, thus persuading the suspect of the futility of denial and inducing a detailed confession. Nevertheless, we must admit that the law officers of Rye acted with remarkable shrewdness in putting the various clues to Robson's guilt together. Furthermore, their readiness to have the victim's corpse 'ripped', together with the dogmatic findings of the surgeons, suggest that medicine was already thought capable of playing a role in bringing murderers to justice.

In 1601 there appeared in print a piece by Robert Yarington, which combined in one play two quite separate murders, one English, the other Italian. The full title was *Two Lamentable Tragedies. The one, of the murther of Maister Beech, a Chaundler in Thames-streete, and his boye, done by Thomas Merry. The other of a young childe murthered in a Wood by two Ruffians, with the consent of his Unckle.* The Beech murder is set in London, the other near Padua. The play is written in blank verse without division into acts or scenes. In their place the writer provides alternating sections on each murder, each being about 100–150 lines in length early on but much longer towards the end. Yarington tells us the first murder was committed in London recently and that 'most here present' will know the details of his play to be true.[72]

Thomas Merry, the London murderer, is a young man of good reputation, probably a Puritan, who keeps an alehouse called The Bull. He becomes jealous of the worldly wealth of a neighbouring shopkeeper, Robert Beech, who, we are told, has little debt, is well stocked and has £20 put by for emergencies. To acquire this last Merry decides to entice Beech to his upstairs room and kill him. He recognises that his sister Rachel, who lives with him, and his servant Harry Williams, could be a problem, but puts his plan into operation regardless. One Friday evening in August he goes to see Beech, who is in his shop reading, and tells him some friends desire his company at The Bull. Reluctantly Beech agrees to come and is directed to the upstairs room. Merry, who follows behind, had earlier placed a hammer strategically near at hand. With it, as Beech reaches the upper room, Merry strikes him fifteen times on the head. He wipes Beech's blood off his own face and looks in the shopkeeper's purse to find but ten groats. Merry's sister Rachel and then his servant come in and are told by Merry that he was forced to kill in self-defence. Harry Williams is reproachful, suggesting his master should have settled his differences 'in the field' – that is, in a duel. He decides to leave Merry's service, but is persuaded to agree to keep silent about Beech's death. Merry then becomes concerned about Beech's young servant, Thomas Winchester, who had been left in charge of the shop and who must know his master had gone to The Bull. Merry thinks he must therefore also be killed. Rachel offers to go to Beech's shop to see what the boy suspects, but instead Merry goes himself and murders Thomas with seven blows of a hammer to the head. Merry flees home without being recognised; the hammer remains sticking out of the dying boy's skull.[73]

By now Merry's lust for murder has dissipated and he becomes somewhat repentant. With Rachel's assistance he moves the body of Beech to a lower room and covers it with faggots preparatory to moving it out of the house. Rachel, who had been cleaning up the bloodstains, and who does not know her brother is the killer of the boy, is instructed to burn the cleaning cloths because Merry expects that, when the boy's murder is reported and Beech's disappearance noticed, houses in the neighbourhood will be searched. There enter three or four neighbours who comment to each other on Winchester's murder and remark that, while some people believe his master did it, others disagree because of Beech's law-abiding life. 'Then let', says one neighbour of unspecified rank, 'commaundement everywhere be given, | That sinkes and gutters, privies, crevises, | And every place where blood may be conceald, | Be thoroughly searched, swept, washt, and neerely sought, | to see if we can find the murther out.' This man also advises that, in case Beech's body has been thrown in the river, the Thames watermen should be told to bring any man's body floating there to Lambert Hill, the location of Beech's shop. The neighbours then go to see if Beech's dying servant can provide them with any information. He is brought forth 'in a chaire with a hammer sticking in his head'; he is still breathing but unable to speak.[74]

The scene shifts to Merry talking to Harry Williams, who is paying him a visit. Williams again promises his silence about Beech's death and is given cash and a cloak for a visit to a local fair. To disarm suspicion Merry pays a visit to Beech's shop and has a look at the dying Thomas Winchester. He asks the neighbours who are present 'Whie pull you not the hammer from his head', but is told this should not be done before death so as to help the coroner. Relieved to find the boy virtually dead and himself not under suspicion, Merry takes steps to dispose of Beech's body. Rachel produces a bag she has been sent to purchase and which Merry intends to use to move the corpse. Since the weight of the whole body is too great, he uses 'the chopping knife' to cut off the head and legs and then sets off with the torso and arms ('this middle mention of a man') by boat to Southwark in order to throw it in a ditch at the Paris Garden. While Merry completes his grisly work, Rachel quakes with fear and tells him he will burn in hell unless he repents. When he has deposited Beech's torso, he takes the bag, now containing the head and legs, to a 'darke place' near Baynard's Castle, where he abandons it. There enters into the play at this point a Master Cowley, who enquires of Harry Williams why he has looked so unhappy of late. He suggests Harry should tell him of his secret grief, since containing it might ruin his health. Harry refuses, but Cowley insists he will share his woes.[75]

The bag left by Merry near Baynard's Castle is discovered by two watermen. The stage directions read, 'Taking the sack by the end, one of the legs and head drops out.' One of the watermen thinks that Bull the hangman, being too lazy to set a traitor's head on London Bridge and his legs on the gates, has simply flung them in the street. The other waterman, however, points out that this identification cannot be correct since the head is badly wounded and hose and shoes remain on the legs; Bull always strips quartered traitors. One of them has heard of Thomas Winchester's murder and Beech's disappearance from Lambert Hill and they decide there may be a connection; so they carry the bag there. On their arrival the contents are immediately identified as parts of Beech; one of the neighbours there gives them a small reward. Then enters a gentleman with a porter carrying a sizeable load. It is the torso of Beech, which the gentleman's water spaniel had discovered in the Paris

Garden ditch. Presumably, he has come to Beech's shop because of his reported disappearance.[76]

The group of neighbours now resolve to investigate his death. They have already found out that the hammer in Winchester's head (Winchester has just expired at this point) was borrowed from a local cutler, but the latter cannot remember by whom. Their interest, very sensibly, is in the bag that carried the body parts. The seller is found, but he can say only that a young woman bought it. He is therefore taken from door to door to see if he can identify any female denizen as the purchaser. At Merry's he sees Rachel, but he fails to recognise her as his quarry. While Merry is much relieved and believes the danger of discovery is now past, Rachel is concerned about Harry Williams and suggests her brother should have brought him to dinner where they might have persuaded him to continue his silence about the slaying of Beech. Merry is not worried, for he has recently encountered Williams returning from a sermon at St Paul's Cross and got him to reaffirm his promise. Rachel asks if he swore to that effect, but her brother points out that Williams never swears oaths. Merry tells her that, if he escapes discovery as the killer, 'I would endevour all my coming dayes, | To please my maker, and exalt his praise.'[77]

He is out of luck. The intrusive Cowley asks Harry Williams a second time to tell him the cause of his grief and, additionally, why he is not living at his master's house. He eventually gets Williams to admit to 'secret torment'; then to knowing who killed Beech. Cowley quickly points out that failing to reveal such knowledge incurs 'the danger of the lawe' and punishment, which causes Williams to let slip that Merry is the guilty one and that he himself had no part in the murder. Cowley tells him, that if he confesses to 'the officers', he will find 'the favour of the lawe' – that is, escape punishment.[78]

At this point the officers of the law arrive in the form of a constable and three watchmen. They make comments about Merry, whom they have come to arrest following the disclosures by Williams to Cowley, then by one of them, presumably, to the authorities. One officer remarks that Merry is reckoned to be the least likely person in London to have committed murder. Says another, 'Is this the fruites of Saint-like Puritans, | I never like such damn'd hipocrisie', while a third comments, 'He would not loase a sermon for a pound, | An oath he thought would rend his iawes in twaine'. The constable arrests Merry and Rachel. Merry immediately confesses to the two murders but protests that Rachel and Harry Williams are entirely innocent.

The muse Truth then comes on stage to inform the audience of the outcome of the subsequent trials, for, despite Merry's protestations, all three are arraigned. Merry is convicted as principal and is to be hanged, and then his body hanged in chains. Harry Williams is convicted as an accessory but allowed benefit of clergy; Rachel is also found guilty as an accessory but as a female she cannot have the privilege and is to hang. Their offence is 'conceal-ment' of murder. The muse Truth interjects to say that doubtless many of those in the audience actually attended the executions.[79]

Finally comes that infrequent thing in sixteenth-century murder reporting, an execution scene. Merry seeks Rachel's forgiveness for embroiling her, and receives it. Rachel laments the shame of her death and hotly denies the rumour that she induced her brother to commit the murders. Merry, addressing the crowd, admits his guilt, says his conscience is now at rest, that he never killed before and that he has never indulged in fornication or adultery. He adds that he never hated Beech; it was only 'desire of money' and that 'foe of man', 'that great Leviathan', that incited him. The ladder is turned, and Merry hangs. 'Rachel shrinketh', and then addresses the crowd in turn. She warns 'all sisters' how they may unthinkingly conceal 'the wicked deeds of brethren or of friends' to their own peril: 'Conceale no murther,' she urges, 'least it do beget, | More bloody deeds of like deformitie.' Rachel too is hanged. The officer in charge asks for God's mercy on her soul and says 'this spectacle' will teach others to shun the dangers of 'misguided taciturnitie'. He orders the bodies cut down, hers to be given a funeral, her brother's to be conveyed to Mile End and there hanged in chains. There the part of the play devoted to the murder of Beech and his servant ends and the author returns to the Italian crime.[80]

The Merry murders in *Two Lamentable Tragedies* were clearly well suited to the Elizabethan stage, although whether the novel idea of alternating the scenes with others about a very different slaying in Italy was welcomed by the audience, or merely confused it, is hard to determine. Perhaps the difference in location and social setting circumvented this, for the Italian murder was of an upper-class boy-heir by assassins hired by his guardian uncle. The setting was landowning Italy and thus very distinct from commercial and artisan London.[81] Possibly, Yarington was trying to offer something that would have a fascination for all the classes in his audience, gentry and nobles (the travelled classes), as well as London citizenry. If the dialogue, or lack of it, disappointed playgoers, the violence and bloodletting must have been emotionally arousing. The twenty-two blows on the skulls of Beech and young Thomas Winchester, and the hammer embedded in the latter's head and remaining there through two further appearances on stage, must have been a particularly emotive feature. The dismembering of Beech's corpse, the transporting away of the body parts, and their return and display on stage were more than good measure. The playwright was so sure of the emotional impact of the dismemberment of Beech's body, even on an audience inured to the sight of brutal judicial punishment, that he has the muse, Truth, immediately enter and reassure the audience, 'I see your sorrowes flowe up to the brim, | And overflowe your cheeks with brinish teares'; but take comfort, 'this is but a playe'. After Rachel's execution Truth again enters and refers to the 'scarce drie eyes' of the watchers.[82]

Religious belief figures in the play but does not dominate. It is the troubled conscience of Harry Williams that causes Merry's guilt to be revealed. In the latter's gallows speech he mentions the devil as being the creator, at least in part, of his greed. Rachel, eager to save her brother's soul, emphasises that God will 'overpasse' his sins if he laments the slaying of Beech 'with true unfained teares' and lives the rest of his life 'In Gods true feare with upright conscience'. As we have seen, Merry, in his neighbourhood, was known as an abhorrer of oaths, a lover of sermons and a Puritan. More generally, the hypocrisy of 'Saint-like' Puritans is the subject of a scathing remark by one watchman. The play is thus a modest example of the theatre hitting back at the Puritans, whose political influence at this time is reckoned to have been in decline.[83]

Yarington handles Rachel's situation with sympathy. She is reproachful of her errant brother, she is conventionally religious and above all she is loyal. The playwright portrays her end on the gallows as the result of the last of these characteristics, and has her deny she was in any way 'the author of this crueltie', as one rumour had it. If we accept the play as being historically accurate, it appears Rachel may have been convicted unfairly. Like Harry Williams she is said to have been guilty of 'concealment', Yarington meaning she failed to report the crime to the authorities. Here the writer must be in error. Such 'misprision' was only a misdemeanour and punishable by fining. Harry Williams, similarly charged, obtained benefit of clergy, which meant their crime must have been held a felony. What Yarington probably intended to mean by 'concealment' of the crime was their giving Merry support after the deed was committed, knowing his culpability. Yet it might be argued neither Rachel nor Williams should have been so charged, since, as Yarington tells it, Merry never admitted to them he had committed murder, claiming self-defence in one instance and another killer in the second. Obviously, neither the Crown nor the jurors believed Rachel and Williams were ignorant of Merry's committing of murder.[84]

A notable feature of the play is the rapid development of the plot. The pace is a hot one, with Merry committing the two murders almost as the play opens and then working feverishly, and with some success, to cover his tracks. The suspense here alone must have made it, for the times, gripping entertainment. There is also an element of mystery: whether Harry Williams can be relied on to keep silent about the death of Beech; whether Rachel will be recognised by the man who sold her the bag. Another element of mystery must have been the matter of whether Rachel would hang, and whether, if she was so sentenced, she would admit at the gallows to a greater role in the murders than appeared at first sight. Another distinctive feature of *Two Lamentable Tragedies* in comparison with other plays and pamphlets about murder is the relatively protracted gallows scene and the speeches therein by both Merry and his sister. Quite unique is Rachel's somewhat feminist warning to all sisters never to conceal 'The wicked deeds of brethren, or of friends'.[85]

Also of prime interest is the machinery of detection where murder is concerned. Most noticeable in the Beech and Winchester instances is the absence of officialdom. This is partly explained by the fact that Thomas Winchester, with the hammer in his head, did not die until two days after he was attacked, and therefore the coroner could not be approached, as indeed he could not be in the Beech case for lack of a body. The enquiring devolved on neighbours, who initiated a search for Beech himself and for bloody evidence of foul play. Hoping to extract a few valuable words about his attacker, they go to see the dying Winchester, but he is beyond speech. It is one of the neighbours who makes and announces the discovery that the hammer was borrowed from a local cutler. It is to the group of neighbours, who rewarded them, that the two watermen deliver Beech's head and legs. The bag containing Beech's torso is found in the Paris Garden ditch not by the watch or a constable but by a gentleman who, helpfully, if surprisingly, has it carried by a porter back to Beech's house. A neighbour who observantly notices that the bag is a new one finds, in true detective style, the seller's mark. He has it identified by another neighbour, which results in the salter's man, who sold it, being brought forth and asked who the purchaser was. He answers 'a maid', but he does not know her name or address and cannot remember what she wore. Since, however, he claims the ability to recognise her again, the group of neighbours sends him to inspect all the young women in the locality, although without success. All these activities by the denizens of Lambert Hill were eminently sensible and, if pursued further, might have revealed the culprit, but the need for further detective work was removed by Williams's admission of his master's guilt. Thus the play suggests that the middle class of Tudor London was willing and experienced enough to participate effectively in the discovery of murderers, and that self-help was regarded as an important first step in the investigative process.[86]

The last pamphlet we have from the reign of Elizabeth I that describes a particular murder seems to be the one concerned with the slaying of a minister of religion. This was William Storre, MA, late a fellow of Corpus Christi College, in the University of Oxford, who, at the time of his death in August 1602, was vicar of Market Rasen in Lincolnshire. The location of the crime was thus far removed from London, with which, unlike the Page case, there was no apparent connection; there was, however, one with Oxford, where the pamphlet was printed. We are told that Storre was asked, after evening prayer at his church, to give his opinion in regard to a dispute between the 'lords' of the town, on the one hand, and the freeholders and other lesser persons, on the other, over rights in the town's common fields. Storre, though speaking with 'discretion', was thought to 'incline more to the right of the freeholders and the rest of the commons', and the son of one of the town grandees, a Francis Cartwright, who had a 'hot stomacke', vented his wrath in verbal abuse of the minister. Later, in the marketplace, he announced that but for the law he would cut Storre's throat, 'tear out his heart, and hang his quarters on the maypole'. Worried by this overt hostility, Storre sought to have the local justices of the peace restrain Cartwright by bonds or recognizances but got little satisfaction. While he was considering if he should make a complaint to the Court of High Commission, the minister, the next Sunday, gave a sermon that Cartwright, who was present in church, believed was a condemnation of himself. Thus he thirsted for revenge the more.[87]

A week later, when he saw Storre out walking in the morning on the south side of the town, Cartwright hurried to a cutler's, retrieved a sword he was having sharpened there, overtook Storre and attacked him. The pamphleteer, unlike the authors of accounts of earlier Tudor murders, then provides an exhaustive description of all the wounds that Cartwright had inflicted. The first blow at Storre 'cutt his lefte legge almost of'. Then 'making at his head, the other casting up his armes to defend it (for other weapons had he none) he gave him two mortal wounds on the forepart therof thorow the brain-pan: cut of three of his fingers and gave him other two grievous wounds on the outside of either arme, betweene the elbow and the hand, the one to the middest of the arme, and the other more then half in sunder, deviding the maine bone about two ynches one part from another'. 'Thus massacred', Storre fell backwards into a puddle, 'and striving to recover himselfe the splinter bone of his legge halfe cut thorow before, knapt in two and his heele doubled back to the calfe of his legge'. Cartwright, not yet satisfied with the results of his assault, 'continued his rage still more fiercely upon him and gave him another gash on the outside of the right thigh to the very bone. And again on the left knee his legge being bended as he lay, he cut him the fashion and compasse of an horse shoe battring to pieces the whirlbone and the nether part of the thigh bone, that it was most grievous to behold.' At this point a girl came by, and cried out, and Cartwright fled. Neighbours came to the scene, saw Storre wallowing in blood and fled back into the town crying 'murder'. Others carried Storre to the nearest house, where a constable dwelt, and made great efforts to staunch the blood. Next day a bone-setter and 'three or four of the best local surgeons' came. They opened up his wounds and forced together his bones, Storre suffering 'their extremities' for more than three hours without fainting. Unfortunately, the blows had 'so perished his braines' and caused so much loss of blood that he died within a week, although not before he had forgiven and prayed for his enemy.[88]

Whereas the great majority of murder accounts of the period conclude with the perpetrators convicted and/or on the way to the gallows, Cartwright is said in this account to have escaped justice. After committing the deed, he hurried to the house of his father, who pacified his pursuers until the constables arrived and escorted him to a justice of the peace. There 'either for lacke of their due information of the truth or by the corrupt and favourable affection of the magistrate, or both, there was very slender bail taken, and the malefactor by this sleight sent away'. Presumably this means that the younger Cartwright quit the town and escaped indictment and trial. The only valid reason for his escaping process of law that is to be garnered from the text is that no one is said to have observed the start of the assault, although several persons could testify to the severity of the wounds as they appeared minutes later. There appears to have been a debate in Market Rasen over the culpability of the supposed murderer. Cartwright's sympathisers claimed he was 'stirred up', provoked, by Storre or that the minister deserved it because of his habit of reproving 'the corruptions in every corner' and his criticism of the behaviour of individuals.[89]

In addition to providing a straightforward description of the crime and its circumstances, the pamphleteer's apparent intention was to prove that the assault on Storre was indeed murder and to bring Cartwright into court. For the latter purpose he annexed to his account what he called the testimony of four substantial 'juries'. The first of these was a group of the 'better sort' of parishioners, the second several ministers of Storre's acquaintance, the third comprised gentry of the region to whom he was well known, while the fourth was made up of 'learned' men of Oxford University, men whom he had prob- ably known before he came to Market Rasen. These men were not, of course, actual jurors or connected directly with the investigation of the crime or the prosecution of the subject. They were men who could, if asked, testify to the 'quiet carriage' and impeccable character of Storre, and the unlikelihood that he had goaded Cartwright into attacking him. Thus, should the Crown find and consider indicting Cartwright, they would ensure the charge would be murder and not the pardonable crime of killing in chance medley, which was manslaughter.[90]

The story is continued in a second pamphlet, one printed in 1613, eleven years after Storre's death. Apparently, when the Privy Council and the Archbishop of Canterbury heard of the crime, the justice who had bailed Cartwright was removed from the peace commission and the constable in whose house Storre had died was bound over to answer for his behaviour, although the nature of his dereliction of duty is not explained. The case was also referred to the justices of assize, presumably so that on their next visit they might look into the crime thoroughly, even if the chances of arraigning Cartwright were slim, since he had soon fled to the Continent. Cartwright's friends were also busy: they managed to obtain a pardon for him. The 'foulness of the cause' (that is, the murder) they disguised by supplying information that was quite untrue, a practice by no means unknown. They then told Cartwright that it was safe to return to England, which he did. However, Storre's widow, who with her five small children was living on charitable relief from well-wishers, took action of her own. She went to a local magistrate and attempted to appeal Cartwright.[91] 'Appeal' was a medieval form of accusation, one that pre-dated presentment/indictment. It was a formal charge put forward by the victim of a felony, or in homicide cases by the next of kin. It was a private action, not one brought by the Crown, even if it could result in the death penalty.

An appeal rather than a bill of indictment was sometimes the felony victim's choice in the later Middle Ages and earlier sixteenth century, when such a bill was unlikely to be approved by a jury of indictment (that is, found *billa vera*) because of local politics. This was probably one reason why Mrs Storre acted as she did. Another attraction of appeals was that they might produce financial reward, a payment by the appellee to get the appellant to drop the action, which was known as compounding. However, as far as we can tell, this was not the intent of Mrs Storre. She was seeking, primarily at least, the punishment of Cartwright; whether this was personal revenge or for the benefit of society is unclear. Cartwright's lawyers informed him that she would not compound and that they had tried to discover a legal flaw in the appeal (a common way of defeating such a suit) but had failed. Cartwright then fled to the Continent once more. He does not seem to have been willing to appear in court and plead the pardon that had been obtained on his behalf. This was probably because there was doubt as to whether, while it excused Cartwright from the Crown's suit against him, it also negated the appeal, the private action of the widow. Apart from that by Mrs Storre, there are no appearances of the process of appeal in the accounts of late Tudor murders, nor do we read of any other murderer, Black Will (the slayer of Thomas Ardern) excepted, fleeing to the Continent.

There is yet another pamphlet that deals with the circumstances and aftermath of Storre's death and has the additional merit of telling us something about the personality and attitudes of the murderer. It is entitled *The Life, Confession and Heartie Repentance of Francis Cartwright, Gentleman* and was published in 1621, showing that the murder was still of great interest almost two decades later. The piece, which purports to be written by Cartwright himself, has as its stated aim the demonstration of the latter's 'uncleanesse' and the giving of satisfaction to the 'offended world'. While admitting that his violent behaviour and his misfortunes resulted from his own turbulent character, which allowed 'the Devil to build a mansion for himselfe to inhabit', and that 'One impiete begat another', the pamphlet is in part excusatory and intended to repair Cartwright's reputation. Thus had Storre used 'milder reprehensions' he would have 'plucked me out of Satan's snare', states Cartwright. The attack on the minister, so he claimed, was intended to be but 'a slight wounding', but the Devil had made his sword 'pierce deep'.[92]

Cartwright tells us that the appeal by Storre's widow was rejected in court on account of an error it contained, but that his pardon was not allowed by the judges (he suggests, at the King's bidding) for five years during which he was bound over. Although prosecution by the Crown had ceased, Cartwright was compelled by the judiciary to make his peace with the Church, which had excommunicated him for Storre's death. This he did by giving a 'testimonie of my Contrition and Repentance' together with 'a true profession of my Religion' in a convocation of the clergy held at the time of parliament.

Cartwright was involved in other violence subsequent to the murder of Storre. When he sought to marry a woman of his own rank, he was attacked by four men with halberds and left for dead. At Grantham in an unrelated incident he encountered a Master Riggs, who insulted him 'beyond the temper of any humane sufferance', and he killed him. For reasons that are not apparent, but possibly because the bench feared he might be acquitted, the jury that tried him for this crime was chosen by the assize justices rather than by the under-sheriff. Cartwright, who was indicted for murder, was, however, found guilty only of manslaughter and sentenced to a year's imprisonment. He tells us that because of his wasteful ways he was unable, at the year's end, to 'purchase freedom'. Presumably he had not the where-withal to pay his prison charges (debts to the jailer for food, exemption from shackling, and so on). However, he was permitted to join the navy on an expedition to Algiers. Even in this military situation he made enemies, so much so that his commander sent him home. His troublesomeness had won him his freedom.

The collective account of the Storre case stands alone in narratives of Tudor murder. It possesses several unique features. The crime had its origins in a dispute in urban politics, apparently a class and economic one. The victim was a clergyman of good background and qualifications. The deadly assault on the victim and the wounds inflicted are described for once in great detail. The miscreant, at the time when the first pamphlet about the crime was written, was not in custody and was likely to escape justice through the slack or corrupt behaviour of local magistrates. Additionally and perhaps most significantly, one pamphlet itself, through the appending of testimonials to the victim's character, was active participation by the writer, and possibly his patrons, in the process of bringing the criminal to justice: an initiative to supplement the defective machinery of the criminal law. Could it have been inspired by the 'learned' of Oxford University, and the appeal likewise? Needless to say, since the murder was done openly and Cartwright, in the account, never comes to justice, there was no reason for the pamphleteer to refer to God's providence. The nearest thing to strong Protestantism in the account seems to be the stern sermons delivered by the victim.

The second pamphlet, the one printed in 1613, which was concerned mainly with the aftermath of the crime and Cartwright's flight, demonstrates that a murderer of some wealth had ways other than acquittal in the courts of escaping the gallows. Money and friends could obtain him a pardon, flight to the Continent was a possibility (extradition was a political matter and very rare), and lawyers might block any criminal appeal of the old sort. One novelty in this piece is the reference to the punishment of negligent officers of the law.

The third pamphlet, that by Cartwright himself, provides ample proof of his volatile personality, his violent temper, which, combined with a sensitivity to slights, made a deadly combination. His emotionality, high profile, social rank and readiness to demonstrate, whether sincerely or not, a strong Protestant inclination, made him of great interest to clergy of similar beliefs. After he had fled to the Low Countries following Storre's death he received 'continuall solicitings for my amendment', daily letters in fact, from 'Master Trigg', 'a godly preacher' of Leadenham (Lincolnshire). After he had slain Riggs, two ministers visited him in jail. One, 'Master Buddie', stayed with him until he had shed his despair and had resolved on repentance. Such clerical interest and diligence had not secured mention in pamphlets, in regard to Elizabethan murders at least, since the Saunders case. The pamphlet concludes with a section entitled 'Resolution and Religion', a statement of his religious beliefs possibly drawn from his 'testimonie' before convocation. This suggests what may have been another reason why he attacked Storre – namely, his earlier favouring of a small number of tenets of the Catholic faith and patronage that he had received from certain of its adherents among the nobility.

When we reflect on the written accounts of murder produced in the late medieval period and the sixteenth century, several tendencies are discernible. The murder pamphlets of the late sixteenth century derived from the practice of Tudor chroniclers of interpolating short mentions of such crimes among their curiosities and other 'low history' components. The Tudor chroniclers in turn inherited this practice from late-medieval London chroniclers, although, since the printing press had allowed them to write at greater length, they were more informative. Pamphlets describing particular murders, which as far as we can tell from other sources were generally accurate in their information,[93] divided right from the time they first appeared into those written by men using them as a means to propagate their particular brand of religion, strong Protestantism, and those written by authors who, although they usually included some religious maxims pro forma, were more eager to entertain than to improve the earthly behaviour of their readers.

If we except murder by poison and the Storre case, there is one notable shortcoming in virtually all the deaths described. It is the lack of detail. Victims are hit on the head with blunt instruments, have their throats cut or their necks broken, and are stabbed with daggers in head, neck or chest, but in most cases we are told this in a single line. The writers do not give us the gory details so much beloved by later describers of violent death. This may be because one of their major sources, coroners' inquests, did not provide such information, but it may also have been because Tudor men and women were so used to killing; not that of human beings, of course, but of animals, which they themselves frequently butchered for domestic purposes. There can have been few men and women, even in London, who did not know how to stun an animal and cut its throat. Flowing blood did not afright. However, murder by poison, which was uncommon (or at least its discovery was), was much feared, and the effect on the victim was usually recorded with more care.

In contrast with the extensive coverage of the executions of traitors in reports of treason cases, hanging scenes were not dominant in accounts of sixteenth-century murder. Several of the latter do not offer one at all because the reporter wrote his piece before the execution; but, even if the account was written after the event, such an episode was not de rigueur. When executions were included, it might be because the murderer had denied his guilt to that point and the crowd (and readership) wished to discover if denial was maintained when death was imminent. It might also be because a murderer, although he admitted guilt, had hitherto shown no repentance, but now was expected to, and in so doing give clues as to why he had committed the crime. There is no example, apart from William Sherwood, of a condemned principal murderer being noted in any pamphlet as refusing to repent before he or she was executed. The reporting of last speeches by murderers seems to have started only with the executions of Ann Saunders and Ann Drury in 1573, although Lord Stourton's few words and prayer at the gallows (1557) have survived. Not all last words had a religious connotation – that is, confessing or repenting of sin in order to get a better deal in the next world – though there are sometimes apologies for past behaviour to relatives and associates, and general concern for dependants they will be leaving behind.

While the executions of murderers got limited journalistic attention, the corpses of their victims might draw considerably more. They might be attributed with supernatural powers. Before burial, or even after exhumation, they were believed to be capable of revealing the culprit through indicating by a wink, a change of facial colour or an issue of blood (cruentation, as it is sometimes called) that he or she was then present. The corpses of murderers also held an interest. The location of the hanging, which was often the site of the crime itself, was always noted. So was whether the body was left, as part of the sentence, to rot in chains as a warning to would-be murderers, instead of being taken down a day or so after execution. What happened to the ashes of female murderers executed by burning, we are not told. Indeed, whereas there is some comment on the scene at several hangings, there is nothing similar in regard to burnings, perhaps indicating that many persons felt that this method of execution was too brutal.

Women murderers were likely to add to the popularity of any pamphlet or even chronicle. The presence of women within an account as either murderers or murder victims may well have been sexual titillation to a readership whose lives were regulated, even dominated, by religion. Neither the chroniclers nor the authors of pamphlets can be said to have been particularly hard on murderesses. They were ready, mostly, to allow excuses for their venture into murder, to indicate, for example, that their motivation was love for a man of lesser wealth than their husband, not economic gain. Forced marriages, it is hinted, were a factor in husband-murder cases. On the other hand, the accounts do not play down the women's duplicity towards their spouses while plotting to do away with them. Pamphlet authors were not averse to writing about wife-murder. The Kynnestar case of 1573 shows that this was true from the beginning of murder-pamphlet production. In the Meaphon and Robson cases the writers are particularly hostile to the culprit husbands; in the Robson case the author is also very sympathetic towards the victim wife, portraying her as being singularly blameless.

No modern-day reporter of murder, producing his account in book form, would dare to exclude the basic cause of the crime; he would, indeed, in all probability devote a substantial section to that aspect of the case. Sixteenth-century pamphlet writers, however, seem to have had few scruples about dealing with causation in the vaguest manner. It is difficult, therefore, for the historian to be sure of the reasons for the murders of Abel Bourn and Richard Hobson, or those committed by Kynnestar and Meaphon, or why exactly Cosby quarrelled with Lord Bourke. Probably it was because coroners' inquests and magistrates' examinations were only incidentally interested in causation. Motive is most clearly displayed in pamphlets and chronicles where wives arranged the murder of their husbands, or where the deed was done in order to acquire the victim's wealth. There is no suggestion in the reports of any of the murders that contemporaries thought that the culprit was mentally deranged, although to modern eyes the behaviour of Kynnestar, especially, seems to have been decidedly odd.

Sixteenth-century writers of murder pamphlets show little interest in the workings of the criminal law. There is virtually no detail provided about the trial of murder suspects. Examining is mentioned, but only briefly, and the same is true of coroners' inquests. The techniques of detection at the operational level get greater mention, but largely in the recognition of clues made available through what was regarded as the providence of God. There is nothing like the description of detection provided in the reports of some witchcraft cases of the period. The fact that the discovery of the murderer was attributed to God's providence suggests not just the religious inclination of men and women at this time but also their lack of faith in the ability of law officers to investigate with success. It may also tell us that people really believed, despite the existence of maxims like 'murder will out', that few murderers were ever detected and charged.

Yet detective skills were not so primitive that miscreants did not feel the need for alibis. We notice that Nicholas Lincoln bought shoes at a market for children he had arranged to have murdered at that very time. Like Mrs Page, he was most careful not to enter premises where he believed the bodies to lie without the presence of witnesses. Ralph Meaphon may well have hoped that his absence from work in the early evening would not be noticed by his fellow workers, and that his house, son and the evidence of murder would be destroyed by fire; he denied that he had returned to his home during working hours. Henry Robson's explanation of his possession of ratsbane was that he intended to use it to kill rats in the jail, and then, when this alibi was refuted, he said it was to break open the locks. The pamphlet writers do not lay any great emphasis on such subterfuges; rather they record them as evidence of the villainy of the murderers and perhaps to show that they were soon exposed nonetheless.

Mystery is an important element in the presentation of modern murders, but, unsurprisingly, sixteenth-century pamphlet writers and chroniclers usually eschewed it. They did not wish to create doubt as to who was the guilty party, nor to question the homicidal intent of the same. However, the play *The Lamentable and True Tragedie of M. Arden of Feversham in Kent*, which appears to be historically fairly accurate, subtly seeks to reduce the responsibility of Alice Ardern for the murder of her husband, a strategy designed perhaps to create ambivalent feelings in the audience about how much she was really to blame, and to cause them to ask themselves whether Thomas Ardern was a cuckold or a bawd. Not dissimilarly, the play *A Warning for Fair Women* seeks to put the blame for the murder of George Saunders largely on the shoulders of George Browne and Ann Drury rather than those of his own wife. Saunders is called 'ancient' and implied to be overbearing towards his spouse, who is portrayed as youthful and being exploited by the other conspirators. Playgoers must have been uncertain how responsible Ann Saunders was for her husband's death, and indeed, until fairly late in the play, whether she was responsible at all. This mystery was doubtless intended. Whether Rachel Merry was a principal, an accessory, or completely innocent in her brother's crime, was also left to the audience or reader to decide. These dramatic presentations of murder, doubtless inspired in part by contemporary pamphlets, were based, we notice, essentially on crimes where there was opportunity for plenty of murderous action on stage because there was either a plurality of slayings or there was more than a single attempt to kill one person, and where women were involved.

Tudor accounts of murder, as is apparent from the cases examined above, were in no way formulated according to a single model, even if there were a number of common elements in their content. Many of the features of murder accounts that, it has been argued,[94] became standard in the seventeenth century are vestigial or lacking in these earlier writings. In the chronicles and pamphlets of the Tudor period there is little emphasis on the certainty of punishment for the murderer, only occasional mention of the devil, and hardly anything about the 'slippery slope' whereby small sins or an irreligious life ultimately lead to great crimes. There is little 'horror of conscience', no reference at all to the dreams of the killer or the victim, and mention of the last words of the latter is rare. Just as exceptional are the occasions when 'nature' reveals the culprit. Cruentation occurs in only three cases and touching of the corpse not at all. Only the contemporary account of the Storre case can be regarded with any degree of confidence as an effort by the pamphleteer to influence justice, which was to ensure that Francis Cartwright was indicted and, perhaps, was prevented from obtaining a pardon for his crime.

While Protestant sentiment is apparent in a good number of Tudor murder accounts, a few others may have been used for semi-covert propaganda of a political as much as a religious nature. The Hall/Grafton report of Hun's death ought, probably, to be included in such a category, and the account of the slaying of Richard Hobson more certainly, since in the year of its printing Jesuit missionaries were beginning to reinforce the faith of the Catholic minority in England and Edmund Campion and seven associates were put on trial for treason. The pamphlet on the murders of Page and the Lincoln children displays the writer's concern about the fair application of the law, while the describer of the Lincolnshire murders in *A world of wonder* seems to be eager to draw attention to disaffection among the London apprentice class.

Similarly uncommon in Tudor accounts of murder, but worthy of notice, is sympathy expressed for those who suffered from the crime. The pain inflicted on the victim is mentioned hardly at all. Only the death by poison of John Brewen and the demise from multiple wounds of William Storre run to more than a few words. On the other hand, Elizabethan pamphlet writers appear to have been the first describers of murder who expressed directly what the victim's death must have meant to his or her dependants. The pamphleteer who wrote on the Hornchurch and Aylesbury murders had strong views on this matter: 'Looke, looke ye murderers how many miseries ye bring to those that live . . . the parents, wives, followers of those you murder'; not to mention, he adds, to your own parents, wives and children. The shock to innocent wives of perpetrators draws similar comment from the writer on the Greenoll murder. There is another expression of social concern by the first writer elsewhere in his pamphlet. He commends strongly the gallows speech of a man who had murdered his stepson, which asked that step-parents should 'remember the children . . . committed to their patronage' and see they were 'used as derely as their naturall children'. The author of the pamphlet about the murder of Mrs Kynnestar by her husband shows in contrast a sensitivity in another direction, namely in regard to marital discord that might lead to murder. He suggests all men should take good care to behave themselves in living with their wives, and separate from them if the partnership becomes recriminatory.

Psychological explanations for changes in society are not usually well received by historians but one such may help us to understand the great interest in accounts of murder in the late Tudor period. Religion may have been a partial reason, but that part was not a dominant one. Nor can we allow more than a tip of the hat to the theory that the genre of murder accounts was fuelled by a desire to aim a blow at the Tudor patriarchy. The later sixteenth century was an age characterised by a noticeable improvement in the material comforts and well-being of the main readership, the middle and tradesmen/artisan classes. Public order had improved since earlier in the century, the threats to law-abiding men and women and their property had receded and some of this section of the population had sufficient time (and skill) to read, and also to watch plays.[95] This amelioration in the rigours of everyday life was probably one reason for the rise in sensitivity in regard to crime and violence, and human tragedy at large. Together they fostered a fascination with the arousal and expression of human emotion to which Tudor crime gave rise; and murder was crime, violence and human tragedy epitomised.

As to sixteenth-century accounts of murder in chronicle and pamphlet, we must admit that, although much more informative than those in medieval sources, they are indubitably exiguous and superficial. Yet without them our knowledge of many murders, infamous in their own decade, would be almost zero. Luckily the circumstances of a small number of murders have left traces in other Tudor writings, notably in governmental and other record sources, and these can be used to supplement contemporary accounts where such exist. What follows, therefore, in each of the subsequent four chapters, is an attempt to provide a longitudinal study of a notable murder case using as wide a range of contemporary sources as possible as well as commentary by writers of later centuries where apposite and well informed. What emphasis there is in these investigations is on legal process, an essential precaution when discovery, indictment and conviction depended then, as accurate modern assessment depends now, on understanding the niceties of the law. Happily, the four murder cases are of such compelling interest that they easily bear the intrusions of the historian.

Chapter 3

THE BILDESTON MYSTERY

In the 1520s Bildeston, in Suffolk, a village about 12 miles south-east of Bury St Edmunds and 10 miles west of Ipswich, had a population, so it has been calculated, of just over 300 persons. The inhabitants had the right to hold a weekly market, and also a three-day fair in late September, but the chief economic activity was the making of cloth. So that they might learn about the making of the staple products, broadcloth and vesses, men came to Bildeston from the Continent. One clothmaker there, John Stansby, had no fewer than twelve Italians working for him.[1] A newcomer of another sort was Philip Witherick, who is at the centre of this story. He appears to have settled in Bildeston in 1528 or 1529, arriving from Hadleigh, Suffolk, 5 miles distant to the south-east, the original home also of his wife Margery. Witherick, ten years later, was a fairly wealthy inhabitant of Bildeston. One of the village constables thought he was worth just short of £20 a year, while another player in the drama that was to unfold said his goods were reputed in the village to be worth about 100 marks. Philip Witherick kept a number of livestock (we know he had three troughs in his backyard) and may have been a dairy farmer, but he is also reported as 'making a cloth' from time to time.[2]

The sequence of events that led directly to Philip Witherick's trial for murder commenced about the end of September 1537, when Ambrose Letyce, a tailor, came to board with him. Ambrose seems to have found a number of customers in Bildeston for whom to work, but on Tuesday, 18 December, at 6 a.m., he left Witherick's house, telling the wife he was going to work for a carpenter, Elmen, for two or three hours, and would return by noon at the latest. In fact he did not return at that time or later; he disappeared. The reason given at a later date for his disappearance was debt. Philip Witherick had demanded from him twelve shillings owed for meat and drink, while another debt, to a Mr Vynes, was also causing Ambrose to become nervous because Vynes was known as a 'hasty gentleman'.[3]

The failure of Ambrose to return to his lodgings at the Withericks, especially as he had left his gear there, caused much concern in Bildeston. A village constable later on deposed that Ambrose's disappearance created a great 'rumour' there. What specifically this rumour was is not apparent, but we can safely infer that it was believed that Philip Witherick had in some way been responsible for Ambrose's failure to return. Significantly, a visitor to Bildeston who had known the Withericks when they lived in Hadleigh claimed, at a later date, that he had heard that Philip Witherick was in trouble over his lodger's absence as early as about a 'se'ennight' before Christmas, which must have been very close to the time of Ambrose's disappearance.[4] We may conclude, therefore, that unless there was a great inventor of malicious gossip at hand Witherick's troubles arose largely from his having a bad reputation in the community. However, later on, when this feature of the case was looked into on the King's Council's instructions, evidence of hostility against him proved difficult to discover. Examinees affirmed that there was no malice between Witherick and any other person in Bildeston except one Robert Downyng, a clothier, who had a definite grudge against him. As for bad relations between Witherick and Ambrose Letyce, William Thrower, one of the two Bildeston constables, stated that he knew of no malice between the pair, and Margery Witherick said the same.[5]

Two days after Ambrose had disappeared Philip Witherick began a personal search for his lodger, although how diligently and extensively we are not told. The likelihood is that he made a determined effort, for he probably knew already that the 'rumour' was a dangerous one: it was that he had murdered Ambrose. At about the same time the two constables of Bildeston, William Thrower and Nicholas Vincent, their suspicions aroused by the abandoned gear, went to seek the advice of a local justice of the peace, John Spring of Lavenham, a man of more than local reputation. The justice advised that if by Christmas Ambrose had not reappeared in Bildeston 'to were his best gere' they should bring Philip Witherick before him. Since Ambrose was still missing on 26 December, they did as Spring had suggested and the justice made Witherick provide two sureties. Philip was now officially under suspicion, but there was probably no restriction on his continuing search for Ambrose, a task he must have attended to with an increasing degree of anxiety. It is possible that the local law officers also conducted a search, but if they did so no record of it has survived. There was another searcher for Ambrose, one about whom, on the other hand, we do possess a fair amount of information. This was an itinerant cooper named John Thompson, who had appeared in Bildeston just before Christmas and lodged at the Crown Inn. While there he had a conversation with Witherick's wife and learned about Ambrose's flight. He promised Margery Witherick he would go 'about the country' and see if he could find him. He set off immediately.[6]

What the law officers, whom we have met, were doing in the two weeks following Christmas is unclear. We do know that another official entered the case at this point. He was William Gawger, the manorial bailiff of Bildeston and thus the local representative of the lord of the manor, who was Henry Bourchier, Earl of Essex. That this bailiff rather than the constables or one or more justices of the peace should soon be the main protagonist in what was becoming an attempt to charge Philip Witherick with the murder of Ambrose Letyce is slightly less remarkable when we notice that his employer, the Earl, had quarrelled with some of the residents of Bildeston in the recent past.[7] He may therefore have expected his bailiff to administer there with a heavy hand, even involving himself in criminal law matters, rather than exercising authority in a more traditional way. If this was in fact Gawger's mandate, it would help to explain how it was that he took not merely a part, but a leading part, in getting Philip Witherick charged and brought to trial.

The first indication that Gawger had made the case his own was around 8 or 9 January 1538, when he called on Margery Witherick when her husband was out. He told her he had spoken with Philip, 'who had told him many circumstances of the matter'. From this he deduced that Philip 'was in a greate faulte'. What these circumstances were, what Witherick said in his defence then and at later stages in the legal preliminaries to the trial and at the trial itself, we are never told. We may surmise that he explained that his threats to Ambrose in regard to money owed had never led to actual violence against the tailor. Gawger then told Margery she should look out for herself 'and playe a wise parte', since, because of her husband's 'comonyng and trifeling in the matter', he believed Philip was guilty. Of what crime he was guilty the records do not state at this point, but it can only have been causing Ambrose's death. The bailiff told Margery that if Philip was convicted of the crime she would at least get her 'raiment' and a third part of her husband's goods. He added, however, that he felt pity for her and her children and therefore if she acted sensibly in the matter he would guarantee to get all her goods returned to her. What he hoped she would do, although he never said so directly, for he was cautious in his speech, was give evidence on examination and in court against her husband. Gawger was unsuccessful in getting Margery to betray Philip on this occasion, but on each of the two following nights he sent a messenger to remind her of what he had said and again to advise her to 'helpe herselfe asmyche as she coulde'.[8]

Once more Margery Witherick seems to have refused the bailiff's requests. We do not know how investigations by Gawger and the constables progressed later that month, but by the beginning of February the bailiff had turned his attention to the Witherick children, Martin, who was 11 years old, and his sister Mate, who was 6. By then Martin Witherick had already pointed to his father as having murdered Ambrose. Indeed, we may suspect that it was Martin's accusations that had caused the birth of the 'great rumour' in the first place. On Candlemas night (2 February) Gawger and his fellow investigators, who now included the clothier Robert Downyng, had Mate Witherick brought to the latter's house to be questioned about Ambrose's suspicious disappearance. The little girl, apparently without any personal knowledge of the event, said her father had killed Ambrose, though she denied seeing a certain Edmund Neve help to carry the body away, as her brother had reported.[9] A little later in the month Gawger took young Martin with him on a journey to 'Dunmow' in Essex, about 25 miles from Bildeston, which was the bailiff's home. Martin, when questioned about this episode at a later date, made a very revealing statement. While there he had seen Gawger go into the church graveyard, locate some 'bonnes [bones] of men that were newly cast up ther', and put a number in his bonnet. These they took back with them to his house in Bildeston, where he locked the doors and burned the bones. His plan, it was later revealed, was to plant false evidence.[10]

From early in March the legal proceedings against Philip Witherick began to accelerate. On Ash Wednesday (6 March) the bailiff took Witherick to his master, the Earl of Essex. Apparently he went with 'good will', that is to say voluntarily, not under arrest. Thrower, the constable, and Robert Downyng also went, their reason being to seek the advice of the Earl concerning Witherick's threat to have from them the costs 'that he had bene put to in this matter'. Such aggressive talk by Witherick suggests he was far from admitting any guilt and believed the suspicions against him were maliciously inspired. As her husband was taken to the Earl, Margery Witherick went to John Spring, the justice of the peace, for advice. When she mentioned to Spring that Philip was the nephew of John Witherick, abbot of the important priory of St Osyth in Essex, the justice told her to go and see the abbot and obtain from him a letter in her husband's favour addressed to the Earl. The inference is that it was believed the latter would be the decider of Witherick's fate. In addition to the letter, the abbot sent one of his servants to see how Philip Witherick 'was handlyed and delte with'. Margery stayed with the abbot for a week, presumably awaiting better news.[11]

In the meantime Gawger and Downyng hastened back from the Earl's to Bildeston, visited the Witherick house, seized all Margery's goods and took Martin to a house known as 'Lynens', which they seem to have used as a base for their operations. We may take it that the Earl was unimpressed by Witherick's denial of guilt and the abbot's letter but warned Gawger more evidence was needed if Philip was to be convicted. To remedy this perceived deficiency the bailiff sought to obtain testimony that would support Martin Witherick's tale of murder. On 9 March when at Lynen's house he instructed the constable, Thrower, to fetch Edmund Neve. This was the man who, as we have seen, was said by Martin (who claimed he was told so by his sister) to have helped his father dispose of the dead Ambrose. The constable also went to the Witherick house to fetch little Mate, but she cried and it was left to Downyng to calm her and bring her to Lynens for a second interrogation. Mate was questioned about the words imputed to her by her brother, but she denied ever uttering them. This was sufficient for Edmund Neve to be sent on his way and Mate taken home. Doubtless Neve had been there to confront the child-testifier should she accuse him.[12]

The boy Martin remained at Lynens with Gawger and Thrower. The men were talking about the case around the fire when Martin asked them to go out into the backyard with him. This they did, and 'there the boy shewed that his father killed Ambros and that John Willson dyd helpe his father to bere hym awaye'. Additionally, Martin gave them some directions about where the body now lay. Thus the three went and searched, with the aid of cromes, pools in several meadows. When they came to a meadow belonging to one Harry Rycroft, Martin assured Gawger and Thrower that this was definitely where the body lay. The men searched two or three deep pools along the river there, but found nothing. Incensed by their failure, Thrower called Martin a 'horson boy' and a 'naughty lying boye'. Apparently unabashed, Martin then offered another version of where Ambrose's body had gone. He said his father had hurled Ambrose into their well, a deed that Gawger and Thrower said was impossible, since there were always women working there. However,

Thrower asked the bailiff to forgive Martin his lies if he now told the truth about Ambrose's death. Martin, given this final opportunity, then launched into an entirely different story. His father, he stated, smote Ambrose down with a staff 'and than pluckyd hym into the bakhouse' where, on a trough, he 'choppyd of his hed' and threw it 'undyr the lede and so choppyd hym all to peeces and so brent [burnt] hym . . . trough and all'. His mother Margery, Martin added, 'with the hot water washed awaye the blode'. We are not told how Gawger and Thrower greeted these latest revelations. Gawger, at least, may have felt that they would serve his purpose.[13]

The bailiff then called on Thrower, Downyng and some other men to go to Witherick's house to assess the amount of corn stored there and to make an inventory of Philip's goods. While they were all in the kitchen there, Thrower noticed a heap of ashes. These, on stirring, revealed some bones, probably the ones acquired by the bailiff at Dunmow and covertly planted. Gawger told his helpers to 'look narrouley for some tethe, for that wylbe good evidens'. At a later date one of the visitors stated he had heard that Robert Downyng did, in fact, find a tooth in the ashes, but another of the group deposed, contrariwise, that there were no teeth discovered there. A day or two later Gawger took Martin Witherick and some of the bones to the Earl of Essex. This was probably to show he now had additional evidence, and to have the boy give Bourchier his latest version of Ambrose's demise. The Earl may have wanted to see Martin directly accuse his father (Philip was still at the Earl's house) and to listen to what words passed between them. A week later the bailiff brought the Witherick father and son back to Bildeston, the former 'like a prisoner', and for the moment kept them in his own home.[14]

Even before Martin was taken to the Earl, the bailiff and the constables had turned their attention in part to Margery Witherick. Threatening to take her too to the Earl, they urged her to tell the truth about Ambrose's death, since her son had told all and, so they said, her husband had confessed a great deal about the matter. Margery persisted in denying she knew anything about a murder, so she was locked in a room in Constable Thrower's house. In the few days she was imprisoned there Margery became so sick that she was given the last rites. At some unspecified point Thrower asked her how it was she knew nothing of a murder that had taken place in her own home. To this she replied, 'Thrower . . . for the passion of God desire me not to saye otherwyse then the truth for hurting of myn own soule.' Moved by this, Thrower ceased to badger her.[15]

On Sunday, 24 March, Gawger came to see Margery and told her that, by refusing to confess, meaning refusing to say her husband had killed Ambrose, she had lost her chance to 'tarry at home' and must now go to the assizes with Philip; 'and then thow shalle see wether thow shalle not be compelled to confessyth the trewthe', he added. So it was. By the next afternoon Margery was at the Bury St Edmunds assizes, where her husband was one of those being arraigned. There one justice came down from the bench, led Margery to a nearby house and examined her about Ambrose's supposed murder, 'whether she knew her husband guiltie therof'. This Margery 'expressly denied'. Then Gawger appeared, bringing with him her son Martin, who said openly in his mother's presence that his father was guilty of murder. The boy gave his account of the crime as he had just given it at the bar of the court to the justices. The justice who had examined Margery then said to her 'thou seyst what evidence is layde . . . therefore loke to thyselve, whether thow wylte dye with hym [i.e. Philip] or save thy lyve'. The implication of these words was that Margery, if she would not provide the required evidence, was to be arraigned as an accessory to murder, a capital offence; for had not Martin said that she it was who had washed away Ambrose's blood? Yet still Margery refused to fall in with their wishes.[16]

Then George Colte, a justice of the peace, took Margery aside to try yet further persuasion. Said an obviously distraught Margery, 'Alas, what shall I do, I wolde fayne save myselve but for the peril of my soll, for if any suche thing was done yt was not done in my howse.' Colte answered that the evidence laid against her husband was so clear that he was certain it must be true; so 'loke to thy selve'.[17] Finally Margery yielded, saying, 'then lett yt be as the boye hath saide for me'. She had decided to agree that her son's tale was the truth, although she knew full well it was all lies. William Thrower also spoke to Margery at the Bury sessions and in a manner similar to that of George Colte and the justice who had examined her. In answer to the Bildeston constable Margery pointed prophetically to the dangers physical and spiritual of agreeing with the charge against her husband: 'Alas Thrower,' she said, 'how shall I do if this matter be proved contry a nother daye [to] that I have said'. Thrower's response was to advise her 'to aske councell'. He also reported Margery's words to one of the justices, and for so doing, and maybe for his advice to her, he was rebuked and committed to the custody of the sheriff.[18]

The details of Philip Witherick's trial have not survived. We do not know how the charge against him was formulated and thus we have no knowledge of how Ambrose was supposed to have died, in the law's eyes at least, and when. We do know that only Gawger the bailiff and young Martin Witherick gave evidence in court. Margery's affirmation of her son's tale may have simply been reported by Colte, the Justice of the Peace, or taken the form of a deposition. It was stated at a later date that 'the bones' found in the ashes at Witherick's house, which the bailiff had transported there from Essex, were displayed as evidence at the trial. With his own son speaking against him and the support given to this tale by his own wife, by Gawger and by the bones, Philip Witherick was convicted of murdering Ambrose Letyce and adjudged to be hanged. The sentence, in accord with sixteenth-century practice, would have been carried out within hours, probably in the early morning of Tuesday, 26 March 1538, and news of it would have reached Bildeston by that afternoon.[19]

Margery Witherick had been taken back from Bury to Bildeston as soon as she had given her agreement to her son's statement on his father's guilt. We do not know if she and her children were immediately turned out of the family home because of Philip's conviction. Concern over their fate on the part of the Withericks, and perhaps of their neighbours also, must have suddenly been pushed aside when, about two weeks after Philip's execution, startling news came to Bildeston. Ambrose Letyce had not been struck down and dismembered by his host, but was alive and well in Essex. The bringer of these tidings was the itinerant cooper John Thompson, who before Christmas, as soon as Ambrose had disappeared, had told Margery Witherick that he would look for her lost lodger.[20]

The account that Thompson gave later on of how he discovered the missing man was as follows. On hearing of Ambrose's disappearance, he went first to 'Ardeley' (Ardleigh), Essex, because, he said, he had been told an Ambrose had also recently disappeared from there. It turned out that they were not the same man and this he reported back at Bildeston.[21] John Thompson seems to have been, as well as a cooper, a semi-professional finder of lost persons, for then he travelled, so he said, down to Essex to look for the Ardleigh Ambrose, not for Ambrose Letyce. On the suggestion of the Ardleigh Ambrose's wife, he set off for the village of 'Wakering' on the Thames estuary. On his way he called at the village of Prittlewell, only about 4 or 5 miles from 'Wakering', both villages being about 45 miles south of Bildeston.[22] There he worked for a few days for another cooper, one John Nele. When moving a pipe of sack for Nele on Friday, 29 March, he 'fortuned to cast his eye asyde' and 'spied the said Ambros Letys'. He went to him 'and toke hym by the hande and renewed his acquentance with him', although without telling him of the troubles Philip Witherick had encountered because of his disappearance. Thompson did, however, tell other men in Prittlewell about Witherick's predicament and ask them to bear witness to Ambrose's presence there. Thompson then left Prittlewell, where he had been for about four days, and travelled to Hadleigh. There he informed Henry Doyle, a justice of the peace, of his discovery. The news came too late to save Philip Witherick, whose execution he heard of from two sawyers on Dedham heath on 1 April, just before he reached Hadleigh. Doyle it must have been who sent Thompson back immediately to Prittlewell to bring up Ambrose. Thompson must have ridden hard, for he was back in Prittlewell on 2 April, but the journey turned out to be fruitless. This was because the constable of Prittlewell refused to allow Ambrose's return, for he had received instructions to ensure Ambrose appeared before the Chancellor. It seems the Council had already heard about the mysterious Witherick case and had decided to investigate.[23]

Undoubtedly, King Henry's chief minister at the time, Thomas Cromwell, was concerned about the case, but it was under the authority of the Chancellor, Sir Thomas Audley, an Essex landholder of increasing magnitude, and the Council, that Suffolk Justices of the Peace John Spring, Henry Doyle and Thomas, Lord Wentworth, conducted several examinations in mid-April 1538 of persons who had investigated Ambrose's disappearance or given evidence concerning the supposed murder. The first of these, conducted on 13 April, was of the executed man's son Martin. Then followed the examining of the Bildeston constables, of John Thompson, Ambrose Letyce and Margery Witherick, all before 25 April; the boy and the constables were each questioned on two separate occasions. By sixteenth-century standards it must have been a thorough investigation. For the historian there is satisfaction in the survival of the depositions of so many players in the drama, but there is also one tantalizing deficiency in the record evidence. There survives no examination of the chief protagonist in the prosecution for the Crown, the Bildeston manorial bailiff, William Gawger.[24]

The interrogatories (questions) that examiners used or were expected to use have luckily survived. They were obviously devised by someone, doubtless connected with the Council, who already had a good number of facts about the case at his disposal. Central to the investigation was the need to discover

Martin Witherick's motivation in accusing his father. The belief was that some adult had given him encouragement, perhaps even suggested the accusation to him. Another question was intended to discover how the suspicion that Ambrose had been killed first arose. Several questions were concerned with the pressure put on Martin and his mother to give the evidence they did, who pressed them, and whether rewards were promised. There was a question that hinted at the irregularity of taking a felony suspect, which Philip Witherick was, to be examined by the manorial lord, the Earl of Essex, who held no judicial commission in Suffolk. There were questions about where Philip was kept in custody, for how long and how he was 'ordered' (treated) there. This suggests there was a suspicion that maltreatment accounted for his inability to defend himself against the charges. Enmities already existing in Bildeston at the time of Ambrose Letyce's disappearance were also to be enquired into, especially any enmities between Gawger and the two constables, on the one hand, and Witherick, on the other. Another line of enquiry was intended to establish the movements of Ambrose after his flight from Bildeston, and when and how he came to hear of Philip Witherick's plight and death. Lastly, there was to be investigated Philip and Margery Witherick's marital relationship, whether there was any malice between husband and wife.[25]

The responses to the interrogatories made by the examinees yielded a good amount of information, but without clearly explaining the motivation of the chief players in the drama. However, several reasons for young Martin's denunciation of his father came to light. Martin himself deposed that a village woman, Margaret Dee, told him to say his father had killed Ambrose with a staff, carried his body to the bakehouse and burned it. Furthermore, she had offered him twelve new 'pounts' (points, ties to support his hose) to do so. He said that the bailiff and one of the constables, when he recounted to them Margaret Dee's advice, told him to maintain the part about the slaying but to alter his tale about the disposal of the body. He said it was the constable William Thrower, the one who called him a liar, who suggested he should say his father had thrown the corpse into the water at the back of Harry Rycroft's meadow. Martin added that Thrower promised him 'divers thinges', including a pennyworth of new red points, and later sent these to him by the hand of Margaret Dee. How Gawger the bailiff had influenced him the boy made plain. He told how, at Lynens, the bailiff had asked him directly if 'I dyd see my father kill Ambrose Letyce or not'; to this 'I sayd nay'. The bailiff then retorted that 'he wolde make me to tell hym' so – that is to say, make Martin say he had seen the murder.[26]

In the depositions of others the malevolent role of Gawger is also clearly delineated. His was the original decision to utilise and reinforce Martin's accusations of his father. He tried to bully Margery Witherick into giving evidence. He it was who appears to have planted bones where they would be discovered and used as evidence against Philip Witherick. When about to take Martin to the Earl of Essex, Gawger instructed the boy to repeat there what Margaret Dee had told him to say, adding that in reward 'thow shalte have part of thy fathers goods when thow comest to age'.[27] We may note in passing that this appeal to the boy's cupidity is confirmed by another source, an authoritative one, which states that the bailiff seized Philip Witherick's goods, and then got Martin to say what he taught him, the lies about his father, through Martin's greed for his father's possessions.[28] The boy's answers to the examiners show Gawger continued his corrupt practices at the assizes at Bury St Edmunds. At his father's arraignment, Martin was instructed by Gawger to say in evidence that Philip had 'choppyd of Ambros hede upon the lye trowffe under his lede'. And, if his father in denying it was to say the trough 'dyd stond styll in his yerde', Martin was to say that Philip 'had three trowffes and that one of theyme is brent'.[29]

The role in the drama of John Thompson, the cooper, is a mysterious one. The council member or lawyer, or whoever was responsible for drafting the interrogatories, was obviously suspicious about his behaviour in Bildeston and his journeys. Thompson's deposition shows that he had known Philip and Margery Witherick well twelve years earlier. He was asked if at one time he had been pledged to marry Margery Witherick; presumably some form of liaison between the pair was still remembered. Thompson denied it, saying he had been married when Margery was a maid and lived in Hadleigh. His appearance in Bildeston at virtually the time of Ambrose Letyce's disappearance and the beginning of Philip Witherick's misfortunes was obviously considered not simply coincidental. His readiness to look for the lost man could not be held against him, but there must have been some suspicions arising among examiners and councillors at his mention of a second lost Ambrose and of Letyce's eventual discovery at virtually the place where the other Ambrose was supposed to be staying. Thompson had travelled 45 miles, as he would claim, fortuitously, in the very direction Ambrose Letyce had gone earlier.[30]

It rather looks as though Thompson had advised Ambrose to flee from Bildeston and his debts, and that he knew Ambrose would travel ultimately to Prittlewell. The second Ambrose seems to have been introduced into his deposition to explain his travelling directly to the Prittlewell area. Whether this man was a total figment of his imagination or a convenient and obliging acquaintance is unclear. Thompson claimed that he first heard of Philip Witherick's execution, and thus doubtless his trial, when he was near Dedham on 1 April 1538, about a week after the event. The only other piece of interesting information that Thompson's examination revealed was that he had to go to London to appear before the Council. He states that this occurred on Maundy Thursday, 18 April, when he went up 'to hear of this matter what shuld [be] don therin'. Interestingly, that night he supped, he said, at one Damarall's house with Margery Witherick, who presumably was about to appear, or had already appeared, before the Council. No evidence survives that suggests that Thompson's behaviour was found criminal, or that he was punished in any way.[31]

One of the interrogatories used by the examiners was about marital relations between Philip Witherick and his wife Margery. Only the depositions of their son, Martin, and Ambrose Letyce tell us anything about this important matter, and what they say is contradictory. In one answer Martin stated that, when Margaret Dee advised him to say his father had murdered Ambrose, she concluded with the words, 'and thus thow shalte helpe thy father owght of the waye and save thy selfe and thy mother from betyng'. Martin was examined a second time, and on this occasion the examiner asked what it was that might have induced Gawger and the constable William Thrower to entice him to cause his father's death. He answered that he 'cowde not tell except it were because my mother had so evyll a lyff with my father'. The examiner was obviously very interested in this response, so much so that he uses the nominative pronoun. However, his subsequent question did not elicit the response expected: 'and when I examined the boye how his father and mother agreed to gether, the boye said well, and told me he never saw his father bete his mother.'[32] The evidence concerning domestic violence was thus equivocal, 'evil life' apparently meaning something else, something that the examiners never delved into; at least, there is no record of it.

We also have the comments of the Withericks' lodger, Ambrose, on the marital relations of his hosts. He deposed that he 'never knewe any variaunce or greate malice betwene the said Withryck and his wife but that they lovyd

honestly together lyke man and wife and dyd very seldome stryfe or fall owte
. . . nor that the said Wetherycke dyd ever hit his said wife, to this deponents
knowing'.[33] Additionally there are the ambivalent words uttered by Margery
Witherick herself at the Bury assizes when she was pressured by the justices to
confirm her son's testimony against her husband. As we have already seen, she
answered: 'Alas what shall I do, I wolde fayne save my selve but for the perill of
my soll.' Alongside this response, in the margin of the deposition is a comment
by an examiner or member of the Council: 'This supposeth that she was pute
in feare of her life before.'[34] Maybe so, but in what reference? Margery's words
may have referred to her fear of her husband, but, equally well, they may be
explained by the threat made to her, at both Bildeston and Bury, that if she was
uncooperative she would be arraigned as an accessory to murder.

If we view the Witherick case from the early twenty-first century, it is
tempting to see the boy Martin as a young person deeply troubled by some
form of abuse within his family rather than as one vindictively attempting to
revenge himself on a father who thrashed him for his lies. The evidence of his
mendacity is plentiful: William Thrower, the constable, who was Martin's
godfather, had no doubts he was a liar. If we seek to explain Martin's
behaviour in ways that exclude beatings, revenge and cupidity, we enter the
realm, it must be admitted, of mere speculation. Was Philip Witherick guilty
of what might be called mental cruelty to his wife or children? Were his
sexual demands on his wife excessive or deviant, Margery's predicament being
noticed by her son, who sought to protect her? Did Philip sexually abuse
Martin or his young sister Mate? Was he known by family and neighbours for
buggery with man or beast; did he have a homosexual relationship with
Ambrose Letyce that became known?[35] The attraction of such theories is that,
if true, they would explain the readiness of so many people in Bildeston to
believe the worst of Philip Witherick and account for the immediate creation
of the 'great rumour' when Ambrose disappeared, a key element in the
rumour being rather a collective desire to be rid of him. Was Margaret Dee,
the woman who gave Martin the new points for his hose and told him what
to say about the supposed death, acting as an agent for many others in the
Bildeston community?

Surprising to the modern mind is the fact that the manorial bailiff, William
Gawger, was so ready to press a charge of murder and get Philip Witherick
arraigned when there was but Martin's word that Ambrose was dead. Surely
he must have seen that, if Philip Witherick was convicted and executed, and

it turned out the boy was a complete liar and there was no murder, he would
be in serious trouble, especially if his own concocting of false material
evidence became known. We can surmise only that he was ready to embark
on such a dangerous course because he believed that his master would
protect him if things went awry.[36] It is even possible that the Earl urged him
on. The bailiff may also have been motivated by a desire to have the
administration of the movable goods of a convicted felon, Witherick. There is
no indication in the records, at least, that Gawger wanted to secure a
widowed Margery Witherick as his wife.

A not unlikely reason for the bailiff's hostility to Philip Witherick may have
been village politics. Bildeston had been racked with internal disputes since
the 1520s, when Richard Stainsby (or Stansby), a clothmaker and at that
time the Earl's manorial bailiff, sought to add to his own lands by dubious
methods. In September 1533, Stainsby was presented (that is, accused and
convicted) at the manor court sessions 'by the whole homage' for abusing his
office and 'misdemeaning his copyhold'. Specifically, this amounted to cutting
timber on the demesne, enclosing some of the latter so as to add it to his own
property, and building a large private pew in the village church. The Earl
removed Stainsby from his office and stripped him of his copyhold lands, but
the ex-bailiff fought back, seeking the intervention of Thomas Cromwell and
Archbishop Cranmer. He even sued the Bildeston tenants in the Star
Chamber. He was successful in his suit and regained his copyhold, which he
held until at least 1542.[37]

The new bailiff appointed by the Earl was probably a man more acceptable
to the majority of the Bildeston population, one no doubt ready to oppose the
practices of Stainsby and his supporters. Given the nature of religious and
familial ties at that time, and the fact that Richard Stainsby was quite likely
the godfather of little Mate Witherick, her father Philip may well have been a
Stainsby sympathiser, and thus no friend of the new bailiff Gawger. Philip, we
may conclude, may well have been on the wrong side, the ousted side, in
village politics.

Whether community hostility towards Philip Witherick was compounded
by his religious beliefs is unclear. He appears to have quit Hadleigh about
1529 or 1530. From 1527 Thomas Bilney, a Cambridge don, was preaching
there and introducing the new religion so effectively that by the time Philip
was hanged the town was introducing English into the mass. Foxe praised
Hadleigh as being one of the first towns 'that received the word of God in

England'.[38] The records, it must be admitted, throw no light on whether Philip's migration from Hadleigh to Bildeston was connected with such changes in religion, but the possibility cannot be dismissed. As a nephew of the abbot of St Osyth's, John Witherick, we might have expected Philip to have been conservative in religion and thus likely to find the new religious climate in Hadleigh distasteful and a reason to migrate. Yet, given the interest of Cranmer and Cromwell in Richard Stainsby's predicament, we ought not to come to this conclusion too hastily, especially when we consider Stainsby's installation of the large pew, a practice later associated with the followers of the new religion.

The inhabitants of Bildeston were much engaged in the making of cloth. Philip Witherick seems to have been a farmer, but what type of agriculture he specialised in is not apparent. As we have seen, Ambrose Letyce, when questioned about any enemies that Witherick may have had in Bildeston, said there was no malice between his host and any other inhabitant, but that Robert Downyng 'being a clothier hath borne grudges' against him 'bycause he dyd some tyme make a clothe or two in the same towne'. Ambrose added 'that he had heard say that Downing hath mulled muche on the matter'.[39] There is no doubt that, as Gawger pursued his investigations into Ambrose's supposed death, Robert Downyng, despite holding no office connected with the criminal law, was at his side most of the time and consorted with and assisted the two constables. We notice that Philip Witherick, when he talked of seeking his costs for the trouble he had been put to, was intending to sue Downyng as well as the constables. In all Downyng appears to deserve a good deal of the blame for Witherick's death.[40]

What happened to those responsible for such a grave miscarriage of justice? What impact did it have on those in high authority? The case was considered of sufficient interest by a judge of the King's Bench, John Spelman, to rate a comment in his law reports under the heading 'Bury assizes, Suffolk, Lent 1538'. What caught Spelman's attention was that the hanged man's son 'being under twelve years of age' gave evidence against his father and this was by the procurement of a bailiff, who got the boy's cooperation by bribing him with a promise of his father's goods. Spelman displays no surprise or regret at the way the administration of the criminal law had malfunctioned. Apart from an interest in testimony given by a child, what moved him was the nature of the crime committed by the bailiff, Gawger, specifically whether it amounted to felony. Apparently, the King's

Council, the investigating body, asked the judges of the two benches for their opinion on the matter. They consulted together and then reported to the Council that the offence was not felonious, since Witherick's death came about by process of law.[41]

Of most interest is the recommendation by the judges that the bailiff should be imprisoned for life 'pur cest hirrible act'. Gawger, however, was a slippery customer, or, more likely, protected by someone of importance, perhaps the Earl of Essex. He was certainly not in prison the following spring, since he was involved at that time in another murder, a real one. In March 1539, the local coroner came to Chelsworth, a small village one mile to the west of Bildeston, to examine the dead body of William Thompson, a miller. At the inquest the jury presented that Thompson had been murdered, the death blow being a dagger stroke to the left side of the head. The murderer, they said, was William Gawger, yeoman, of Dunmow, and he had been assisted by Margaret Coley of Bildeston.[42] The latter may have been the wife or daughter of the Roger Coley who had been associated with Gawger in the search for evidence against Philip Witherick.

Gawger was put on trial in the Court of King's Bench at Hilary Term, 1541. Very likely the presentment by the coroner's jury had caused him to be sent for trial at the Bury assizes. However, he was not arraigned there. Perhaps by the influence of his friends, he was able to be remanded back into custody and then, doubtless through a writ of certiorari, have the case removed into the King's Bench. When arraigned there, and prosecuted by the Attorney-General, he successfully argued that the indictment was 'insufficient', that is to say inaccurate. He pointed out that in it he was named as being of 'Dunmow', Essex, when in fact there was no 'Dunmow' in that county, only a Great Dunmow and a Little Dunmow. After a number of men had testified that this was true, Gawger was discharged.[43] He had had to endure less than two years in jail for the murder of Thompson.

The reason for the slaying of William Thompson does not appear in the records. The fact that Margaret Coley assisted Gawger suggests she had a personal quarrel with Thompson. Maybe Gawger was not the principal but simply supporting Margaret in her confrontation, even if he struck the blow; we cannot tell. If, on the other hand, William Thompson was related to the cooper John Thompson, then the murder may have been connected with the Witherick case. We may speculate that Gawger was aggrieved by John Thompson's discovery of Ambrose Letyce, which ultimately led to Gawger's legal troubles. It may even have been that Ambrose had been persuaded or bribed to disappear permanently by a group in Bildeston so that Philip Witherick could be accused of his death. Annoyed by what he considered to be John Thompson's interference, Gawger may have uttered hard words to Thompson's brother or kinsman, which led to blows and the death. In Queen Mary's reign, in February 1556, when the inhabitants of the town of Great Dunmow petitioned the Crown successfully that they might henceforth be a body corporate and have a common seal, twelve men, tenants and inhabitants of the borough, were nominated to be the first burgesses. The sixth name on the list was a William Gawger, probably the ex-bailiff of Bildeston.

Chapter 4

THE MURDER OF THOMAS ARDERN

O n Sunday, 14 February 1551, at seven in the evening at his home in Faversham, Kent, Thomas Ardern, ex-mayor of the town, current jurat and probably the greatest property owner there, was brutally murdered. The crime, which was perpetrated by a group of conspirators led by the victim's wife, Alice, and her lover (a tailor), was the culmination of much plotting and several aborted or unsuccessful earlier attempts. The detailed account of the conspiracy, the murder, and the fate of the murderers which is to be found in Holinshed's *Chronicles*, is the first in-depth description of domestic murder in English history. This in itself testifies to the impact of the crime on contemporary society. John Taylor, the Water Poet, tells us it was a slaying that was still being talked about eighty years later and was likely never to be forgotten.[1]

Although Holinshed in the *Chronicles* makes a cursory apology at the outset that the story 'may seeme to be but a private matter, and therefore as it were impertinent to this historie', he was obviously in little doubt of its great interest to his audience, since he devoted over six pages (about 4,500 words) to its recounting. This was as much space as, for example, he might devote to such events as major wars or rebellions. He had obviously taken considerable trouble to collect accurate information about the case: he tells us that he had had 'the instructions delivered by them that have used some diligence to gather the true understanding of the circumstances'.[2] The tale as set out is a model of factual compression yet at crucial points it possesses sufficient direct speech by the participants to maintain a high level of emotionality. Some of the reported speech is quite memorable and helps to demonstrate the character of the utterer, particularly the criminal mentalities of those involved. What is notable as the story unfolds is the degree to which all facets of the crime are explained: there are no loose ends. The motives of all the players are neatly if concisely laid out, as is the social situation of each and his or her own degree of commitment to the commission of the crime. The conspiracy, the precognition of the homicide and the failure of several attempts to kill are set out in detail, as are the circumstances of the actual death, the detective work of the local authorities, the confession of the principal culprit and the eventual punishment of virtually all the conspirators. Yet there is at least one notable lacuna. The chronicler tells us very little about the victim except that he was a gentleman 'of a tall and comelie personage' but covetous, avaricious and unpopular in his own locality.[3]

According to a version of the tale in papers attributed to the historian John Stow, to be found in a Harleian manuscript, Thomas Ardern originated in Norwich, the son of a woman of miserly inclination who made a good living by begging. However, according to Edward Jacob, the Kent antiquary, he came from a substantial family that lived in Wye, 9 miles south of Faversham.[4] Of Thomas Ardern's education we know nothing. He makes his first appearance in the records when, in July 1537, a warrant was issued for payment of his wages as a clerk of Edward North, at that time the Clerk of Parliament. The task on which Ardern had been engaged was the recording of statutes that touched on property purchased by the King and on the lands of the suppressed monasteries. His employment as clerk to North must have been of prime assistance in gaining for him the hand in marriage of Alice Mirfyn, North's stepdaughter, but it did not lead to him obtaining, as far as can be ascertained, an official position under North when the latter moved to the Court of Augmentations, first as Treasurer (1540–4), then as Chancellor (1544–8).[5]

In June 1540 Ardern was referred to as being of Faversham, Kent, where for about £90 he purchased from the Crown land and tenements that had recently belonged to the abbey of Faversham as well as the site and house of the Carmelite priory at Sandwich in the same county. When settled in Faversham, Ardern seems to have found himself in need of business partners and, indeed, new patronage to supplement the good offices of his father-in-law. We find him (1540) as co-beneficiary in regard to ex-monastic property (in Huntingdonshire) with Sir Richard Long, Steward of the Royal Household. This grant established a relationship for him with William Whorwood, the Attorney-General, and more particularly with his clerk William Walter, for whom Ardern appears to have acted as agent-procurer of other property, also lately monastic, in subsequent years.[6] From no later than 1541 Ardern in addition to his other employment was serving as steward of the manor of Hothfield (Kent) for its lord, Sir Thomas Cheyne, Warden of the Cinque Ports and Treasurer of the King's Household, and it may have been Cheyne who was instrumental in enabling him to acquire lands that had until recently belonged to Faversham Abbey. It was from Cheyne that in December 1544 he apparently purchased the house and site of that monastery, but there is no mention of a price.[7] During the same period Ardern acquired several other pieces of property formerly belonging to the abbey but there is no evidence of Cheyne's involvement. Thus in March 1545 he obtained from the Crown a score or so messuages (houses with their yards) in Faversham town for £117 3s 4d, while in September 1543 for £202 16s 2d he secured a grant of land and tenements in north Kent. Another part of the latter purchase was the marshes of the manor of Lyesness stretching along the south bank of the Thames near London, for which his co-grantee and the ultimate recipient was Henry Cooke, a London merchant tailor.[8]

These acquisitions must have made Ardern the most important person in Faversham. They were probably financed by his acting as broker between those seeking the lands of the religious orders from the Court of Augmentations and his stepfather. If in the early 1540s he secured appointment to the customership of Faversham, as one source has it, this would have provided him with additional income to invest.[9] Whose patronage it was that provided him with the comptrollership of the port of Sandwich in November 1546 is not evident. He lost the position at the end of Henry's reign three months later but was reappointed in June 1550 and awarded the profits of the office from the time Edward VI succeeded to the throne.[10] Here the hand of North is more likely than that of Cheyne, since North was a partisan of the rising Duke of Northumberland. In the first parliament of the new reign (1547) Ardern was returned as member for Sandwich, though whether he actually sat is uncertain. The suggestion has been made that Sir Thomas Cheyne may have promoted Ardern's election. In the months preceding his death Ardern appears to have made regular visits to the home of this patron and employer, or so Holinshed's tale tells us.[11]

Ardern's prominence in his home town of Faversham is not to be taken as indicating harmonious relationships with his peers there. Although his name appears on a list of Faversham freemen of July 1541, he was not apparently made 'free' until 1543, when he became a member of the 'twenty-four'. In 1546 he was made a 'jurat' (alderman), and when, in 1548, the Mayor of Faversham died during his year of office Ardern was elected to serve for the remainder of the term. However, on 22 December 1550, because, as it was said, he had infringed the liberties and freedoms of the town, he lost his position as 'jurat' and was 'utterly disenfranchised for ever'.[12] The story of Ardern's death in Holinshed's *Chronicles* would seem to indicate that the loss of office was connected with an avaricious Ardern somehow arranging matters so that the town's first fair of the year, the St Valentine's fair, should be held on his own land and thus benefit his coffers rather than those of the town. Amongst his neighbours in Faversham Ardern had at least one enemy. The field in which his corpse was eventually deposited by the conspirators he had 'most cruellie taken from a woman', the widow of one Cooke (probably the Henry Cooke mentioned above) and now married to the 'mariner' Richard Reed, who had cursed him to his face.[13]

The mind that planned the murder of Thomas Ardern was that of his wife Alice. She was the child of the union of Alice Squire of Hampshire, widow of John Brigandon, with Edward Mirfyn, citizen and skinner of London and son of Sir Thomas Mirfyn, Mayor of London in 1518–19. Alice, the mother, on the death of Edward Mirfyn (around 1528) married Sir Edward North, who was then aged about 32 and as yet unwed. By North she had issue two sons and two daughters.[14] Through her mother's third marriage Alice the daughter became the stepdaughter to a man of much importance in mid-century politics, a connection that Holinshed, unlike the author of the Harleian account, omits. North, as well as being a great power in the Court of Augmentations, was an executor of Henry VIII's will and a Privy Councillor (1546–53). He was particularly noted for his skill as an auditor of governmental accounts. It is usually assumed that North was able to finance his considerable purchases of land from the wealth brought to him by his wife, but his offices as Treasurer and later Chancellor of the Augmentations must have been very lucrative; not, admittedly, on account of his salary but because of the opportunities for peculation. Indeed, early one morning in 1544 Henry VIII summoned the recently promoted North from his bed to explain a £3,000 deficit in the court's finances from his time there as Treasurer. North only exculpated himself by agreeing to an exchange of lands that was profitable to the King. There was also a story told of North being accused by Edward VI of cheating the Crown out of certain lands.[15] From no later than January 1545

North had the authority to appoint stewards, woodwards, bailiffs and collectors in lands currently under the rule of the Court of Augmentations, which was likely to have profited him greatly through gratuities of appointees or a percentage of their straightforward purchase of office. We know little about relations between North and his stepdaughter. It may well have been he who arranged her marriage to Ardern. We do know he planned for her eventual widowhood; Ardern's will of December 1550 shows he stood bound to North in 1,000 marks to make Alice a jointure of £40 a year or else provide for her that annual amount in his will. In the event he named Alice as his sole executrix and left her property in Faversham including his house; North he made overseer of the will, which shows a continuing connection between them.[16] The parallel source to Holinshed tells us that in their married years Ardern and Alice often had 'recourse to my lord northes', although the purpose of the visits is not stated.[17]

Alice's marriage to Ardern may have been childless; Ardern's daughter Margaret was probably the product of an earlier union. In the account of the murder in the *Chronicles* there is also reference to 'one of mistres Ardens owne daughters', indicating that she must have had at least one child by a partner other than her current husband. A source of somewhat doubtful reliability, the so-called Dolphin Inn manuscript, notes that when Ardern and Alice settled in Faversham he was 56 and she 28. Holinshed, writing of the time of the murder, says they were a good-looking couple: he was 'of a tall and comelie personage' while Alice was 'yoong, tall, well favoured of shape and countenance'.[18]

The stability of the marriage was ultimately threatened by Alice's infatuation with Thomas 'Mosbie', who is described in the *Chronicles* as 'a tailor by occupation, a black swart man, servant to the lord North'. Yet it seems Mosby was somewhat higher on the social scale than a tailor. The version of the murder in the Harleian manuscript calls him 'one of the chefeste gentlemen about the lord northe'.[19] Certainly in the *Chronicles* Ardern treats Mosby as a social equal. This may have been because in the two or three years before Ardern's death Mosby had the greater influence with North, and Ardern wished to avail himself of it to acquire benefits. Ardern's avarice was so great, we are told, that he turned a blind eye to the adulterous relationship his wife maintained with Mosby: he perceived 'their mutuall familiaritie to be much greater than their honesty', but because it was to his financial advantage to do so 'he was contented to wink at hir filthie disorder' and, indeed, frequently invited Mosby to 'lodge' in his house. For clarification Holinshed adds that Mosby 'obteined such favour at hir hands, that he laie with hir, or (as they terme it) kept hir, in abusing hir bodie'.[20] Edward Jacob, who does not reveal his source but seems to have been drawing on the Faversham wardmote book, provides information that Alice Ardern fed Mosby with 'delicate meats' and clad him in 'sumptuous apparel'. Their affair had begun some years earlier. One source states that it originated before Alice's marriage to Ardern. The liaison had been disturbed at one point by a quarrel between the lovers, but Alice successfully revived Mosby's interest, we are told, by a gift of silver dice.[21]

The conspiracy to murder Ardern was initiated by Alice after her tolerated adultery with Mosby had continued for what is described as 'a good space'. The relationship seems to have waxed hot and furious for over two years in this phase. Alice had become 'inflamed' in her love for the tailor and this caused her to loathe her permissive husband. Her ardour and possessiveness were such, it seems, that she could brook no delay in marrying her lover, although Mosby may not have been consumed by passion to the same degree. When exactly the idea of murdering her husband took firm shape in Alice's mind we have no way of knowing, but it seems not unlikely that she determined to hasten Ardern's end once he had made provision for her in his will, which was dated 20 December 1550.[22]

Alice's first move in her murderous design was to ascertain from a local painter, William Blackborne, whether, as report had it, he was knowledgeable about poisons. When he confirmed that he was, Alice, quite openly, requested the concoction of one that would have the 'most vehement and speedie operation to dispatch the eater thereof'. The painter, displaying no scruples, made the poison and instructed Alice to put it in the bottom of a porringer and pour milk on it. In the event, Alice put the milk in first and the poison after, with the result that the consumer, her husband, 'misliked the tast and colour' and told his wife so. Thereupon she poured it away, saying that it was impossible to please him. Ardern then rode off on business towards Canterbury and on the way 'fell into extreme purging upwards and downewards' and thereby escaped death.[23]

Soon after this episode Alice happened to come into contact with 'one Greene of Faversham', a servant of Sir Anthony Ager and an enemy of her own husband. Apparently, Thomas Ardern had deprived Greene of a piece of land behind Faversham Abbey, and threats and blows had resulted. Greene may have had a closer connection with the Court of Augmentations, and thus Edward North, than did Ardern. A 'John Grene' was deputy usher of that court in 1547 and was also the purchaser of provisions there.[24] There is a reference to a freeman of Faversham of the same name in January 1546, and this man, like Ardern, may have had a connection with the town of Sandwich: a John Grene was mentioned in February 1550 as being the founder of a recently dissolved chantry there.[25] Well aware of the enmity between Greene and her husband, Alice offered him £10 to find someone who would kill Ardern. Some time later (we are not told when, but it was during a visit by Ardern to London) Greene set off from Faversham for the capital on the business of Sir Anthony Ager. On the way he encountered on Rainham Down, near Rochester, a suitable assassin. This was one Black Will, 'a terrible cruell ruffian'. Greene was told by a travelling companion, Bradshaw, a Faversham goldsmith who had met Will before while soldiering at the siege of Boulogne, that the latter had committed many robberies and murders in the vicinity of that town and was as 'murthering a knave as anie . . . in England'. When members of the company in which they were travelling greeted Black Will and asked where he was bound, he answered in graphic fashion: 'By his bloud I know not, nor care not, but set up my staffe and even as it falleth I go.'[26]

Greene arranged a private meeting with Will and there it was agreed that the latter should kill Ardern and be paid £10 for his labour when the deed was accomplished. Will asked Greene to identify Ardern for him, and it was decided this should be done in St Paul's churchyard in London, which Ardern frequented, the next day.[27] Greene thereupon wrote a letter to Alice Ardern to inform her of the arrangement and credited Bradshaw with recruiting Black Will. The goldsmith himself carried the letter back to Faversham. This was a detail of importance for Holinshed, who was much exercised by Bradshaw's eventual fate. When Greene pointed out Ardern to Black Will at St Paul's, the latter asked who it was who walked behind Ardern. When told the person in question was his servant, Michael, it only raised Will's enthusiasm for the task in hand. 'By his bloud I will kill them both,' he said, but was dissuaded by Greene, who revealed that the servant was in cahoots with the plotters. Michael's support had been bought by a promise to arrange a marriage for him with a kinswoman of Mosby's. Will then sought to kill Ardern in St Paul's churchyard but was unable to find the opportunity because his quarry was never alone: 'there were so manie gentlemen that accompanied him to dinner that he missed his purpose.'[28] Rather foolishly, Greene revealed Black Will's eagerness to kill to Michael, who thereafter was in great fear of being murdered himself. This affected the next plan, which was for Will to slay Ardern in the parsonage where he was staying in London, as he slept, the doors having been left unfastened by Michael. Michael, however, when his master was gone to bed, went back on his word and made sure the doors were bolted. Thus Black Will, when he arrived to commit the murder, was completely thwarted. Next day he came to Greene in great annoyance, 'swearing and staring because he was so deceived', and threatening, with many terrible oaths, to kill Michael. Michael's untrue explanation that Ardern had risen from his bed and bolted the doors himself pacified the plotters, who then decided Will should ambush their quarry on Rainham Down as he returned home to Faversham. Once again Black Will failed. This time it was because before he reached the place of ambush Ardern was overtaken by several gentlemen of his acquaintance and thereafter travelled in their company.[29]

On his return home Ardern sent Michael to the Isle of Sheppey with a message for Sir Thomas Cheyne, at this time, as we have seen, Ardern's employer and perhaps also his patron. Cheyne sent a letter to Ardern in response, but Alice took it from Michael on his return, hid it and gave instructions that he should tell his master he had lost it. Michael was to suggest that, since he knew nothing of the contents of the letter himself, Ardern should pay a personal visit to Cheyne. Apparently, Ardern accepted uncomplainingly this display of fecklessness by his servant and said he would go. The conspirators' plan, doubtless devised by Alice, was for another ambush, this time between Faversham and the Sheppey ferry. Black Will, now with a companion who bore the name George Shakebag, was at this time lodged, thanks to Greene, in a storehouse belonging to Sir Anthony Ager at Preston, a hamlet a mile to the east of Faversham.[30] There Will was frequently visited by Alice, who brought him meat and drink. She instructed him to rise early and lie in wait for her husband in a certain broom close through which he would pass on his journey to Cheyne's. Will managed to stir himself early in the morning but yet again failed to achieve his design, for he took the wrong direction and set up his ambush in the wrong place. When he realised his error of location, Will attempted to intercept Ardern on his return but all to no avail.[31]

Although we are supplied with no time frame for these machinations they probably occurred in January and the first half of February 1551. Just before

The Tower of London. *(Private Collection/Bridgeman Art Library)*

The Lollards' Tower can be seen at the south-west (i.e. left) corner of St Pauls. *(© The British Library)*

A map of Elizabethan London. The Beech–Winchester murders occurred at Lambert Hill, just north of the Thames at centre right. *(Guildhall Library, Corporation of London/Bridgeman Art Library)*

Greenwich Palace, which George Brown visited soon after murdering George Saunders. *(Ashmolean Museum, Oxford/Bridgeman Art Library)*

THE COPYE OF THE SELF SAME VVORDES; THAT MI LORDE
Sturton spake presently at his Death, beyng the.vi.day of March, in the yeare
of our Lorde.1557.amonge the people as his Confession, desiringe the people to take
Example by hym, and to kepe no Enuy in their hertes
for that is the roote of all euylles.

GOOD people, I am come hither to dye, I am come hither to dye, and iustly Condempned for mine offences by the law, what myne offences were I
am sure you vnderstand, whiche was for a most cruell and detestable murther by my commaundement don and comitted, wherfore I shal desire you
al for goddes sake to let mee be an Ensample to you al, and to al the worlde
and beware that yee lette no malice take roote in your hertes, for that is the vtter dys-
fit oter of al vertue, I shal desire you al, and al the worlde, to forgiue me, and speciallye
those poore women, Children, and kinsfolke, of them whom I haue caused so cruelly
to be murthered, that God may put it into their hertes, for Christes sake, & for Charite
to forgiue me, and if there be any here, or els where, whom I haue offended, I shal desire you al for charite sake to forgiue me, & if there be any of you who hath offeded me,
I do from the bottome of my hert forgiue them, as frely as I trust God of his mercye
hath forgiuen me being moost sory and repentant, & when I shall departe out of thys
worlde, that you wil say al, Lord take his spirit into thy handes, & I shal also desire you
for christes sake to say with me on your knees our Lordes Praier, which is the Pater
noster, & so turning him to the East, & sayd the Lordes Praier, which done, he desired
Sir John Sowch to forgiue him, who answered that he dyd forgiue him fro the bottome of his hert, & then going higher on the Ladder said, good people pray for me, & so
wynkyng with his eyes sayd, I charge the O Satan in Goddes name to depart from
me, and suffer my soule to rest in the lord, & than sayd, Domine accipe spiritum meum. And so
departed this worlde:on whose soule God haue mercy.

¶The Praier of the Lord Stourton which he spake kneling on his knees desiring
the people to praye for hym and also say with him.

LORD herken to my wordes, consider the thought of mine hert, behold howe
lowde I cry vnto the, let my iust Praier enter into thine eares which vnfay-
nedly commeth from myne hert, here me lord for I am poore and distitute of
mans helpe, take care for my soule, saue me thy seruaunt which wholy trust
in the, haue mercye vpon me O Lord, for I wil neuer ceafe cryinge to the for helpe for
thou art my lorde, and more merciful than my tonge can expresse, as aduersite assaileth
me I wyll cry and cal for helpe vnto the, I wil cal vpon the in the day time, and in the
night my cry shal not be hid from the. O thou god of heaueus, the maker of the waters
and lorde of al creatures, here me a pore synner callyng vpon the, and putting my hole
trust in thy mercy, O lord what great pleasures thou haste prepared for me in heauen,
that I should delight in no earthly thynge but in the, my most pleasure is to cleue faste
vnto the, and in the to set my hope and trust, haue mercy vpon me O Lord, O Lorde,
God haue mercy vpon me for thy manifolde mercies sake forgiue me al myne offences:
I comit my spirit into thy handes, deliuer me fro the power of darknes of this world,
thou hast redemed me O Lord God of trueth.

In te domine speraui non confunder in eternum,in iusticia tua libera me.
¶Inclina ad me aurem tuam accelera.et,c,

FINIS.

Imprynted by Wyllyam Pickeringe dwellynge
vppon London brydge.

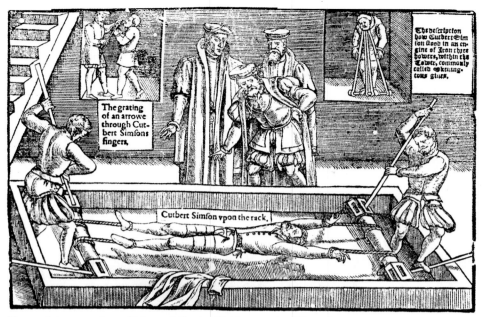

The rack in operation. *(Private Collection/Bridgeman Art Library)*

The death of Thomas Arden according to a seventeenth-century woodcut.
(Reproduced by permission of The Huntington Library, San Marino, California)

Arden's house as it is now.
(The Faversham Website)

A seventeenth-century portrait of a mid-sixteenth-century execution scene: burning at the stake. *(Private Collection)*

The slaying of Nicholas Lincoln's three children. *(Lambeth Palace Library)*

A hanging showing a typical gibbet and the ladder on which the condemned person, unbound, usually stood. *(Mary Evans Picture Library)*

Anne Brewer's death at the stake as portrayed on the title page of Thomas Kyd's pamphlet. *(Lambeth Palace Library)*

the Faversham St Valentine's fair the plotters resolved on another but quite different attempt. First Mosby, whose taste for murder seems to have been the weakest among the conspirators, sought to challenge Ardern to a duel so that he might kill him in fair fight. Although greatly provoked, Ardern refused. The conspirators, Alice, Mosby, Greene, Michael, Shakebag, Will and one of Alice's maids, then held a meeting at the house in Faversham of Mosby's sister, Cicely Pounder, to devise a plan that, from what transpired afterwards, we can see was designed to exercise stricter control over Will so as to ensure he was at the right place at the right time.[32] The scheme decided on was the one eventually used with success, but Mosby, initially at least, was unhappy with what he considered to be a cowardly way of dispatching Ardern. He quit the meeting in a huff, intending to make for the Faversham inn, the Fleur de Lys, but before he got there he was overtaken by a messenger from Alice begging him 'of all loves' to return and play his role in the enterprise. He returned, and Alice went down on her knees before him and begged him to participate if he truly loved her; she assured him there was no danger, since no one would care, and thus enquire closely, if Ardern was killed. Alice's importuning was successful (the *Chronicles* notes that just previously she and Mosby had promised each other 'to be in all points as man and wife together' and indeed had received the sacrament openly together in London), for eventually her lover 'was contented to agree'.[33]

The conspirators then implemented their plan. While Ardern was away from his house, they sent out all the servants not privy to the plot and then concealed Will in a closet at the end of the parlour. When Ardern, who had been settling certain debts with a neighbour, came home between six and seven o'clock in the evening, Mosby, in a silk nightgown, was standing at the door.[34] Ardern asked him if it was supper time and was answered in the negative. He therefore suggested 'a game at the tables' while they were waiting. As they passed through the hall on the way to the parlour, Ardern greeted his wife with 'How now mistresse Ales', but, adds the *Chronicles*, she 'made small answer to him'. In the parlour Ardern sat down on a bench that faced the closet wherein Black Will was concealed. Michael stood by his master, holding a candle but in such a way as to keep Black Will in shadow when, as intended, he should emerge. At a particular point in their game Mosby said to his opponent, 'Now may I take you sir, if I will', words, says Holinshed, intended to tell Will that the moment had come. Ardern, obviously puzzled by what he took to be Mosby's exclamation of victory, asked, 'Take me

. . . which waie?' At that moment Black Will stepped forward, threw a towel around Ardern's neck and proceeded to strangle him. Mosby assisted by striking the victim's head with a 14lb pressing iron that he carried on his girdle. Ardern fell to the floor emitting a great groan, which was taken by the murderers as a sign he had expired. They carried him out of the parlour to his counting house, but, as they were putting him down, 'the pangs of death coming on him', he uttered another groan and his limbs moved. Thereupon Black Will gave him a great gash in the face, which killed him. Will then took the money in Ardern's purse and the rings from his fingers and asked Alice for his pay: 'Now the feat is done, give me my monie.' Alice gave him the promised £10, and Will, having obtained a horse from Greene, rode off.[35]

The conspirators then had to dispose of the body, but first Alice gave it seven or eight 'picks' in the chest with a knife. This was probably to divert attention away from other marks and wounds but possibly out of sheer hatred; Holinshed does not make the matter clear. They wiped away the blood in the parlour and 'strewed againe' the rushes on the floor that had been disturbed in the struggle. The knife with which Alice had stabbed her husband was deposited, with the cloth that had been used to wipe up the blood, in a tub at the side of the well. This must have been located within the grounds of Ardern's house. Alice, by no means emotionally drained or upset by the perpetration of the murder, but quite composed, then sent for two London grocers, business acquaintances of her husband who were lodging near at hand, to come to supper as had been arranged earlier. When they arrived, Alice and Mosby's sister, Cicely Pounder, who had also been summoned, provided them with entertainment while pretending to be mystified by Ardern's delay in returning home. They all had supper and afterwards Alice had 'hir' daughter play the virginals 'and they dansed, and she with them', but there was still no sign of Ardern returning. Said Alice, 'I marvell where he is so long; well, he will come anon I am sure', and she suggested they should play a game 'at the tables' in the meantime. The Londoners, however, excused themselves on the grounds that their host would soon be locking them out, and left.[36]

After their departure those servants who were in the conspiracy were sent out, some to pretend to seek Ardern, others on errands. Remaining in the house were the actual perpetrators of the crime (Black Will excepted), Cicely Pounder, a maid named Elizabeth Stafford and one of Alice's 'owne daughters'. These carried the body of Ardern out of the house, through the

garden gate (after a delay to find the key) and, into the field adjoining, and
deposited it after going a mere ten paces further. While they were so engaged,
it began to snow. Ardern's body, which was placed face upwards, was clad in
nightgown and slippers. All had been done in the greatest haste; inside one of
the slippers was a long rush or two. The time was about midnight. The
carriers then retraced their steps through the garden and into the house,
where the doors were then opened. The servants who had been sent out
returned, but were sent off again to try to locate Ardern amongst the
wealthier townspeople, 'where he was woont to be'.[37] Alice next began to
weep and affect great distress at her husband's disappearance, news of which
had now reached her neighbours. As a result the Mayor of Faversham and
others undertook to search for him. This must have been in the early
morning. They looked first at the site of the town fair and then at the area
next to Ardern's house. There Prune, one of the London grocers, discovered
the corpse. The searchers looked closely at 'The maner of his bodie and hurts'
and noticed the rushes in the slipper. Most importantly, they observed
footprints in the snow from the body to the garden gate of Ardern's house, for
the snow had stopped falling almost as soon as the conspirators returned to
the house, leaving their footprints clearly outlined. The Mayor then sent some
members of the search party to retrace their steps and enter the garden from
the other side. They found more prints in the snow, which showed that the
body had been brought to its present position in the field out of the house
and through the garden.[38]

The Mayor and his companions therefore entered the house to examine the
victim's wife, Alice, 'knowing hir evill demeanor in times past'. In response to
their questions she strongly denied being implicated in the murder: 'I would
you know I am no such woman,' she declared. They next examined her
servants, asking each about some human blood and hair found near the
house, and the knife and piece of cloth, which had been found in the tub.
Faced with this incontrovertible evidence, all the conspirators present
admitted their guilt, but none more dramatically than the dead man's widow:
Alice, 'beholding hir husband's bloud', cried out, 'Oh the bloud of God helpe,
for this bloud have I shed.' When the suspects at Ardern's house had been
arrested and put in jail, the Mayor and his assistants went to the Fleur de Lys
inn, where they found Mosby in bed. Near at hand they espied his hose and
purse, both stained with Ardern's blood. He asked why they intruded on him.
They held before him the bloody hose and purse. Like his confederates, he

immediately confessed and was taken to jail. By this time the only members of the conspiracy who were still at large were Greene, Black Will, his companion George Shakebag and Blackborne, the painter who had originally provided Alice with poison. The latter pair fled and were never heard of again.[39]

After providing much detail about the crime and the perpetrators, the *Chronicles* becomes terse in the extreme when dealing with the judicial aftermath: 'Shortlie were the sessions kept at Faversham where all the prisoners were arraigned and condemned.' Edward Jacob, without giving his sources, states that the conspirators were tried under a special commission, that is to say, one of oyer and terminer, which would have allowed the justices appointed both to conduct enquiries about and then to try the suspects themselves.[40] It would also have ensured that the court was empowered to try petty treason, which was how husband-murder and employer-murder were technically classified. The only additional information about the trial provided by Holinshed is that, when examined as to whether there were any other accomplices, Alice named Bradshaw, the Faversham goldsmith, a neighbour of Greene's and, according to the *Chronicles*, 'a verie honest man'. All he had done was to bring her, from Greene, a letter that said, quite erroneously, that the recruitment of Black Will was thanks to Bradshaw when, in fact, he was never a member of the conspiracy and all he had done was to describe Will's dark past. On Alice's information Bradshaw was arrested, but he was allowed to confront those who had already been convicted. When he asked them if they knew him, they said they did not. Greene's letter was then produced against him and he explained the circumstances. But it was to no avail. He was arraigned, convicted and sentenced like the others.[41]

The judgment against all the conspirators was death, and Holinshed carefully lists where the executions took place. Michael was drawn to the gallows (as befitted a traitorous servant) and hanged in chains at Faversham. Mosby and his sister, Cicely Pounder, were hanged at Smithfield, London. Alice Ardern, for husband-murder, was burned at the stake at Canterbury, and one of her maids suffered similarly, but for the murder of her master, at Faversham. Greene, says Holinshed, returned to his old haunts some years later and was arrested, tried and convicted.[42] He was hanged in chains by the highway between Ospringe and Boughton (that is, very close to Faversham). Black Will, the *Chronicles* tells us without further explanation, was burned on a scaffold at Flushing in Zealand, and Adam Foule, who had carried the silver dice from Alice to Mosby, was arrested and put in the Marshalsea prison in

Southwark. This was because Mosby was heard to blame his misfortunes on the same dice. He was, however, able to show that Foule knew nothing of the conspiracy and thereby save him from the gallows.[43]

Holinshed finishes his account of the Ardern murder with a tale of a curse and something 'verie strange and notable'. Apparently, in the place where the corpse had been laid in the field by the murderers no grass would grow for more than two years. This attracted the attention of many strangers as well as townspeople. Disclaiming irrefutable information, the *Chronicles* adds that Ardern had 'most cruellie' taken the field, before the lease expired, from the widow Cooke. In retaliation she cursed him most bitterly, wishing 'manie a vengeance to light upon him'.[44] When he was murdered, many people thought this had indeed come to pass. Here the chronicler finishes with happenings at Faversham 'thus far touching this horrible and heinous murder of maister Arden. To returne then where we left', and he moves his focus to the 1551 session of parliament.[45]

For details of the murder of Ardern and the machinations of the conspirators we are dependent very largely on Holinshed, Harleian MS 542, and the wardmote book; the short accounts by other Tudor writers provide no additional information. Governmental records, on the other hand, do offer one or two extra details of interest. We learn whom Ardern may have visited to settle debts on the day of the murder. More important entries in official records concern those of the conspirators who escaped immediate arrest, namely Black Will and Greene. To capture the latter the government organized a manhunt. A letter from the Council of May 1551 mentions that Greene was initially spirited away by an ally; he was 'conveied awaie' by 'one Bate'. Bate was arrested, put in the London Counter, and compelled to enter into an agreement with the Privy Council. He was to be set at liberty in order to recapture Greene, but he had to give surety he would return to jail if he failed in his purpose. Aided by some assistants, he appears to have been successful, since in mid-July 1551 a warrant was issued for payment to the hunters of a sum of 20 marks for bringing Greene before the Council and then conveying him to Faversham to be hanged in chains, an event that probably occurred at the end of July or early in August 1551.[46]

The conspirator who escaped English justice was Black Will. After the murder he may well have sought a ship to take him to the Continent. This is suggested by a letter from the Privy Council to Sir Thomas Cheyne eight days after the murder, instructing him to release a French ship that had been detained in the harbour at Faversham. Will was eventually captured by Sir William Godolphin in June 1551, but later, at a time and in a manner unknown, he made his escape.[47] Yet the Council did not abandon the chase. We know that Will eventually reached the Low Countries, for it was at Flushing in May 1553 that he was arrested for a second time. He was captured, so another letter of the Council tells us, by the 'procurement of certain servants of the treasurer of his majesty's household'; the latter, of course, was Sir Thomas Cheyne. Having 'stayed', as it was put, the murderer, the next step was to have him extradited.

Thus the Council wrote to the English ambassador at the Imperial Court, Sir Philip Hoby, instructing him to request of the Emperor that Black Will, 'who of long times has been a notable murderer and one of the most wretched and vile persons that lives', should be sent to England to be punished 'for many divers causes', but one in particular, 'the shameful murder of one Arden of Feversham in Kent'.[48] The Council also sent letters to the bailiff and other magistrates of Flushing, doubtless to explain its concern about Will and his crimes. Hoby was instructed to try to get the regent to order the Flushing magistrates to hand over Will 'to those who shall be appointed to convey him to England'. The imperial authorities did not do exactly as was requested of them, but they obliged the Council in another way, for Black Will was 'burnt on a scaffold' in Flushing.[49]

Such is the dramatic tale of the demise of Thomas Ardern. No doubt we ought to rejoice in the insights it gives into Tudor domestic violence and household relationships, to say nothing of the literary merits of the text itself. Modern-day historians, however, are rarely ready to accept any historical source as one totally true, even where none of its data, as with this case, is contradicted by other writing of the period. What historians seek to discover are the origins of the writer's information, and the 'spin', as it is called in current popular parlance, that he imparts to it: that is to say his use and abuse of his sources, the aspects of the information he plays down or emphasises, or chooses to interpret in what seems an illogical or biased manner. Additionally, just as important for the historian is why the writer chose to insert the material in his work at all. Only when these questions have been answered can the validity and social significance of the piece be assessed with any accuracy.[50]

The first question, therefore, is from where did Holinshed obtain the Ardern story. He provides us with an answer of sorts himself: he got the details from those 'that have used some diligence to gather the true understanding of the circumstances'. This cryptic comment, particularly the words 'diligence' and 'true understanding', demonstrates that Holinshed had considerable respect for the integrity and intelligence of his informants. Of the story he states. 'I have thought good to set it foorth somewhat at large, having the instructions delivered to me . . .', but whether this means he requested and then received these 'instructions' or whether, so to speak, they arrived on his doorstep without specific request is not clear.[51] His phraseology, however, seems to preclude unsolicited reception such as, for example, from among the materials collected by the original projector of the *Chronicles*, Reyner Wolfe. He may have used Stow to dig out the material, but the odds are against this thesis since crime and its handling were hardly Stow's *métier*.

One possible supplier of the details of the Ardern case was the school-master and antiquarian John Twyne. From the late 1520s Twyne was master of the grammar school at Canterbury. He was also sheriff there in 1544–5, alderman and member of parliament in 1553, and mayor in 1554. Having been sheriff he obviously knew something about crime and criminal law and may well have noted with interest the burning in his home city of Alice Ardern on 14 March 1551 and the unfortunate hanging of George Bradshaw at the same time. The concern over the unjust fate of Bradshaw in the text gives strength to the argument that Twyne was the key informant. Twyne was well known to those responsible for the *Chronicles*. Holinshed's employer, Reyner Wolfe, was a benefactor of Twyne, and Holinshed himself commended Twyne's skill as an antiquarian.[52]

Another possible supplier of the murder details was Sir Thomas Cheyne, an employer and patron of Ardern, who was not only Warden of the Cinque Ports (1536–58) but also Lord Lieutenant of Kent (1551–3). His authority must have been dominant in north-east Kent. Holinshed took a great deal of interest in Cheyne's career. In the *Chronicles* he was bent on showing Sir Thomas in a most flattering light. He inserts under the year 1546 a copy of letters patent to Cheyne that appointed him the King's representative at the christening of the Dauphin's daughter. The reason he gives for this is the necessity of correcting a report that Sir Henry Knevet had been given that task. Then, in his coverage of the first year of Elizabeth's reign, which was when Cheyne died, Holinshed inserts a long encomium of the man. This praises Sir Thomas for his 'love of chivalrie', the size of his household, his liberality, his good wages and food for servants and his careful provision for them in his will. Finally, Holinshed extols Cheyne's 'wit, experience, courtesie and valiantnesse' while at Court for sixty years under five different rulers: he was 'so worthie a gentleman, and such a necessarie member in the common-wealth as his want cannot but be lamented of all good and true English harts'.[53]

Why Holinshed should be so eager to praise Sir Thomas Cheyne is not apparent from either the content of the *Chronicles* or what we know of the knight's career from other sources. The life of his son and heir Sir Henry Cheyne, on the other hand, does seem to offer some clues. The son was particularly concerned to achieve elevation to the peerage, and to this end, apparently, he entertained Queen Elizabeth in 1563 and 1576 at his newly built mansion at Toddington (Bedfordshire), paid for by the sale of much of his landed inheritance in Kent. He was created Lord Cheyne in May 1572.[54] Excessive praise of the type that Holinshed heaped on the elder Cheyne is to be found in regard to other persons in earlier chronicles, and the reason for it is usually political: the writer's monastery, the writer himself, his family or his community has benefited from the patronage of the subject of the flattery or is expecting to do so. Sir Thomas Cheyne died in December 1558 and there is no evidence he had a connection with Holinshed or Wolfe. Similarly without supporting evidence, but a good deal more likely, is the theory that Sir Henry Cheyne, in an effort to advance the glory of his family while or after seeking ennoblement, became a benefactor of those engaged in compiling the *Chronicles* and supplied Holinshed with the letters patent and the biographical details mentioned above. Perhaps in the course of their communication Holinshed discovered that the younger Cheyne had in his possession an account of the Ardern murder, once his father's, and asked to see it. Sir Thomas would have had every opportunity to hear the details of the case. As we have seen, it was to him as Warden of the Cinque Ports that the Privy Council sent the letter ordering the freeing of the French ship at Faversham, and it was his servants who pursued Black Will to the Low Countries and got him arrested.[55] The Council took a great interest in the punishing of the murderers, and as one of its members Cheyne would probably have had access to whatever information came its way. He may well have kept an account of the case as revealed by the confessions of the culprits, an account that his son inherited and passed on to Holinshed.

Among other possible suppliers of information to Holinshed must be placed the law officers involved, or at least those who had the keeping of records.

The clerk of the court would probably have had custody of the pre-trial examinations, which in this instance would have been overt confessions, although it is possible some details came from gallows speeches. Holinshed's reference to having the 'instructions' delivered by those that 'have used some diligence to gather the true understanding of the matter' is too vague a statement from which to decide which of these possible sources should be given most emphasis. All, however, are preferable to the suggestion that Holinshed acquired his material from his erstwhile employer, Robert Burdet, a gentleman of Bramcote, Warwickshire, and subsequently his son Thomas. Robert, it is believed, sat with Ardern in the parliament of 1547, but there is no evidence they were on cordial or familiar terms, which might have provided him with an interest in the latter's fate.[56]

Why did Holinshed think it important to include the Ardern murder in the *Chronicles*? He shows us he expected criticism on the grounds of it being 'impertinent to this historie' because it was 'but a private matter'. Yet there is no such apology for including the murder of the two Hartgills on the order of Charles, Lord Stourton under the year 1557.[57] What Holinshed was apologising for in part was probably the inclusion of a murder that was a purely domestic tragedy, whereas the several other murder cases he mentions were in a sense public matters in that they involved persons of gentry status or above, or involved threats to public order, as for example did the crimes of Lord Dacre and Charles Gavaro.[58] Holinshed's main excuse for his close attention to the Ardern murder was 'the horriblenesse thereof'. This term he does not define and it is left to the reader to decide what particular elements of the killing he regarded as especially heinous. Was it the large number of the conspirators, the machinations and leadership of the wife of the victim, the involvement of the servants, the repeated and varied attempts at slaying, the fact that the leading conspirators were motivated by sexual desire or because the crime was committed in a man's own house by his household; and if it was a combination of these facts, then which ones? And, further, if there was indeed moral revulsion on Holinshed's part, was this the real reason for the inclusion of the misdeed in the *Chronicles*?

Some light is thrown on this matter if we consider the *Chronicles* through a wider lens. Despite the majestic nature of Reyner Wolfe's original plan and Holinshed's commitment to it overall, it is obvious the latter was essentially a middle-class historian with London inclinations. He was writing to a considerable degree for the urban bourgeoisie, especially those in the capital, among whom he presumably believed the greater part of his future readership lay. His standard offering was therefore a shrewd mixture of the curious and vulgar, what we might call low history, on the one hand, and the high history of royalty, Church, magnates, diplomacy, wars, parliament and legislation, on the other, the latter being tailored to ride the political pressures of his own times. Within the low-history parts of the English section of the *Chronicles* is to be found a fair amount of writing on crime and justice. Holinshed appears to have been the first chronicler to provide considerable detail about serious crimes committed by the middle and lower classes, although we notice that such offences had to be sufficiently different from the general run to be newsworthy.[59]

When dealing with either crime or criminal law, Holinshed was obviously at ease. Unlike most monkish and urban historians of earlier periods, he had a good understanding of legal process and how the felonies and treasons were defined. He was, therefore, very capable of judging how accurate were the reports of notable crimes and trials that came into his hands. His competence is well demonstrated by the emphasis he gives to the trial in 1554 of Sir Nicholas Throckmorton. Recognising, apparently, the legal and constitutional issues involved, he provides us with what appears to be the first verbatim report of the proceedings in a criminal trial, an account of the greatest value to modern historians.[60] Despite his knowledge of the criminal law, Holinshed, unlike many among the professional judges, justices of the peace and even lawyers, does not appear to have relished the infliction of punishment on offenders. On the other hand, he cannot be regarded as an advocate of moderating the penalties. Except in the odd instance, he was objective and neutral in reporting their infliction. He was, however, obviously moved when there was a miscarriage of justice, as in the conviction of George Bradshaw, or gross judicial bias, as in the treatment of the petty jurors in the trial of Sir Nicholas Throckmorton for his role in Wyatt's rebellion.[61]

Holinshed saw nothing wrong with the judicial procedure or the punishments inflicted (Bradshaw's apart) in the Ardern case. He may have wished to make the point that 'masterless men', especially ex-soldiers like Black Will, were a menace to society, or to emphasise the validity of the maxim 'murder will out'. He does not, however, seem to have been bent on suggesting that Ardern was a grasping 'nouveau riche' in government employ picking over the carcass of the medieval Church. He would have known that a good number of his readers or their fathers could be described in the same way. Doubtless Holinshed was well aware of these aspects of the tale and recognised that they would increase interest in his writings, but there is no indication that he sought to give them particular emphasis. His chief concern in presenting the material that had come into his hands was to demonstrate how vile could be the crime of petty treason.[62]

Murders labelled as petty-treason cases in which the wife killed her husband figured only very rarely at the assizes in the later sixteenth century. The extant home-circuit records for the reign of Elizabeth provide a mere half-dozen examples, and how many women were actually burned at the stake, the traditional punishment, is unclear. Thus a Surrey woman who killed her husband by poison in September 1599 was sentenced to be burned but was remanded on a plea of pregnancy, and there is no evidence of her eventual execution. Literary evidence shows there were one or two other women sentenced to be burned, but the details of their crimes are scanty.[63] In the fourteenth and fifteenth centuries, where court cases of husband-murder were similarly rare, the records also hint at a reluctance to categorise such crimes as amounting to petty treason.[64] Even in an instance of May 1438, a murder by assault in Suffolk, the indictment modestly stated 'she feloniously killed him', not 'she traitorously killed him', nor even 'she feloniously murdered him'. Not surprisingly, with such a mildly worded indictment the woman was acquitted. In contrast, at the same sessions a carpenter who had committed petty treason by killing his employer was charged with having traitorously and feloniously assaulted and killed him and was sentenced to the traitor's fate of being drawn to the gallows before being hanged.[65]

A case that does seem to have had something in common with Ardern's occurred in Northamptonshire in June 1420. Thomas Beeston, a justice of the peace and clerk of the King's Bench, was murdered by his wife Katherine. She was sentenced to be burned at the stake. Here the victim was a man of gentry status and an office holder of importance such as was Ardern. Furthermore Katherine, like Alice, had a male accomplice, who, as was often the case in female felony, was very likely her lover.[66] The records of the Beeston case suggest that the victim's family made strenuous efforts to see the two perpetrators were punished and that eventually it succeeded in its quest. A case closer in time to the Ardern murder provides an example of a woman of knightly class being executed for murder. This was Agnes, Lady Hungerford, who was executed at Tyburn in February 1523 for the murder of her first husband, James Cotell, after the death of her second husband, Sir

Edward Hungerford. The latter had bequeathed Agnes the whole of his estate, and presumably his son and his supporters revenged themselves by bringing about the prosecution.[67] Agnes, however, unlike Alice Ardern, was hanged, not burned, but whether this was because of her status as the wife of a knight, or some other factor, is not apparent. In these cases family members must have been active in prosecuting, but this was not so with Ardern's murderers. As far as we know he had no relatives capable of bringing effective pressure to bear for inflicting the severest punishment on the miscreants. Alice Ardern and her confederates owed their conviction to the overwhelming evidence against them. The footprints in the snow and the bloodstains, but primarily Alice's confession so soon after the event, made impossible any defence. An example from this period of an acquittal at trial after a principal in a felony had already confessed to a justice has yet to be discovered. Had there been no confession by Alice or any of her confederates, and if she had had no evil reputation and no confederates, an acquittal, or more likely a verdict of killing in hot blood, might have been a possibility. The offence had been committed in Faversham, a member of the Cinque Ports confederation, and thus the arraignment had to take place there. Since Ardern at the time of his death was out of favour with his peers in his home town, the trial jurors might have been persuaded to give Alice the benefit of any doubt, though her 'evil reputation' militated against it.[68]

The indictments of Alice and her co-conspirators have not survived, but since she was burned the crime cannot have been categorised as mere felonious killing. The burning in the Ardern case is somewhat surprising, since, although Alice was not of knightly status, we might have expected her wealthy origins and her stepfather's position to have saved her from the stake, if not from execution.[69] The answer to this problem seems to be found in the political position of Sir Edward North at the time: his degree of importance in the Privy Council and his power to intervene in the case. North, who had suffered a setback in his career in 1548 when the Duke of Somerset was in the ascendant among the ministers of the King, joined the opposition to him in 1550. In religion he was to be classified with neither the Henrician Catholics nor the committed Reformers.[70] He could not therefore be considered to be particularly close to the new ascendant minister, the Earl of Warwick, serving at that time rather as an ally. He remained so, it appears, in 1551. When his stepdaughter confessed to murdering her husband, his own erstwhile protégé, he had to decide if he should try to intervene in some way.

Having only modest influence in Kent in general, and Faversham in particular, he would not have been in a position to intervene in the trial proceedings; but, because of the confession, the only viable move anyway was to try to procure a pardon. Yet the difficulties in this direction would also have been great. There was increased severity in the implementation of the criminal law during the Edwardian period, and the heinousness and notoriety of the offence were tremendous obstacles.[71] At the very least a pardon would have been inordinately expensive and would have lowered North's political credit. As one who had risen to power in the reign of Henry VIII, he would have learned that when a member of one's family committed a notorious crime it was politically advisable to distance oneself from the culprit, or even take a leading part in demanding his or her punishment. What he said in the discussions over suitable punishments for the Ardern conspirators at the Council meeting on 5 March 1551 we do not know, but he was certainly present.[72]

At this distance it is impossible to gauge the emotional ties between North and his stepdaughter. She may have resented his arranging of her marriage to someone of Ardern's lesser status, particularly as North may have owed a great deal to the wealth that her mother had brought into the marriage with her stepfather.[73] If Alice had little love for North, his attitude may have been similar. It is, on the other hand, possible that North did exert himself in search of a pardon for her, but that other Privy Councillors blocked his attempts. The distance in time between Alice's confession when she was first questioned (15 February) and her execution (14 March) was a month, which would have been just sufficient for the necessary lobbying and formal and informal payments, but, as North would have known, the chances of success were very small. This was because Alice was a principal in the crime rather than an accessory, and, secondly and most importantly, because 'special' (that is, specific to one person) pardons for husband-murder, if they ever existed at all at this time, were the rarest commodity – rarer than pardons for high treason.[74]

One person of importance who might have stood between North and a pardon for Alice was Ardern's employer and more recent patron, Sir Thomas Cheyne. We cannot discern if he was of greater weight in the Privy Council at this time than North; probably not, but his power in the locality of the crime was paramount, and, as he was Warden of the Cinque Ports, the justices sitting at Faversham would have been very respectful of his interests. Cheyne, as we have seen, was personally involved in the pursuit of those conspirators not arrested at the scene of the crime. However, other evidence of active participation by Cheyne in proceedings subsequent to the murder is lacking, and it would probably be best to conclude that the Council, knowing that two of its members had conflicting interests in regard to the fate of Alice Ardern, decided to supervise the processes of the law rather closely. It is probably quite significant that, later in the year of the murder, Sir Thomas, not North, was given the custody of Ardern's daughter Margaret, then aged 13.[75]

Following a decision taken at its meeting on 5 March 1551 the Privy Council sent a letter to the Kent justices of the peace instructing them to 'take order for the punishment of those that slew Ardeyn'. By this time, therefore, those of the conspirators who were in custody had been arraigned and found guilty on their confessions. The methods and places of execution had, however, been referred to the Privy Council, which now gave its commands. Their effect was as Holinshed stated, but with two differences: Michael, the servant, being guilty of petty treason towards his master, was to be drawn to the Faversham gallows before hanging, after which the body was to be quartered, and George Bradshaw, whose fate Holinshed omitted, was to be hanged in chains at Canterbury.[76] As we have seen, chains were normally used so the skeletal remains would continue to hang on the gallows, as a warning to others, for months after the execution, and also to thwart souvenir hunters. The Privy Council's interest in the case on the judicial side continued after the executions of March 1551; we have already noticed the efforts it made to extradite Black Will. When Greene, in flight or hiding, was captured in June or July 1551 it ordered (20 July) the Chancellor to send a special commission of jail delivery to the Mayor of Faversham for the 'attainder', as it was put, of the prisoner.[77] Greene had already been indicted and the purpose of the commission was that he should be tried in the immediate future instead of waiting for the next regular sessions. The only two persons involved in the conspiracy in whom the Privy Council took no interest and who escaped the gallows were therefore George Shakebag, Black Will's confederate, and the daughter of Alice Ardern who was in the house at the time of the murder.

Along with the unrelenting villainy of Alice, the several bungled attempts at murder and the ritualistic nature of Ardern's slaying in his own parlour, the case was memorable because of the execution of so many participants. Holinshed and the other writers of the age who mentioned the episode do not seem to have found the punishment in any way excessive. It is often forgotten that the Tudor age was one of great severity in the administration of criminal justice, a severity that considerably surpassed the standards of the later Middle Ages in England.[78] The conviction rate for felony was noticeably greater, torture was employed in the later sixteenth century on a regular, although not frequent, basis for felony as well as for treason, and punishments of physical disfigurement multiplied. Had Alice been successful in her attempt to poison her husband and this had occurred four years before her execution in 1551, she might well have been put to death by boiling, the punishment invented in 1531 and still in force in 1547.[79]

Where Holinshed appears to have been an innovator in his account of murder is in his portrayal of Alice's motivation. She is propelled into the murder of her husband by her sexual desire, her lust for another man, a factor noticeably absent from earlier chronicles.[80] There is no suggestion of her being abused in any way by her husband; rather the reverse. Thomas Ardern, whatever his reputation in business matters, seems to have been long-suffering and tolerant in regard to his wife, while Alice regards him with unremitting hostility, even contempt, and has suborned the loyalty of the household servants as a necessary preliminary to her design. Alice is not just one of a group of conspirators: she is the moving spirit and actually stabs her husband, a deed that ended the possibility of her being tried merely as an accessory. Her choice of Greene as her lieutenant was of doubtful benefit to her plan, for it was he who recruited the bungling Black Will whose aberrations resulted in the murder being done in Ardern's own house. Her failing as a planner of murder lay much in her rashness: her brazen request of the Faversham painter for a poison 'which should have most vehement and speedie operation to dispatch the eater thereof' and the decision to slay Ardern in his own house on an evening when guests were expected do not suggest a cool head. Nor had she and her co-conspirators made a careful plan for disposing of the body, believing, perhaps, that since it was the time of the town's St Valentine's fair there would be strangers in the locality towards whom suspicion for the murder would gravitate. In short, Alice was far too emotional to achieve a successful murder and was not suited to the command of such a conspiracy. Nor can we escape the suspicion that her impatience was increased and her judgement warped by her sexual desire for Mosby and the thought of becoming his wife.

Around 1590 the story of the Ardern murder was recycled. This time it took the form of a play, the full title of which was *The Lamentable and True*

Tragedie of M. Arden of Feversham in Kent. Although he followed the original accounts closely for the most part, the playwright altered and expanded their tale in several directions, seemingly so as to provide more excitement and emotional involvement for his audience. For the historian these modifications are of interest for two reasons. First, it is possible that the dramatist had access to information about the circumstances of Ardern's murder that were not available to Holinshed, the compiler of the account in Harleian MS 542, or the writer of the comments in the Faversham wardmote book. This we need to test, and, if proven, we then need to establish whether the additions are soundly based historically or there for dramatic purposes. Secondly, the playwright's modifications may throw more light on society's attitudes to murder, particularly to husband-murder, in the late sixteenth century.[81]

Perhaps the most noticeable addition the dramatist makes to the Holinshed/Harleian account is to insert the character called Franklin. Presumably this is supposed to be his surname rather than his status, although a secondary intention may well be to show that Ardern's natural peers in society were to be found in the highest ranks of the lower classes rather than among the lesser gentry. The main purpose of Franklin's insertion, however, is to provide greater demonstration, by means of conversation between the pair, of Ardern's emotions and thoughts in the period of the conspiracy. The playwright obviously believed his audience would find the portrayal of a gentleman on good terms with his wife's lover hard to believe. Furthermore, the murder of an acquiescent husband would increase the villainy of Alice, thereby jeopardising the image of dual responsibility for the consequences of a failed marriage that the dramatist seems to have been intending to project. Thus Ardern is made to utter, in Franklin's presence, disparaging remarks about Mosby's social origins ('a botcher' who crept into a nobleman's service), to hope for his death, to get into an affray with him and to speak as if he is merely suspicious of his wife's fidelity, not totally cognisant of her adultery. Such acceptance of his wife's behaviour as the play allows is explained as being the result of Franklin's advice that he should be sweet to Alice and not scrutinise her life too closely.[82]

A second group of additions concern Black Will and Shakebag. So as to make them more believable and vicious as criminals (for the former in the Holinshed/Harleian accounts is nothing more than an incompetent oaf and braggart), the playwright seeks to place them in an underworld context.

'Protection' and the murder of whores, flight to sanctuary, the hue and cry, the assizes, the name of a notorious horse-thief, the receiving of stolen goods and Newgate jail therefore appear in the dialogue. A notable feature of Elizabethan social life was the general interest in criminal activity. This gave rise to a number of pieces of popular literature that were concerned not only with infamous crimes but also with the tricks and organisation of the criminal fraternity – the first criminological studies in English history.[83] Another invention of the playwright is his characterisation of Ardern's servant Michael as being homicidal by nature. Unlike his depiction in the historical accounts as one who has to be promised a bride to obtain his participation in the conspiracy, he is shown as eager to slay his master, even his own elder brother if it will improve his earthly fortunes. When the murder has been done, he is even prepared to poison his mistress, Alice, if she appears to be ready to confess to the crime.

Whereas the Holinshed/Harleian accounts tell us little of the everyday relations between Ardern and his wife, in the play Alice speaks of his 'froward looks, Hard words and blows'. She portrays herself as being even by sixteenth-century standards in an uncomfortable situation, perhaps fearing for her life. Furthermore her husband, she says, is given to whoring: he keeps 'in every corner trulls' and in London 'revels it among such filthy ones'.[84] There is nothing pointing in this direction in the accounts, and we may suspect that, unless there was a strong popular tradition that the playwright tapped, his intention was simply to even up the score, so to speak; to relate again to the popular marriage experience of blame lying on both sides. The aim would be to create ambivalent feelings about Alice's crime and fate, to play to different sympathies within the audience.

To convince his audience that the events and characterisations in the play are historical, the playwright indulges in a fair amount of name dropping – names that are absent from the accounts. There is the horse-thief Jack Fitten, a Jack of Faversham who served at the siege of Boulogne, and a London 'queen', Widow Chambley; there are important men like Protector Somerset and Sir Anthony Cooke (a tutor of Edward VI). Lord Cheyne (that is, Sir Thomas Cheyne), merely mentioned in the accounts, appears in person. Ardern's lodgings in London, simply a parsonage in Holinshed, are located specifically in Aldersgate Street. However, Lord North (that is, Sir Edward North as he was in 1551) is not named in the play at all. The name given to Mosby's master (and Ardern's former employer who now 'loves not me') is

Lord Clifford.[85] Why, at the time the play was written, the dramatist wished to keep Alice's important stepfather's name away from the notoriety of the case can be explained in two ways. It may have been done out of respect for her stepbrother, Sir Thomas North, the translator of Plutarch, the source of so many classical allusions of late-sixteenth-century dramatists. Thomas North, however, had died in 1584 and a more likely cause may have been the prestige, at the time the play was constructed, of another stepbrother, Sir Edward's eldest son and heir, Roger North, who at that time was an intimate of the Queen, a hero of the Dutch battlefields and a great patron of players. The 'Lord Clifford' of 1551 was Henry Clifford, second Earl of Cumberland and sixteenth Lord Clifford (d. 1570), a relative nonentity and of Catholic inclination who had favoured Mary, Queen of Scots and dabbled in alchemy. He had no known connection with the Ardern case. His son George, the third earl, was a naval commander, buccaneer, gambler and favourite at Court, whose links, if any, with *Arden of Feversham* and its author do not show, although he was a patron of the stage.[86]

Certain situations in the Ardern murder story that are treated but briefly by Holinshed and the author of the Harleian manuscript are developed at considerably greater length by the playwright. This, no doubt, is because they are natural material for the stage in that they provide the audience with a change of pace. A chance medley, as such affrays were properly called, between Ardern and Mosby is one such. Another is the attempt on Ardern's life in London. They offer a host of opportunities for movement and action, and for general stage 'business', such as when an apprentice drops the shutter of his store on Black Will's head as he waits in ambush. The plan to assassinate Ardern by having Michael leave open the door of the lodgings so that Black Will may fulfil his murder contract provides many entrances and exits and amounts to a notable 10 per cent of the whole play in length.[87] As we might expect, the climax of the play, the murder scene and the immediate aftermath, is also inflated, with virtually all the dramatis personae making a stage appearance. The Mayor of Faversham, visiting the Ardern house in search of Black Will, is accompanied by the town watch 'with glaives and bills', not simply 'others his companie' as in Holinshed. The authoritarian aspect of this visitation is enhanced by the Mayor having a Privy Council search warrant. The ostentatious showing of documents also occurs in the opening scene of the play when Franklin brings letters patent of Ardern's grant from Protector Somerset. The detective work leading to the discovery of the vital evidence against the conspirators is not an anonymous effort, as in the accounts, but done by Franklin, Ardern's only friend.[88]

For Holinshed Alice is evil. 'Thus this wicked woman,' he writes, 'with hir accomplices, most shamefullie murdered hir owne husband, who most entirelie loved hir all his life time'. For the playwright Alice is by no means so vicious. While Holinshed tells us that Alice was the purchaser of ratsbane from the painter for the purpose of poisoning her husband, the dramatist makes Mosby the prime architect of this plan. Elsewhere the play implies that Alice and Mosby had been lovers at an earlier time, and, although there is no reference to the hazards of arranged marriages or of substantial difference in age between man and wife, this mention of earlier intimacy provides a slight excuse for Alice's adultery and intention to murder. Age, however, is made a factor in another manner. After her arrest, when Mosby calls her a strumpet, Alice replies that she was too young to recognise his villainies. Earlier, immediately after the slaying, she tells Mosby that it was he 'that made me murder', her reasoning being, presumably, that he created such sexual desire in her that she had to do away with her husband so she could marry him. Another amendation by the playwright designed to soften Alice's image concerns Bradshaw, the goldsmith. Whereas in the accounts he is cleared of involvement by the conspirators as a whole, in the play it is Alice who declares him guiltless.[89]

A notable difference between the accounts and the play is the strong emphasis in the latter on social rank. Mosby is disparaged as a mere butcher, as a 'base peasant' and as a groom. There is also reference to his bodkin, Spanish needle and pressing iron, but the playwright fails to call him a tailor as such. When the murder is being committed, the playwright has Mosby stabbing Ardern, not belabouring him with a plebeian pressing iron as in the accounts.[90] Alice's derogatory comments and taunts on the subject of her lover's social status are the dramatist's fabrication, but he may have been near the mark in emphasising her great concern with gentle blood. Alice's mother, twice previously married, produced four children for Edward North, two sons and two daughters. The two sons made names for themselves, as we have seen, and married well. Significantly, Alice's two half-sisters married even better, one to William, Earl of Worcester, the other to Henry, Lord Scrope of Bolton. The first of these marriages, that of Christiana, we know for sure had taken place before the murder, possibly a year or so before that time; she was about to give birth when Alice was executed.[91] With these two fine matches on her mind, Alice may have come to believe that her stepfather, in providing her with only his ex-clerk as a husband, had failed her in the matter of marriage, particularly so as she was reputed to be a beautiful woman and her mother had brought considerable wealth into the marriage with North.[92]

Although the play provides no hint, it seems not unlikely that Alice was a widow, or Ardern a widower, when they were married. There is, admittedly, only one piece of evidence pointing in this direction, but it is hard to discount. In recounting the behaviour of the miscreants after the crime has been committed, Holinshed uses the words 'one of mistress Ardens owne daughters'. This is rather different from the Harleian manuscript's simple 'hir daughter'.[93] It is not to be passed off as a slip or loose language on Holinshed's part, for he was most precise in his writing, probably through legal training. The question is what emphasis we should put on the word 'owne'. Perhaps the adjective is superfluous, but there is the possibility that Alice had brought one or more daughters into her marriage with Ardern and that 'owne' was intended to distinguish this or these from any she had had by Ardern or he by a previous partner. In his will of December 1550, it will be remembered, Ardern referred to only a single daughter – Margaret, probably not born of Alice. It therefore appears possible that Ardern was not Alice's first husband and that she was an experienced woman. This would help to explain her independence of mind, ability to plot and manipulate, and her readiness to pursue her own interests to the uttermost.

There can be little doubt that to include the Ardern murder in the *Chronicles* was a shrewd move on Holinshed's part. The tale must have had an immediate relevance to many middle-class men with younger wives (as most probably were), especially where their sexual loyalty was uncertain. The involvement of the household servants on the murderess's side must also have caused them more than momentary discomfort. As we have already noticed, the content of the *Chronicles* was designed to appeal to a particular readership, a readership whose common element was wealth sufficient enough to purchase one or several copies of the work. 'Great' history, the history of royalty, nations, wars and nobility, was mixed with mere curiosities such as natural calamities, freaks of nature, executions, and the spectacles and disturbances particular to the capital, things that in essence were the everyday interest of the London citizenry. The thinking behind the production of the *Chronicles* cannot have been simply or even mainly the recording of a noble English past for future generations to mull over or the preservation of half-forgotten incidents and ephemeral records.[94] Surely the motivational force behind the compilation of both the first and the second editions of the *Chronicles* was to produce a good, even majestic history of the British Isles with which intelligent people would want to be associated. Association might be merely by purchasing a copy or copies, or, more importantly, by having one's ancestors, community or group figuring in a meritorious way in the text. It goes without saying that it was necessary for the authors to write in a very neutral way where dynastic claims, religious differences and still living political issues were involved, not simply to avoid governmental displeasure and censorship but to ensure that potential purchasers of the work were not alienated because their ancestors got a bad press. Indeed, one suspects that the compilers were very ready to insert biographical material in the text either because the families in question had patronised them at some time in the past or were likely to do so in the future, or simply because, being people currently in the news, they would benefit sales. As well as being known as subscribers and thus popularising the work, they might, where they had the authority, be of assistance in heading off government censorship.

In conclusion we must examine what appears to have been a connection of Thomas Ardern with the county of Warwickshire. As we have noticed above, Ardern in the earlier 1540s figured in land transactions made on behalf of the then Attorney General William Whorwood and also his clerk, William Walter. Whorwood from 1540 onwards purchased ex-monastic land in the West Midlands, a small part of which he held jointly with Walter.[95] Ardern may well have helped them secure the grants, for he acquired rents from the same properties, probably by their gift. Thus in May 1544 there was a grant to Ardern and Walter, in fee to the latter, of pasture called 'Hethcote' in Wasperton and Hethcote, Warwickshire. The manor of Wasperton, lately belonging to the priory of St Mary, Coventry, had been acquired, minus certain rents charged on it, by Whorwood and Walter in April 1540.[96] Whorwood also acquired rents of small value in Wasperton from the former property of the Franciscan house at Thellesford and by 1547, together with Ardern, from similar land in Hethcote. By late 1547 Ardern had also obtained a rent on the manor of Brewood Hall, near Walsall, of value 30s 4d from the lands of the former monastery of St Mary de Pratis, Leicester.[97] All Ardern's other property appears to have been located in Kent or London. Walter and Whorwood also held some land in the south-east, so why, therefore, Ardern should take his reward and retain it in the West Midlands is a mystery. It seems as though Ardern particularly wanted to have a tenurial or at least a financial connection with the Warwickshire region. Such a desire may have been connected with his origins. It is not uncommon for those of mature years to want to have a tangible and enduring connection with their ancestral locality. Although it cannot at the moment be traced, Ardern may have been related to a Warwickshire family. The pasture in Hethcote in Wasperton was only about 6 miles from Stratford-upon-Avon, and those who wish to do so may imagine a distant connection with Shakespeare, who, some critics believe, could have been the author or part-author of the play of *c.* 1590, *Arden of Feversham*. Ardern's small tenurial interest in the West Midlands may have passed unnoticed by historians because of the existence of the prominent Warwickshire military family with the same name. The latter, the Arderns of Castle Bromwich and Park Hall, do not, however, seem to have had any connection with Hethcote or Brewood. On the other hand, Shakespeare's mother's family, the Ardens of Snitterfield, lived but 4 miles from Hethcote. Furthermore, the bailiff and collector of rents in Wasperton in April 1540, at the time when the manor was granted to Whorwood and Walter, was a John Hill; and Robert Arden, Shakespeare's mother's father, took as his second wife Agnes, widow of John Hill (died 1545), supposedly of Bearley. These John Hills were probably one and the same.

Chapter 5

LORD STOURTON AND THE HARTGILLS

Possibly the most notorious case of murder in England in the sixteenth century, among the upper classes at least, was the slaying of the Somersetshire esquire William Hartgill and his son John on the orders and in the presence of Charles, Lord Stourton. The date of the crime was 12 January 1557 and the place was that nobleman's home, Stourton House, located in the extreme south-west corner of Wiltshire.

In one regard the murder was the climax of a feud, smouldering and burning brightly by turns, between two upper-class families. Yet the crime was atypical of the many land wars of the gentry and nobility of the period in that, although the decade of preliminary hostilities before the slayings involved nothing more than violence to property, broken heads and flesh wounds, the denouement was the coldest of cold-blooded murders, the victims having been taken captive by treachery and only done to death, still pinioned, thirty-six hours later. Furthermore, the murder was not simply done, as happened in these feuds very occasionally, by the servants of a nobleman in the course of a confrontation with their employer's enemies, but secretly on his direct instructions and under his personal supervision.

A contemporary account of the murder commences in dramatic fashion. Soon after the death of Lord William Stourton, we are told, his son and heir Charles 'fell utterly out' with William Hartgill (the year was 1549) and on Whit Sunday morning appeared near Kilmington church door, two miles from Stourton, with a great many men armed with bows and guns. Whereupon William Hartgill's son John, 'being a tall lusty gentleman', who was inside the church at the time, went outside, drew his sword and ran amid a shower of arrows to his father's house, which was situated adjacent to the churchyard. He went there to get weapons in order to protect his parents, who, with several servants, had taken refuge in the church tower. Having armed himself with a longbow, he caused a woman 'to carry the crosse bowe and gonne after hym' and drove away Stourton and his men from around the house and the church. When he then asked his father what they ought to do next, he was told he should take horse and 'ryde upp to the Court and tell the honorable Councell how I am used'. Having first arranged for meat and drink to be pulled up into the church tower for the sustenance of the occupants, he set off. The evening of the next day he told the Privy Council in London of his father's plight. The Council sent the Somersetshire sheriff to remove the 'captyves', as they were called, to safety and to bring Charles Stourton up to London. This he did and Stourton was incarcerated for a short period in the Fleet prison. After John Hartgill's departure for London and before the arrival of the sheriff, Stourton and his men had resumed their siege of the church tower and also killed William Hartgill's valuable gelding. They did, however, allow his wife Joan to return home unmolested.[1]

'Thus', continues this account, 'the sayd Lord Stourton contynued his malice styll durynge all kynge Edwarde's regn'. Then, after providing a single example of violence between the parties in Mary's reign, it breaks off. Happily the tale is continued in another fragment of narrative but when this commences the date is December 1556, a mere month before the murder.[2] However, the storytelling is more dense and the circumstances of the Hartgills' deaths are provided in detail. Were this all the material we had on the murders, it would be difficult to discern the continuance and ultimate escalation of the feud from 1549 to 1556, or to be able to assess the characters and backgrounds of the principals and their families. Fortunately, in the early 1860s J.E. Jackson, who as librarian to the Marquis of Bath had sorted and indexed many of the manuscripts at Longleat House (a mere 6 miles from Stourton), took an interest in the tale and drew attention to various letters and papers there that threw much light on the nature of the quarrel.[3]

The family of the victims, the Hartgills, belonged to the squirarchy. In the mid-fifteenth century a Thomas Hartgill of Stourton, who sat as a burgess in parliament for three different boroughs, was described as a servant of Lord Stourton.[4] The Edward Hartgill who was a yeoman of the Crown from 1460, usher of the King's Chamber from 1476, and sheriff at various times in the 1470s and 1480s for Wiltshire, Hampshire and Somerset–Dorset, was probably his son. Edward was also steward of the manor of Mere, which was very close to Stourton; at a later date Charles Stourton held it by lease. Edward must have been a direct ancestor of the two Hartgill victims.[5] William, the father, served as a tax collector in 1545 and escheator (in Somerset–Dorset bailiwick) in 1542–3 and 1548–9, offices that were traditionally the perquisites of the lesser gentry. At the beginning of Edward VI's reign he was made a justice of the peace in both Somerset and Wiltshire, and was a chantry commissioner in the former in 1548. In 1545 he sat in parliament for the Wiltshire borough of Westbury.[6] By the last decade of Henry VIII's reign the Hartgills were substantial landholders at the southern end of the Somerset–Wiltshire border. William Hartgill, we are told, held 650 acres in Hardington and other land around his residence at Kilmington, 8 miles to the south. He was also steward of the lands of William, Lord Stourton.[7]

Other references to the Hartgills in this period may have a more particular bearing on the feud. Among Thomas Cromwell's personal memoranda for the years 1529 to 1531 is mention of depositions against a John Hartgill, possibly a brother of William, for words spoken against the Lord Chief Justice, Sir John Fitz-James.[8] This is significant because it suggests a readiness in the family members to quarrel with the great men of this land, and, since the depositions suggest the matter endured for some time, an intransigence or reluctance to concede or compromise. Indeed, a seventeenth-century rector of Kilmington, Francis Potter, claimed William Stourton, the father of the murderer, recruited William Hartgill into his retinue because he was 'a mighty stout fellowe' who was recommended for his valour. More significantly, he had 'lately killed a man'.[9]

The same conclusion can be drawn from an episode that occurred in March 1540. Four men of Kilmington complained of the behaviour of William Hartgill. The complaint seems to have been made to the Privy Council, but it was apparently moved to the Court of Star Chamber. At issue was the criminal career of John Webbe, a servant of Hartgill's, the crime he had committed nine years previously, the shelter he was given subsequently by his late employer and his recent escape from custody because of Hartgill's intervention. Those involved in the attempt to capture Webbe claimed Hartgill had had them arrested, and the other men who testified to the truth of these accusations recorded how Hartgill's sons, William the younger and John, or his servants, had on various occasions assaulted and wounded them and maimed their animals. Star Chamber depositions show the Hartgills were

involved in poaching on a large scale and demonstrate very clearly the ability
of William Hartgill the elder to manipulate the law to his own advantage and
to maintain, as the term was, those of his servants who were in conflict with
it. Two of the men who complained about him had once been in his employ
and thus knew much about his strong-arm methods and partiality for
poaching. One, indeed, claimed he had quit Hartgill's service in anger because
of his illegal activities. Another of those who testified, a Kilmington yeoman,
referred to the Hartgills as quarrelsome men of evil reputation and stated
that, because he had demanded back a sow stolen by their servants, they had
attempted to murder him. Yet another said that there were many persons in
the county of Somerset who were much upset by the behaviour of William
Hartgill, his sons and his servants, inferring that concern was not confined
only to their home area.[10] On the face of it the Hartgills, and William Hartgill
especially, were grasping, possessed of few scruples and given to violence. Yet
it was not an uncommon practice to denigrate opponents in land-war
litigation at this time. Certainly the mention of their being of evil reputation
and so known throughout the county was a mark against them, but whether
they were any more than 'surly, dogged, crosse', as a seventeenth-century
report characterised the elder Hartgill, is debatable.[11]

The instigator of the murders, Charles, the seventh Baron Stourton, came
from a military family. His uncle had served in Henry VIII's navy and his
father, William, as a soldier in France (1523) and Scotland (1544–5), where
he was in command of substantial forces and earned commendations. From
June 1546 until his death in September 1548 William, the sixth Baron, was
Deputy-General of Newhaven (Ambleteuse, a small fort in the Boulonnais)
and, by the standards of the time, an efficient officer.[12] His military spirit was
inherited by Charles, who served in the Pinkie campaign in 1547. Both father
and son had an imperious disposition but in the case of the latter it
sometimes reached plain arrogance, as his correspondence clearly shows.
Charles was also possessed of a quick and terrible temper, a trait he was well
aware of, and, at times, lamented.[13]

Lord William Stourton was able to add substantially to the family property
in the earlier 1540s. He paid a total of about £4,500 to Lord Ferrers and the
King for lands in Dorset, Wiltshire and Somerset, an expensive purchase that
suggests he made a profit from his wars. The particular purchase that seems
to have had a direct connection with the murders was made in January
1544. William Stourton paid the Crown over £1,260 for lands lately

belonging to five monasteries. Included were the properties that Shaftesbury Nunnery had once possessed in Kilmington. Among these were the chief messuage and farm of Kilmington, pasture for 400 sheep on the heath there, and a barton and two closes then in the tenure of William Hartgill. Two days after this grant Stourton obtained a licence to alienate the properties to the same.[14] It is possible that Hartgill, however, did not pay the full price immediately, and either delayed subsequent payment or tried to avoid it altogether. Francis Potter, the rector, believed Hartgill had 'cosined' Lord Stourton out of 'Kilmington'. Stourton remained lord of Kilmington Manor as well as lord of the adjacent one of Norton Ferrers, where William Hartgill was also a tenant, and the manor court records suggest that not long after Lord William Stourton's death there was friction over the non-payment of dues and rents and the illegal occupation of land by the Hartgills, as well as over their unneighbourly conduct in shutting off the highway, pasturing sheep on the rectory lands, failing to clean a well and assaulting local inhabitants. Why William Hartgill persistently failed to meet his manorial obligations is unclear. The accusations were made by the manorial jury of presentment. It is quite possible these jurors were recording the beliefs of Charles Stourton, the manorial lord from September 1548, that Hartgill was defrauding him. Hartgill appears to have claimed exemption from some manorial obligations under various leases that Stourton had not seen and that dated from his father's time or the years when Lord Ferrers held Norton Ferrers manor. This matter was still not settled at the time of the murder.[15]

Disagreement of another sort between the Hartgills and Stourtons had started before Lord Charles's time. William Hartgill served as the steward of William Stourton for some years in the 1540s. While his master was away at the wars, he sold various of his lands, receiving at least £2,000 for them. There is no indication that Hartgill acted other than properly in these transactions. A letter from William Stourton to Hartgill of around 1546 is devoid of criticism about financial matters. However, another letter, written perhaps a year later, is brusque and accusing. Stourton stated that he had heard Hartgill was seeking his 'owne gayne more then my comdytie and honor' and therefore he had determined he should make account, 'whyche I never yet dyd', when he next returned from Newhaven; 'then shall I trye your honestie,' he added rather menacingly. He also complained about Hartgill taking new men into Stourton employment and his giving authority to two others who were suspected of having a greater loyalty to the steward than to their employer.[16] The implication was that these servants would either be dishonest themselves or connive at any peculative practices on the part of William Hartgill.

Another comment in William Stourton's earlier letter brings us to what may have been another basic cause of his quarrel with the Hartgills. This was Lord William's marital situation. In the letter he curtly told Hartgill, 'I am not contented that my wife doth goo so farre a brode as I here saye she dothe'. He had married Elizabeth Dudley, daughter of Henry VII's minister Edmund Dudley and half-sister of John Dudley, Duke of Northumberland, but it does not seem to have been a happy match. Perhaps he had left Elizabeth in his steward's care when he went off to the wars. One of the narratives of the circumstances of the murder reveals that just before William's death, and probably for a good while before that, she had been staying at William Hartgill's house in Kilmington.[17] There is no suggestion of any extramarital liaison between Lady Elizabeth and Hartgill. She was probably at Kilmington on her husband's instructions, or at least with his consent. She may have been there because she enjoyed the company of the Hartgills' wives, but there are two more likely reasons. First, she was at odds, even before her husband's death, with her eldest son Charles. Secondly, she was alienated from her husband and they were separated; for Lord William had a mistress. Her name was Agnes Ryce and she was the daughter of Rhys ap Gruffydd, a Welsh magnate who had been executed for treason in 1531.[18] In a chancery case in 1553 Agnes was to claim that she had in fact married Lord William in January 1547 in the chapel of Stourton House. If so, this was a bigamous marriage on Stourton's part for there is no evidence that he had divorced Elizabeth. Years earlier Elizabeth had been betrothed to William's elder brother Peter, who died soon after.[19] Perhaps William came to believe (as had once his royal master) that the marriage had contravened God's law and he was not truly married to Elizabeth. Yet it is much more likely that this 'marriage' was at Agnes's insistence, for the sake of her conscience. Agnes appears to have had a strong hold over William: she seems to have travelled with him wherever he went and to have been instrumental in obtaining from him a home for her mother, Katherine, Countess of Bridgewater, at Stourton Caundle.[20]

Lady Elizabeth Stourton's sojourn at William Hartgill's home suggests that he was sympathetic towards her. His support was more clearly demonstrated when, shortly after Lord William's death in 1548, Charles Stourton went to the Hartgill house to ask William Hartgill to persuade his mother, Elizabeth, to enter into a bond with him 'in a great some of money' that she would never marry again. Upper-class heirs to property in this period knew only too well that widows were entitled to a third of their husband's lands for their own lifetime and that if they remarried this dower portion was often difficult to reacquire at their death. William Hartgill's account of the episode is in his letter to Sir John Thynne of Longleat of October 1548. He noted Charles Stourton had fallen out with him because he would not 'untreuly deseave my lady his mother from all her right and tytle of porcion that shall cum to her by reason of my Lorde's [i.e. William Stourton's] death'. He had, however, caused Lady Elizabeth 'to goo from my howse against her will to Stourton to be onely at his mynde ordered'. Lord Charles's plan was that his mother should release to him all her titles to land and that she should reside permanently in his house at his expense, receiving an annuity of 100 marks and not being charged with the wages of servants. Should unresolvable differences arise between them, then she could reside at Stourton Caundle manor and have 200 marks a year. If she contracted to marry, there was to be no annuity. Stourton, apparently, asked Hartgill to draft this agreement, but the latter claimed he was not skilled enough to do so, and in any case he believed it should contain a clause allowing Lady Elizabeth to distrain on certain of the Stourton lands so as to ensure payment if Charles should die. The nobleman was much upset by this and called Hartgill a 'false vyllaine'.[21]

William Hartgill was also closely involved in the fortunes of Agnes Ryce at this time. Under Lord William's will she was bequeathed most of his goods and chattels as well as money owed to him. It was probably in order to defeat these provisions that Charles, whom his father had named as his executor, refused to act. He was able to have his father declared intestate and himself the administrator of the estate, thus getting the provisions of the will set aside.[22] He then sued Agnes for the jewels, plate and cash she had taken from Lord William's house at Lambeth, Surrey, immediately after his death, but was unsuccessful. When Agnes, presumably with her servants, tried to take possession of some farm stock at Stourton, she was resisted by Charles Stourton's wife, Anne, but Agnes was still able to achieve her purpose. The resistance was probably on Charles's instructions, for at about this time he was bound over in the large sum of 1,000 marks to appear before the Privy Council twice a week until discharged.[23] In 1550 Charles Stourton was able to remove Agnes from Stourton House, which she occupied, but not before

William Hartgill had appeared to encourage her resistance to the tenant Stourton wished to install there. In this encounter Agnes showed herself to be an able defender of her own interests. She locked the gates and placed servants to guard them with bows, guns and other weapons. She kept charge of the gates herself and allowed into the manor house only the sheriff, his servants and her ally, Hartgill. She told the would-be tenant that if he, or his followers, tried to enter, none of them would ever go out again alive, language what was matched in its aggressiveness by Hartgill's rejoinders to the complaints of the frustrated leaseholder.[24]

Charles Stourton had dismissed William Hartgill from the stewardship of his lands soon after he inherited. Hartgill then became steward of the property of the Duke of Somerset, the Protector, at Maiden Bradley, which was within 3 miles of Kilmington. This position he held until October 1552, when these lands went to Somerset's grandson Edward and the stewardship to Charles Stourton's brother William.[25] In July 1549 Hartgill complained that a large number of gentlemen, all friends or followers of Stourton, had been hunting deer illegally on the Duke's lands and destroying hedges and ditches. Stourton, at about the same time, told Somerset that Hartgill had assaulted and threatened with death some of his servants. He asked the Duke to be his 'good lord' and prevent his being subjected to such harassment. He was apparently expecting Somerset to mediate between Hartgill and himself, as patrons were expected to do for their clients. Whether his hopes were fulfilled, we do not know, but the incident is more important in showing that Stourton was not able to dominate his opponent at this point. The reason may have been political: Hartgill had spread a story that Lord Charles was a supporter of the current rebellion in the west, which, given the latter's known conservatism in religion, must have put him on the defensive.[26]

An important factor in gaining the edge in any feud was the ability to manipulate legal process to one's own benefit.[27] At this Hartgill was no slouch: he had a shrewd if untutored legal mind. Early in 1549 the woman newly married to Hartgill's chaplain at Kilmington was indicted of poisoning her former husband and the priest himself indicted as accessory. Possibly to demonstrate his Protestant inclinations and his loyalty to Protector Somerset, Hartgill had been instrumental in arranging the marriage in the face of opposition from other Somerset gentry. Charles Stourton may well have been behind the indictment, for he sent a servant to secure the goods of the priest and kept them for his own use. Hartgill quickly wrote to the Somersetshire sheriff, Sir John Thynne, succinctly drawing attention to the weaknesses in the Crown's case and thus how it could be defeated. He pointed out that the coroner had done his job incorrectly, that female witnesses had been set in the stocks to force them to testify against the woman suspect, and that the jury had been packed, being composed of 'papists'. Since sheriffs, in practice, made the juries, Hartgill made sure at this time that Sheriff Thynne was his patron and ally; the undersheriff, Gamege, he treated as a confidant and confederate.[28]

If the 'fixing' of juries was a key element in success in upper-class feuding, so also was a reputation as a strong 'maintainer' at law of allies and followers. In June 1549 Hartgill and his servants confronted some of Lord Stourton's men, who were hunting hares in the fields. He told them that, should his servants happen to kill any of Stourton's in the expected struggle, he would 'bare them out', and that although he was 'sworn to the peace yet would he borrow a point of the law for he had two or thre hundrith pounds to spend in vayne'. By this he meant he would ensure his men were not punished and would do so by either bribery or the purchase of pardons. Hartgill's words remind us that both he and Stourton were members of peace commissions.[29] Feuds also meant the use of distant courts to outflank and embarrass one's opponents. On some unknown date in 1547 or 1548 William Hartgill obtained from Lord William Stourton a lease of Kilmington rectory, a lease that caused Charles Stourton much annoyance after he had inherited. In December 1549 some of his servants forced their way into the house and injured a shepherd in Hartgill's employ and one other person. Hartgill, doubtless because he did not expect satisfaction in local courts where Stourton's influence might prevail, took the matter into the Star Chamber and obtained writs of subpoena against the intruders. When, however, his servant John Butler attempted to deliver these at Stourton parish church door on Christmas Day, he was beaten and wounded by retainers of Charles Stourton. The interrogatories of his Star Chamber case show Charles Stourton had extended his aggression to Hartgill's local supporters. Thomas Chaffyn of Mere, who called himself Hartgill's cousin, suffered assaults on his servants and the seizure of his sheep and barley in the year subsequent to September 1550.[30]

After the death of Lord William Stourton, William Hartgill had cultivated the friendship of Sir John Thynne of Longleat, whose service as sheriff we have noted. He addressed him in correspondence as 'my moste singular goode

Master', and thus may have been in Thynne's employ; certainly John Hartgill, William's son, was a servant of Sir John. In April or early May 1549 Sir John seems to have tried to mediate, as patron, in the quarrel between Hartgill and Charles Stourton. He did this by a letter to the nobleman, but the bearer, Hartgill's son John, reported Stourton took offence at the message, many times calling the elder Hartgill 'varlett and veleyne'. A further letter by Thynne, asking for moderation on Stourton's part, brought an aggressive refusal to accept the proffered advice and the suggestion that Thynne was not mediating but supporting Hartgill against him and doing so out of spite. In July 1549 a correspondent of Thynne's, noting that Stourton had complained to the Duke of Somerset about Hartgill, asked that Thynne should try to persuade Hartgill 'to lyve in more quyetnes'; if he would not 'yt were better for hym to dwell in Turkey'. This presumably meant that even the Ottoman Turk would be less hostile to Hartgill than was Stourton, and it was the first intimation that Hartgill's life might be in danger. In another letter the same correspondent asked Thynne to tell Somerset of Stourton's 'extreme doyngs' against Hartgill in order that the former might see to it that 'his servant [i.e. William Hartgill] could live in safety'. Relations between Thynne and Stourton continued to deteriorate during the second half of 1549. At a later date Thynne recorded that that autumn Stourton entered and rifled his houses when he was at Windsor with the King; yet he continued to pretend neutrality in the feud. In Mary's reign, when advised by an associate to assist Hartgill against Stourton, he thought fit to answer that he never meddled 'in any man's matters but myne own', even though he pitied Hartgill's 'manyfeste injurie and almost utter undoing' and hoped the Privy Council would intervene.[31] Perhaps Thynne had come to recognize that both parties were incorrigible, but more likely his reluctance to intervene was prompted by Stourton's rise and his own decline in influence with the change of monarch.

Of considerable importance in regard to Stourton's ultimate fate were his actions immediately subsequent to the death of King Edward, actions that had nothing to do with William Hartgill. His behaviour must have made him enemies in high places. Two days after Edward VI's demise Charles Stourton was appointed Lord Lieutenant of the three shires of Wiltshire, Somerset and Dorset. This post carried with it the duty of raising forces on the Queen's behalf and, probably, of proclaiming Queen Mary's title to the Crown. The commission itself has not survived and we must rely on private papers for its content and date, a matter that was to have embarrassing consequences for

Stourton later on. Who it was who sent him the commission is not clear. It may have been a pre-emptive move by the Catholic faction within the Privy Council. It may have come from Mary as she retreated into East Anglia. Stourton was the nephew of the Duke of Northumberland, who at that time was engaged in trying to secure the throne for his daughter-in-law, Lady Jane Grey, and the appointment may have been intended to detach Stourton from their cause. In the event Stourton delayed for nearly two weeks before making proclamation of Mary's title.[32] Naturally enough this provided ammunition for Stourton's local foes, who drew attention also to other suspicious behaviour on his part. It was noted that one Thornhill, who had stayed the night of 17/18 July at Stourton's house, had then ridden to Shaston in Dorsetshire where he proclaimed Jane Grey as queen. This was but 5 miles distant. On 19 July Lady Jane was proclaimed queen at Frome in Somerset, 5 miles to the other side of Stourton's residence. These occurrences were viewed as being in some way connected with Charles Stourton's political sympathies or at least having his tacit approval; and his failure to prevent another proclamation of Jane's title (this time at Wells, Somerset), and to secure the immediate arrest of the Bishop of Bath when he preached a sermon there against Mary's claim to the throne, was also seen to prove disloyalty to the new monarch.[33]

Lord Stourton's suspicious inactivity caused one member of the Wiltshire gentry, Sir John Bonham, to write to him pointing out that, when these proclamations on Jane's behalf were made, Stourton had 'nothing doon to the contrary'; more accusingly still he referred to Stourton's 'nereness of blode to th'arche traitor fawtour [i.e. Northumberland] of all this mischieve'. Then he challenged the nobleman to a duel. In answer Stourton said that if Bonham referred the matter to Queen Mary she would fully answer him, and he added: 'I let the witt, Bonham, ther is nether the blood of uncle nor brother which shall make me forgett my naturall aleageaunce.' Taking up the challenge to a duel, he dared his critic, 'therefor set thy foot to myne when thou wylt'.[34] There were other, more weighty, opponents. The appointment of Charles Stourton as lieutenant in the counties of Somerset, Wiltshire and Dorset must have been a blow to William Herbert, Earl of Pembroke, who had held the office previously, and must have been one reason for the clash between their servants, which gave the Privy Council some concern in August 1553. John Aubrey states that Stourton, for his part, envied Herbert's status as earl and, whenever he rode past Wilton, where Herbert resided, he would 'sound his trumpetts and give reproachfull challenging words'.[35] The political standing of both noblemen improved somewhat early in Mary's reign. By September 1553 Stourton appears to have been in favour at Court, for it was he who instructed the Sheriff of Wiltshire as to those who should be returned to represent that county and its boroughs in the upcoming parliament, and, more particularly, those 'spottyde persons' who should not.[36] But in January 1554 the Earl was reported as being 'in great credyte and restored to all his former authorytie' in the area, a development that may have had a bearing on Stourton's eventual fate.[37]

The accession of Mary and the improvement in Lord Stourton's fortunes seems to have done little to assuage his feud with William Hartgill. In August 1554, as a result of Hartgill's complaints, Stourton was summoned before the Privy Council and was compelled to enter into a recognizance for £1,000 either to justify himself to the Council or to settle with his accuser, which suggests the patience of the counsellors was wearing thin. The offence seems to have been his seizure of corn and cattle belonging to Hartgill, an event the latter mentioned in his will of January 1555. Hartgill also sued Stourton in the Queen's Bench, and at Trinity Term 1556 won £368 6s 8d in damages.[38] In August 1556 Hartgill secured the indictment of several of Stourton's followers for forcible entry in January of that year into property in Kilmington, lands that Lord William Stourton had apparently sold to Hartgill in 1543, but out of which Charles Stourton for some reason believed he had been cheated. The case was to be tried in the Queen's Bench in January 1557. A contemporary account tells us that, because he had failed to pay the damages that Hartgill had won in the earlier case, Stourton was put in the Fleet late in 1556 but was released on £2,000 surety just before Christmas. He was supposed to surrender at the Fleet again on the first day of the next Hilary Law Term (20 January 1557).[39] He must have returned home on about 22 December 1556. Then, within three or four days, 'he devised . . . to send certain parsonages to the said Hertgilles to declare unto them that he was readye to paye unto them the said somes of money according as yt was ordered in the Starre chamber, and to commune with them also for a further ending and quyeting of all matters between them: for the which purpose he desyred a place and tyme to bee appointed of meeting togithers'.[40] This was pure deceit. He intended to kidnap if not murder them.

'Th'order of my lord Stourton's proceedings with the two Hertgilles' is the title of the fragment of manuscript that deals specifically with the murders.[41]

It tells us that the two Hartgills, William and his son John, were suspicious of Stourton's sincerity in offering to pay his debts, but agreed to meet him at Kilmington church on Monday, 11 January 1557. On the day Charles Stourton arrived at 10 a.m. with about fifteen servants, several of his tenants and 'some Gentelmen and Justices'. In all the entourage numbered about forty persons, which made the Hartgills 'veary moch to dreade'. He asked them to come from the church, where they were at the time, to the church-house 40 yards distant where he and his party were waiting. The Hartgills did so but on arrival William complained he could see many of his enemies in Stourton's group. His fears were somewhat assuaged by two Justices of the Peace at Stourton's side, Sir James Fitzjames and Thomas Chaffyn, who assured him that he and his son should suffer no bodily hurt. Stourton told William Hartgill the money was inside the church-house and suggested he should go in and collect it, but William refused. Therefore it was arranged that the payment should be made on a table on the village green. Lord Stourton placed a cap-case and a purse on the table and announced he would pay every penny of the sum the Council had commanded. Then he added that he would first know them to be 'true men'. This, apparently, was a cue for his servants, who immediately seized the two Hartgills 'with all crewelness'. Simultaneously Stourton declared that he was arresting them for felony. The source does not suggest he identified the particular crime.[42]

The father and the son were dragged to the church-house, their purses taken from them, and then they were securely bound with tape that Stourton had purposely brought with him. Stourton gave one of his servants two 'greate blowes' because he failed to perfom this task properly, and another great blow he gave to John Hartgill when he said 'the crueltye shewed unto them was to much'. When he saw John's wife, Dorothy, by the door of the church-house, he kicked at her, tearing her hose with his spurs; then he struck her between the neck and the head with his sword. So heavy was the blow that for three hours it seemed she was dying. The father and son were then transported to Kilmington parsonage, where for the rest of that Monday they were confined without food, their arms bound behind their backs. Stourton, apparently, considered killing them then and there, but was dissuaded by one of his servants. At between one and two o'clock of the next morning (Tuesday, 12 January) they were moved to a house referred to as 'Bonham' situated close to the village of Stourton. There they were imprisoned in two separate places, still bound and without sustenance.

Around three o'clock in the afternoon two justices of the peace were sent by Stourton to examine them, having been told by the nobleman that he would dispatch the prisoners to the proper jail next day.[43] The justices had the two Hartgills freed of their bonds and told Stourton's servants to leave them so, but what they discovered about the supposed felony and what they thought about the peculiar nature of the arrests we are not told.

When the justices had departed, Lord Stourton had the Hartgills bound once more, and then he sent away nearly all the servants who had been involved in guarding them.[44] He had already informed those allowed to remain of his intent to slay the captives, and had promised them that they would be required to do no more than he himself did. At ten o'clock in the evening that same Tuesday Stourton sent four men to move the prisoners from 'Bonham', having given instructions to kill them immediately should they make any noise. The Hartgills were taken to a close called 'Le Worth' near the garden of the nobleman's chief residence. There the brutal deed was done. While on their knees, with their arms bound behind their backs, they were struck on the head with clubs several times until the assailants thought they were 'starck dedde'.[45] While they were being clubbed Lord Stourton stood at the gallery door of his house, less, we are told, than a quoit's cast distant. Then the killers wrapped the two bodies and carried them through the garden to the gallery, whence Stourton led them to a 'lytle place' near his own chamber. There the bodies gave signs of life: 'they groned very sore', especially the elder Hartgill.

Thereupon William Farre, apparently the chief of Lord Stourton's henchmen, at his master's bidding took out his knife and cut both their throats; 'my Lorde standing by with the candel in his hande'. One of the other servants who was present was moved to say: 'Ah my lorde! This is a pytiouse sight: hadde I thought that I now thincke before the thing was doon, your hole land could not have woon me to consent to soch an acte.' 'What, fainte harted knave!' responded Lord Stourton. 'Ys yt anny more than the rydding of two knaves that lyving were troublesome bothe to Goddes lawe and man's? There is no more accoumpt to bee made of them then the kylling of ii [two] sheepe.'[46] The bodies of the Hartgills were then thrown down into a dungeon, after which two servants, Henry Symmes and Roger Gough, were lowered by rope to bury them with earth topped with 'two coursses of thicke paving' and two cart-loads of timber chips and shavings. While they worked Lord Stourton strode up and down and urged them several times to hasten, as the night was nearly gone.

As soon as the Hartgills were carried off from Kilmington by Stourton and his men, the wives and friends of the prisoners must have hastened to inform the Privy Council. On 14 January 1557, three days after the meeting at the church-house, the Council sent a letter to Stourton ordering him to hand over the Hartgills, whom he was known to have arrested for felony and to be keeping in his own custody, to the Sheriff of Somerset. He was also required to come and explain the reasons for those actions. Lord Stourton's movements immediately subsequent to the murder are something of a mystery. By late January he was apparently in the Fleet prison, although on whose authority is unknown.[47] From there he was summoned into the Star Chamber for the assessment of his fine for causing riots against the Hartgills. The latter were named as plaintiffs and the fine must have been the result of Stourton's misdeeds in 1556, not the murder. In court, when a fine of 300 marks had been assessed, he said bitterly to the Lord Chancellor, 'I am sorie to see that Retorick doth rule where law should take place.'[48] The Chancellor said the words were slander of the Court, but he respited punishment for them until the Queen had been told, a decision that suggests either that Stourton enjoyed Mary's particular favour or, conversely, that she wished to be informed immediately of any further misdeeds by the troublesome nobleman.

The matter of Lord Stourton's more recent behaviour then came up. The Chancellor told him he had been accused in an information of other misdemeanours against the Hartgills. The tenor of this information, which the Chancellor then read out, was that Stourton, pretending 'a friendly ende' was to be made to the disputes between them, 'drew them to meete', and then 'imprisoned them in his own house, bound hand and foote, and after that never heard of'. The Privy Council asked Stourton where the Hartgills were. He answered that he did not know for sure but thought they had escaped from the constable into whose custody he had delivered them. His questioners obviously disbelieved him, for he was committed, with three of his servants, to the Tower as a close prisoner. Some of his other servants were incarcerated elsewhere. Stourton was also removed from the peace commission.[49] At this point, while the ultimate fate of the Hartgills was unknown, a Sir John Fitzwilliam was noted in the Privy Council records as having been arrested with some of his servants and also committed as a close prisoner. In this instance the reason for suspicion was clearly stated: it was of murdering the Hartgills.[50] The name of Sir John Fitzwilliam must have been inserted erroneously in place of that of Sir James Fitzjames, who had been present at the meeting at Kilmington church. Why the Privy Council should have believed Fitzjames was a murderer is a mystery. He may, however, have given Stourton support at Kilmington, for the Council eventually fined him a substantial sum and made him pay another to the Hartgill widows.[51]

What led to the discovery of the Hartgills' bodies and thus the indictment of Lord Stourton we can only surmise. Possibly further information from the families and friends of the murdered men resulted in the Privy Council ordering the Wiltshire sheriff or justices of the peace to make local investigations. Just as likely is the thesis that one or several of Lord Stourton's servants imprisoned in the Tower decided to confess either willingly, because of conscience or the hope of saving their lives, or because of threats, probably of torture, by the Privy Council. In Mary's reign there were several instances of men suspected of heinous felonies being threatened with, or actually put to, torture on the rack in the Tower for the purpose of obtaining information about their offences. The manuscript of the murder seems to imply that it was the examination of Stourton's henchmen that brought results. This is suggested by the revelation at this time of a number of crimes committed earlier by the nobleman or on his orders. These included setting fire to Thomas Chaffyn's barn, taking a whole team of oxen from another local gentleman, Christopher Willoughby, and, most notably, a number of 'routs, ryottes, robberyes and murdres', 'which were to long to wright'.[52] It was the Sheriff of Wiltshire, Sir Anthony Hungerford, who actually found the bodies at their burial place in the dungeon.

For Lord Stourton and his minions there was an extra stage in proceedings before they were indicted of their crimes. Henry Machyn, the London chronicler, tells us that Stourton and one of his men appeared before the Privy Council 'and juges' at Westminster on 17 February, where the evidence was declared 'a-for ys owne face' and he was unable to rebut it. The subsequent day there were sent from the Tower to appear before certain members of the Council four of Stourton's servants.[53] It is possible that the Privy Council, because of the strength of the evidence against him, expected Stourton to confess his offence then and there. It was ready perhaps, if he did so, to extend to him the possibility of the Queen's grace. However, Stourton did not co-operate, and the government was compelled to give him a common-law trial before his noble peers.

Two days later, on 19 February, Charles Stourton was indicted. The inquest was held at Salisbury before John Prideaux, a serjeant-at-law, and three

Wiltshire justices of the peace. The jury of indictment comprised four esquires and sixteen gentlemen, drawn, in theory at least, from the locality where the crime was committed. By this period the jurors of indictment were not expected to have a personal knowledge of the circumstances of the crime. The bill of indictment contained about 750 words, and thus was very much longer than was usual. The sequence of events from the meeting at Kilmington church to the burial of the bodies was described in detail, even providing some of the words spoken by Stourton to his minions. Undoubtedly the bill had been drafted by the Queen's law officers.[54] Emphasis was placed on Stourton's mortal hatred of the Hartgills, so enduring and undeviating, and on the treacherous nature of the meeting. The malicious pretence that the Hartgills had committed felony was mentioned, as was their seizure, binding, imprisonment and conveyance from Kilmington to Bonham, and from there to 'Le Worth'. As to the actual killing, Charles Stourton was stated to have secretly conspired the murder with William Farre and four other servants (Henry Symmes, John Davies, Roger Gough and Macute Jacob) and with malice aforethought procured and ordered Farre and the others to take the Hartgills to Stourton with the intention of murdering them. This they did and clubbed the victims, with Lord Stourton present. They carried them in through the gallery door of his house to a chamber over a dungeon, with Stourton leading them, and in his presence Farre then cut their throats. Thus, notes the indictment, Charles Stourton, William Farre and the others murdered William and John Hartgill. They buried the bodies and, 'exulting in this most heinous murder', Stourton said: 'It is but the rydding of a coople of knaves oute of the waye, which have longe troubled us in Goddes lawes and the Kinges.'[55]

The indictment was coloured with many phrases of afforcement designed to emphasise the exceptionally dastardly nature of the crime. Thus, so it was stated, Lord Stourton had been 'led on by the devil' and had 'planned with the most sinful malice', and was 'continuing in the vilest malice', 'for executing that terrible villainy'. These words of disparagement were intended primarily to impress the jurors, both those of indictment and of trial, thereby to persuade them to affirm the charges. Another reason for a heavily afforced indictment was probably to make more difficult the obtaining of a pardon from the monarch. Perhaps the most significant feature of the indictment was that Lord Stourton figured in it as a principal and not as an accessory, even though he struck no blow himself. If the crime had been committed in the fifteenth century, he would probably have been accused only as an accessory. However, as we have seen, Fitzherbert's treatise shows that by Henry VII's time anyone who ordered a murder to be committed, and was present when the deed was done, was to be held a principal, even if he or she took no part in the actual slaying.[56] Nevertheless, we might have expected the Crown to name Stourton only as an accessory; that it did not suggests there was no sympathy at all for him in high places. Had Stourton been indicted as accessory, he could not have been tried until his servant Farre, who actually slit the Hartgills' throats – the crucial wound that brought death – had been arraigned and found guilty. Farre and the other three servants directly involved were not in fact tried until the second week of March and were executed in the third.[57]

As a peer, Lord Stourton, although he could be indicted by a jury largely composed of local gentlemen, had the right to be tried by his fellow noblemen. For this purpose the Earl of Arundel was made Lord High Steward for the occasion so he could preside in the court, whose jurors or assessors comprised fourteen lords, a marquis, a viscount and an earl. The court sat in Westminster Hall on 26 February 1557, and proceedings were very brief. Lord Stourton was brought from the Tower by the constable of that fortress and, when the indictment had been read out and he had been instructed to make a plea, he initially refused to make any response, so says Henry Machyn.[58] Therefore, as was normal in felony trials, he was told that, if he would not plead either guilty or not guilty to the charge, he would be pressed to death. There was one attractive feature about such a miserable death: it did not involve the forfeiture of the miscreant's property, a consideration that may have prompted Stourton's hesitation. The warning, however, had the desired effect. He offered a plea, and, doubtless to the surprise of the court, it was an admission of guilt. Therefore he was immediately found guilty and judgment was given. He was to be hanged. No place of execution was named at that time; for the moment he was returned to the Tower. The plea of guilty demands further comment. Stourton, although brutal and reckless, did not shirk his responsibility: he did not say his servants were the actual slayers. The court record tells us that he expressly acknowledged the murder and put himself on the mercy of the king and queen.[59] Possibly he believed that if he made a clean breast of the crime he would be the better able to obtain a pardon.

To obtain a pardon the convicted felon needed, above everything else, time. As we have seen, he or she needed a delayed date of execution so that in the interim friends or patrons might approach persons who knew those who had personal access to the monarch and who, in return for financial reward, would put to the latter the case for royal mercy in as beguiling a way as possible. Time, however, was what Lord Stourton did not have. Only three days after the trial the Privy Council sent a letter to the Sheriff of Wiltshire ordering him to receive and execute Stourton, the decision having been made to put the murderer to death at Salisbury in his own county. Four of his servants were sent with him, in their case to face a delayed arraignment there. Stourton rode with his arms pinioned and his legs tied under his horse, and his journey, through Staines and Basingstoke, took three days.[60]

He was hanged in the marketplace at Salisbury on Saturday, 6 March. At the gallows he made a brief speech, which was copied down by a bystander. His words were similar to those of many members of the upper classes who were executed for treason in the sixteenth century: he had come there to die; he was justly condemned under the law for his offence; his fate should be an example to all those present; he was most sorry and repentant, and was asking forgiveness of everyone. Anyone who had offended him he readily forgave. Where he differed from those who were executed as traitors was in that he made reference to the circumstances of his crime. Traitors, because their offences were politically inspired, were warned not to do so, but Stourton spoke of the 'most cruell and detestable murther by my com- maundement' and asked his hearers to ensure 'yee lette no malice take roote in your hertes', since such a sentiment was the destroyer of all virtue.[61] After the execution there was some debate as to its manner. Bishop Burnet, writing late in the next century, recorded a tradition that Stourton, as a nobleman, was hanged not by a rope but by a silken cord. There is some evidence that for a time over his tomb a silken string was suspended, but the matter cannot be determined with any satisfaction. As to the servants sent down to Wiltshire with Stourton, they were arraigned and convicted in mid-March and then three of them, on the orders of the Privy Council, were hanged in chains by the Sheriff of Somerset and Dorset. The location of their execution was not specified, but the fourth servant suffered similarly at Mere, about 3 miles from the scene of the crime, and we may assume the three were put to death in the same area.[62]

It was Bishop Burnet who recorded that local tradition had it that Lord Stourton's friends were able to obtain a pardon, or at least a stay of execution, for him, but that it did not reach the Sheriff in time to save his life.

According to this version of events, the Earl of Pembroke was the cause. John Aubrey points out there was a great rivalry in Mary's reign between Charles Stourton and Pembroke.[63] Given the latter's sudden rise, his inclination towards the new religion and the loss of his lieutenancy to Stourton in 1553, this is understandable. Burnet states that the Wiltshire Sheriff, Sir Anthony Hungerford, heard that a pardon or reprieve for Stourton was to be sent to him and immediately informed the Earl of Pembroke, then at his house at Wilton. Pembroke ordered his gates to be shut and when Stourton's son with the pardon arrived from court he could not enter to find the sheriff. He therefore rode on to Salisbury to tell his father the news and then left, thereby missing the sheriff, who rode there secretly during the night to supervise the execution, which then took place.[64] Jackson, no doubt correctly, cast doubt on the veracity of this tale, pointing out that Stourton's eldest son was only 4 years old in 1557, and that neither Pembroke nor Hungerford was reprimanded for any misdemeanour at this time.[65] We also notice that Stourton's family, stripped of title and lands, never raised the matter of his being pardoned, which they surely would have done if true.

When we consider Charles Stourton's fate, it is his intentions when he arranged the meeting at Kilmington that seem to need most analysis. Did he intend to kill the two Hartgills from the outset, or did he merely intend to take them captive? The inducement to the pair to meet him at Kilmington, then the arrest on suspicion of felony, suggest a rational mind rather than an unbalanced one, since these tactics enabled him to get the father and son into his power on the pretence of proper law enforcement. Once they were in his custody, he probably intended to extort from them or frighten them into making whatever concessions he desired, notably to help him annul the Star Chamber decree. Similar occurrences were not infrequent in the later Middle Ages. We do not know if Stourton, in the several hours of their imprisonment, spoke with his captives, seeking acquiescence to his demands in return for their freedom, but such a course of events seems quite possible. If he did talk with them and they spurned his terms, which the singularly stubborn elder Hartgill might well have been inclined to do, he might, in his rage, have decided to kill them – but only then.[66] Since it was common knowledge that the Hartgills were in Stourton's custody, his murder options were limited. His best plan would have been to arrange matters so it could be claimed they were killed when assaulting their guards in an attempt to escape. His answer to the Privy Council when it asked him about the Hartgills' disappearance, to the effect that he had entrusted them to a constable and presumed they had escaped, was foolish, because it was bound to be found untrue if the matter was investigated. Had the men who disappeared been of lowly status there was a chance, given Stourton's rank and thus the cursory nature of any investigation, that the murders would not be discovered; but the Hartgills were gentry who had held significant public office, and their friends and relatives would press hard to discover the truth.

The thought of a pardon, should he be brought to book, must have figured in Stourton's calculations when he decided to kill his captives. With his strong adherence to the old faith and his victims' inclination towards the new, he may well have believed that, if the bodies were discovered and all revealed, he would still benefit from royal mercy. Statute law decreed pardons were not to be available to murderers, but they were granted nevertheless.[67] General pardons, which in the sixteenth century were often conceded by the monarch in parliament in return for the granting of a subsidy, commonly excluded murder, but special (that is, to a particular person) pardons for such were not infrequent in Mary's reign. Thus, at around the time of the Hartgills' deaths, we notice several notorious murderers escaping the gallows in this way. In June 1556 one pardon was granted to a woman who had instigated a murder by two male confederates; in December 1556 one was given to a gentleman and his many associates who had ambushed and murdered Lewis West, a substantial Yorkshire esquire; in February 1557 two went to men who had burgled a house and murdered the owner and his wife while they were at rest, and in June 1557 one was received by a woman who had murdered her husband by poison, lacing his beer with arsenic.[68] The last three of these offences could be considered particularly heinous murders, as dastardly as the slaying of the Hartgills. Thus there must have been special factors that caused the Crown to deny mercy to Charles Stourton.

The chief factor had to be Stourton himself and, more particularly, what those in authority thought of him. The members of the Privy Council, because of that body's many dealings with Stourton involving broken promises and downright lies, arrogance towards themselves, aggressive behaviour towards his neighbours and a generally abusive tongue, were doubtless loath as a body or as individuals to intervene to preserve his life. When such a grave crime was committed by a nobleman, the matter must have come to the monarch's attention. It is impossible to believe that Queen Mary did not know about the murder of the Hartgills and of Stourton's conviction and sentence. The conviction of a noble for felony was an exceptionally rare thing and always had been. The Queen's own inclinations and prejudices must also have played a part, even a dominant part, in Stourton's failure to get a pardon. Bishop Burnet connected the latter to Mary's avid persecution of those she viewed as heretics. His argument was that, because of the severities she visited upon the Protestants, she felt obliged to insist on full punishment for a murderer.[69] This thesis is not a strong one, as the substantial number of enrolled murder pardons of the period demonstrates. A more cogent reason for the Queen's refusal of clemency may well have been her personal distaste for Stourton's behaviour. His career certainly did not flourish in her reign. From the feminine point of view, his treatment of his mother on his father's death may have seemed particularly despicable, as may also his wounding of Dorothy Hartgill at the time her husband and son were arrested. Political memories may have been a third factor in ensuring Stourton went to the gallows. The incidents in July 1553, when Stourton took almost two weeks to proclaim Mary as queen and seemingly gave assistance to those who proclaimed Queen Jane in his region, were not things a ruler could totally forget.

A more prosaic reason for the Queen's refusal to pardon Stourton may have been simply a desire to keep the nobility in its place. The upper classes in general and the nobility in particular were well aware they could be executed for high treason, and this was accepted, but death as a punishment for them for felony was virtually unknown. Their power in the counties had traditionally made their indictment there very difficult to achieve. In any case, when they wished to murder someone, they could rely on their followers, who would be similarly protected. The few instances where members of the upper classes were brought to trial for felony involved, almost exclusively, robbery, rape or manslaughter, and those charged were of no more elevated status than gentry. Much has been written on the disciplining of the nobility in the Tudor period (a crucial aspect of its 'power') by means of the various juridical forms of the King's Council. Imprisonment and large fines ordered by these agencies as punishment were not uncommon, but incarceration was not usually long-lasting and fines were rarely exacted in full. The way Charles Stourton was repeatedly called before the Privy Council, and his cavalier attitude towards its interrogations and decrees, show the limits of conciliar authority when dealing with the truly recalcitrant members of the magnate class.

Trial for felony at this time, which meant in a court of common law, since that category of offence was beyond conciliar jurisdiction, must have been greatly feared amongst them. One reason was that conviction carried the death penalty (there was no alternative judgment); another was that it involved the escheat of all property not entailed. Additionally, it carried the indignity of being hanged on the common gallows like the lowliest of criminals. In the fourteenth and fifteenth centuries any member of the upper classes who was convicted of felony as a principal, or, more likely, as an accessory, was apparently able to obtain a pardon. Only from Henry VIII's reign can we detect a resolve to make an example of some of the most notorious offenders of this class by seeing the death sentence was carried out. As we have seen, on 5 February 1523 there was hanged at Tyburn Agnes, the second wife of Sir Edward Hungerford, for murdering her first husband, James Cotell, in 1518.[70] In June 1541 Lord Dacre of the South pleaded guilty before fellow peers to a charge of conspiring to kill anyone opposing his hunting party and was sentenced to be hanged for the subsequent murder of a park-keeper. As with Charles Stourton, it was thought the monarch was likely to pardon Dacre, especially since (unlike Stourton) it was believed his folly and death were brought about by his companions, 'some light heads that were then about him'.[71] But it was also a time when the King was in a particularly unforgiving mood, being vexed by the rebellion in south Yorkshire and suspicious of the sexual loyalty of his queen. Furthermore, Henry's ministers had had a confrontation with the Dacre family and its associates in 1534 over an enfeoffment to uses and accompanying will, and the bitterness may have still lingered seven years later.[72]

While Queen Mary's predilection for visiting the severest of sanctions on those she viewed as heretics is well known, her attitude towards secular crimes has never been given much attention. The conviction rate for felony at the Middlesex jail delivery sessions in her reign was a notably high one, being surpassed in those sixteenth-century periods for which we have record evidence only by the rate that prevailed in her brother Edward's time as king.[73] This, of course, cannot be directly attributed to Mary, but she did allow almost all the professional judges who served under Edward to retain their offices. On the other hand, she was not averse to granting pardons even for the most reprehensible of murders, as we have seen, and in August 1554 stopped for a time all executions for manslaughter and felonious larceny.[74] It was in her reign that there were promulgated two notable statutes concerned with criminal procedure. They ensured that suspects of felony, those who had arrested them and witnesses should be examined by justices of the peace, the results set down in writing immediately, and dispatched, together with the witnesses, to the next assizes for evidential purposes. Examination of suspects under the common law was no novelty; it had been in existence for nearly 100 years, as probably had the use of witnesses. What was new was the systemisation and standardisation of the pre-trial collection of evidence.[75] It may, perhaps, be objected that Mary, like a number of monarchs, would have been little concerned about such developments. In her case, however, we know she had an interest in the way in which the criminal law functioned, specifically in the use of witnesses in criminal trials. She is reported to have told Morgan, the Chief Justice of Common Pleas, to end the erroneous practice of not allowing witnesses to be heard on the defendant's behalf in Crown cases: that it was her pleasure 'that whatever can be brought in favour of the subject may be admitted and heard'. Even more strikingly, she added on this occasion the admonition that the judges were to sit on the bench, 'not as advocates for me, but as indifferent judges between me and my people'.[76] These were remarkable comments for a monarch, partly because of their technical nature but especially because of their endorsement of the notion of judicial impartiality, a concept other English rulers to this time were loath to support in actual practice.

On the other hand, torture, which had been used from time to time in her father's and her brother's reigns for the purpose of extracting information concerning notorious crimes, especially conspiracies of treason, continued to be used under Mary, and, like examination, became regulated. Formal torture, as distinct from duress by jailers and the like, was a highly centralised operation because at this time there were probably only two sophisticated instruments of torture in England, the most frequently referred to being the rack in the Tower of London.[77] In Edward VI's reign the orbit of torture was extended to men accused of such different crimes as murder, stealing hawks and robbery, and in Marian times of other felonies also. After 1555 authority to use torture to assist examination was allotted to a small number of notables who were to be regularly available to deal with persons charged with particular categories of felony; these were called the commissioners for the examination of prisoners.[78] What part Mary or her husband, Philip of Spain, played in this development is unclear, but they must have known about it. What clues we have, therefore, suggest Queen Mary was quite knowledgeable about the operation of the criminal law. She may well have been sensitive to the need for better public order, and her regime in that respect was generally severe. Yet she allowed pardons for the most heinous of crimes, which suggests her mercy was prompted by factors other than the mere category of the offence; for example, a known proclivity for evil, as in the case of Charles Stourton, might mean a refusal.

Is it possible at this distance in time to account for Stourton's arrogance, aggressiveness, brutality and deceit? Fathers who were professional soldiers, as was Lord William Stourton, saw their children but rarely. Soldier-fathers in all periods have frequently had a tendency to over-discipline their offspring or starve them of affection. In July 1539, in a letter to Thomas Cromwell, William Stourton compared his 'unthrifty' son Charles to a 'false hypocrite' and noted his recent involvement in an 'outrage'. He suggested Charles should be punished by a spell in jail.[79] A strained relationship might well have helped to produce a son who would try to distance himself from his father's attitudes and behaviour patterns. Yet Charles seems to have wanted to follow in his father's military footsteps despite Lord William's low opinion of his offspring. A more likely pernicious influence on his youthful personality may have been the aftermath of an event that occurred in April 1528. William Stourton, for £800, sold the wardship of two sons, Charles and Andrew, to Sir Walter Hungerford, an esquire of the body to Henry VIII and fellow Wiltshire magnate. The purpose of the deal was that Charles, or if he should die then his brother Andrew, should marry one of Hungerford's three daughters. At this point Charles Stourton was about 8 years old and the daughters mere babes. We do not know the outcome of these arrangements. The penalties for breaking the contract were severe, but no marriage seems to have occurred.[80]

The feature of this agreement that is of particular importance in seeking to discover the personality of Charles Stourton is the part whereby his father William contracted to deliver his son to Sir Walter before Christmas (1528). For a young male of the upper classes to live in a future father-in-law's household prior to marriage was not an uncommon practice. Since we know that at least one of the Hungerford daughters survived infancy, Charles Stourton may have remained in the Hungerford household for several years. If he did, then his personality may have been scarred for life as a result of his being an observer of Sir Walter's behaviour towards the members of his own family. Sir Walter Hungerford was an ambitious man and was able to secure advancement by becoming agent for Thomas Cromwell in his home region. He showed an ability to look after his own interests early on in life. As the son of Sir Edward Hungerford by his first wife, he it probably was who accused his father's second wife of murdering her first husband, which led to her trial, conviction and execution.[81] Sir Walter himself married three times. His third wife was Elizabeth, daughter of John, Lord Hussey, whom he wedded in 1532.[82] Marital difficulties soon arose. Elizabeth's account of Hungerford's behaviour towards her is a fearful one. In a letter she told Thomas Cromwell that for more than three years she had been imprisoned in a tower in Hungerford castle by her husband, who allowed only servants he had selected to communicate with her. She particularly feared her jailer, Hungerford's chaplain, believing the food he sent her was poisoned. Often she drank only water; sometimes her own urine. She would have died had not some poor women of the locality gratuitously brought food and drink to her cell window at night. She could not have paid them, because her husband had given her only four groats in four years. She claimed Sir Walter was trying to force her into a divorce on the grounds of 'incontinence', the Tudor term for sexual voraciousness, which she denied in herself but attributed to her husband; she was probably correct, as we shall see.[83]

In mid-1540 Thomas Cromwell fell from power, was attainted by Act of Parliament and was executed. Walter Hungerford, his agent in Wiltshire, was also attainted in parliament, not for high treason but principally for unnatural crime; Holinshed bluntly called it buggery. The French ambassador, Marillac, more explicitly told a correspondent that Hungerford was attainted for practising magic, invoking devils and sodomy: he was guilty of forcing his own daughter.[84] The reason for this excursus into the history of the Hungerford family is to consider what influence its domestic difficulties may have had on a teenage Charles Stourton if, indeed, he was still a member of that household when they occurred. The disputes between Hungerford and his wife Elizabeth, her brutal imprisonment, and particularly, if he knew of it, Hungerford's incestuous and unnatural relations with a girl who might have become his bride, were surely likely to disturb the equilibrium of a youth whose emotional stability may not have been particularly strong. If Sir Walter's inclination towards buggery extended to young males, then Stourton may have suffered even greater stress.[85]

What happened to the dependants of the victims and of the miscreant Charles Stourton? Of the shame and sympathy accruing we know little. As we have already noticed, a suspected confederate of the nobleman, Sir James Fitzjames, was forced by the Privy Council in April 1557 to make a payment of £25 to each of the Hartgill widows. Thirteen months after the murder Joan and Dorothy were granted a small annuity of 5 marks from the lands of William Hartgill, which were in the hands of the Crown because of the minority of his heir. This was Cuthbert, aged 10, the son of John Hartgill. The two wives were also able to secure the custody of Cuthbert pending their obtaining his marriage. The inheritance the boy was to receive on attaining his majority was worth less than £9 a year. This must have been because by his will William gave his wife Joan her dower lands, £100 of the money that Charles Stourton owed him, and his house at Kilmington. To his surviving sons, Thomas and Edward, he gave £40 each, as well as leases and title to land.[86]

On the Stourton side, Charles's wife Anne was able to purchase back his escheated goods from the Crown about two months after his conviction. The wardship and marriage of John Stourton, Charles's 4-year-old son and heir, the Crown sold to Sir Hugh Paulet for £340 (the value of the property that escheated to the Crown was just over £319). However, Anne Stourton petitioned Queen Mary that, as John's mother, she be allowed to see to the education of her son and have him with her until he was 10. She also requested she be allowed to choose his partner in marriage. The wording of the petition shows it was designed with some cleverness. It referred to Lady Stourton losing her greatest comfort in the world, 'her loving, trew and faithfull husband'.[87] Here Anne was doubtless trading on Queen Mary's own yearning for marital bliss but it also suggests, unless his wife was lying, that, although Charles Stourton was a most troublesome member of society, he was a satisfactory husband. This petition was apparently acceded to by the Queen and, furthermore, Lady Anne was granted an annuity of £40 from the Stourton lands at that time in the Crown's hands. She was not without a husband for long. She married a Cornish knight early in Elizabeth's reign, and John Stourton's wardship and marriage were granted to his maternal grandfather, the Earl of Derby.

Chapter 6

A FEMALE CONSPIRACY: THE MURDER OF GEORGE SAUNDERS

I n recording the chief events of the first decade of Elizabeth I's reign the chroniclers made scant reference to murder. Not until July 1571 in his text do we find Holinshed introducing the details of such a crime, the first occasion indeed since Lord Stourton's slaying of the Hartgills. The event was the poisoning of Thomas Chamber of Harrietsham, Kent, by his wife Rebecca. In his coverage of the subsequent year Holinshed devoted most of a page to the murder by Martin Bullocke of Arthur Hall, a would-be purchaser of some silver plate that Bullocke had stolen.[1]

The descriptions of these two crimes heralded a number of similar entries in Holinshed's and Stow's coverage of the 1570s and early 1580s.[2] However, additionally, alongside these accounts there appeared a new form of literature describing notable murders: the cheap pamphlet, soon to become the chief supplier of information on these crimes.

The murders of George Saunders and of John Kynnestar's wife in 1573 seem to have been the first such crimes, if we exclude the death of Richard Hun, to have been celebrated by pamphlet. Saunders was a London merchant-tailor, a well-off middle-aged man apparently well respected in London financial circles. One of the conspirators responsible was his wife, Ann, mother of his several children. Another conspirator was her friend, the sinister widow Ann Drury, notorious for her palmistry and 'surgery' (practice of medicine). The actual killer, George Browne, a 'gallant' with Court connections, was identified by a servant whom Browne believed he had slain at the same time as Saunders. Ann Saunders seemed to many to be innocent of the charges until she was virtually at the gallows, which added to the notoriety of the case, as did the interference after trial of a Protestant minister who, hoping to marry her, tried to persuade Ann Drury to take the whole blame on herself. In all it was a heady brew.[3]

Stow clearly obtained his knowledge of the murder from a pamphlet, *A briefe discourse of the late murther of master George Saunders*, printed in the same year as the crime and now thought to be the work of Arthur Golding, a translator of classical texts, who has been identified as a Puritan in his religious orientation. Stow's short account is drawn from *A briefe discourse* virtually verbatim, with one small addition.[4] The *Chronicles* probably used the same source.[5] The full title of the pamphlet on the murder is *A briefe discourse of the late murther of master George Saunders, a worshipfull Citizen of London: and of the apprehension, arreignement, and execution of the principall and accessaries of the same*. It is about 6,500 words in length, a third of which are homiletic in essence and add virtually nothing to our knowledge of the crime. The pamphlet commences by noting that the murder has attracted a great deal of attention both in London and throughout the realm and has set people talking: 'every man debating the matter as occasion or affection leades him.' The intent of the author is religiously didactic: to give a 'playne declaration of the whole matter . . . that thou mayst knowe the truth to the satisfying of thy mind and the avoyding of miscredite and also use the example to the amendment of thy life'. He does not purport to explain every facet of the case. 'Thou shalt not look for a full discoverie of every particular bymatter appendant,' he writes, justifying his censorship by arguing that such details 'might serve to feed the fond humor of such appetites as are more inquisitive of other folkes offences than hastie to redresse their owne'.[6] Moral improvement and a Christian desire to bury the fault with the condemned offender may have been the author's stated reason for omission here, but equally likely was his probable ignorance of the exact relationship between the characters in the tale in the period before the misdeed was committed. For having listed who the principals in his story are he plunges straight in.

On 24 March (Tuesday in Easter week) 1573, he tells us, George Browne was informed by a letter from Ann Drury that George Saunders would be staying the night at the house of Mr Barnes in Woolwich, from where he would go next morning on foot to St Mary Cray. Browne intercepted him near Shooters Hill and slew him, killing also Barnes's servant, John Bean. As he died, Saunders, who did not recognise his assailant, asked for God's mercy on him. John Bean, despite ten or eleven wounds, survived for the moment. He was found by an old man and his daughter, and conveyed to Woolwich, where he was able to identify the murderer, Browne, before he died. As soon as he had committed the deed, Browne sent word to Ann Drury, visited the Queen's Court at Greenwich, and then went back to London to Drury's house, where he obtained money to provide for his flight away from the capital. However, because of a search speedily conducted on the orders of the Privy Council Browne was apprehended soon afterwards, in Rochester, staying at the house of a man with the same surname. He was taken to Greenwich and on examination 'by the Counsell' confessed to the murder and admitted he had intended to kill Saunders on several previous occasions. He said the murder had been instigated by Mrs Drury, who had promised that, if the attempt was successful, she would arrange a marriage for him with Mrs Saunders, with whom he was totally infatuated. He denied that Ann Saunders herself knew of, or had consented to, the murderous design. Browne was arraigned in the Queen's Bench, pleaded guilty and was executed in Smithfield three days later, maintaining to the end Mrs Saunders's total innocence.[7]

Meanwhile Mrs Drury and her servant, 'Trusty' Roger Clement, had been examined and had confessed their involvement in the murder. They were sent to jail, as was soon afterwards Ann Saunders, who had just been in childbed. She was implicated by Trusty Roger's confession 'and upon other great likelyhoodes and presumptions'. Early in May Saunders and Drury were put on trial at the Guildhall charged with being accessories both before and after the fact, the evidence being a letter to Browne and a gift of money. Trusty Roger was a witness against Ann Saunders; the Crown Prosecutor showed that the evidence against her innocence was overwhelming, yet she maintained a 'stoute deniall', so much so in fact that some observers believed she had been in ignorance of the conspiracy and innocent of helping Browne to flee. The jurors thought otherwise, for both women were convicted and adjudged to death; they were hanged a week later. Roger was tried two days after the women. He too was convicted and was hanged at the same time as his mistress.[8]

The executions, which took place in Smithfield, drew an enormous crowd: 'so great a number of people, as the like hathe not bene seene there together in any mans remembraunce'. The writer, having provided details of this great concourse, then proceeds to the part of his piece that interested him the most. This was the course of events from the time of the culprits' apprehension to their execution. It would bring him to his admonition, 'which is the conclusion and fruite of this whole matter'. He tells us that the executions of those convicted, originally intended for 9 May, were delayed for four days: certain account books of the murdered man, showing those who owed him money, had to be found for the benefit of his children, and also the condemned persons had to be 'reformed to Godwarde' and persuaded to confess their guilt.[9]

The judicial proceedings had in no way been out of the ordinary, but there now occurred something quite peculiar, and this was a third reason for delay. A suspended clergyman by the name of Mell had accompanied Ann Saunders from the Guildhall, where he had been present at her trial, to Newgate jail in order to give her spiritual counsel and comfort, or so it seemed. In fact, despite the evidence, he had come to believe she was totally innocent of the charges. He had also fallen in love with her. Therefore, he planned to persuade Mrs Drury to take the whole of the blame while he would seek a pardon for Saunders. He succeeded for the moment with the first part of the scheme by dwelling on the 'horroure of mischarging and casting away of an innocent' and by promising money for the marrying-off of Drury's daughter. Thus before a number of notables, including the Dean of St Paul's, and contrary to what she had said at the trial, Drury completely exonerated Saunders of consenting to or being involved in the commission of the crime. Mell, however, then queered his own pitch by telling 'an honest Gentleman', whom he thought might help in obtaining a pardon for Saunders, of his 'purpose and whole platforme' – presumably, his intent of marrying her. Because of this 'and also by other follies of his owne', which the writer does not detail, Mell's scheme foundered. The Privy Council, which had also learned of his intentions, saw to it that no pardon was granted and also adjudged him to be put in the pillory for a period at the time of the execution of the two women. Pinned to his chest was a piece of paper bearing the words, 'For practising to colour the detestable factes of George Saunders wife'. The writer approved strongly of this as being necessary to stop those who would 'deface or discredite' the proceedings of the Privy Council or any public trial and judgment.[10]

Whether Ann Saunders was immediately aware that Mell's efforts on her behalf had failed we are not told. She seems to have recognised she must now fend for herself, a recourse made more imperative when she overheard by chance two workmen talking about a gallows that was then being erected.

Fearing she and Ann Drury were to be hanged that very day, she went to the latter, who was also in Newgate, told her what she had heard, and asked her if she would keep her promise, that is to say, assume the entire blame for the murder. Drury, however, had by this time changed her mind. She told Saunders she would 'not dissemble' nor 'hazarde her owne soule eternally for the safetie of another bodies temporall life'. Ann Saunders now realised she was doomed and decided to tell the truth. Before four members of the clergy, including once again the Dean of St Paul's, she admitted she had indeed given her consent to her husband's death and helped to bring it about. She also confessed to the 'unlawfull lust and liking' that she had for George Browne, 'hir sinfulnesse of life committed with him', and asked for spiritual comfort and counsel. This 'unfayned repentance' and willing yielding to death drew the plaudits of the writer as did Saunders's reconciliation with her murdered husband's kin, whom she sent for the day before she died. 'On hir knees, with abundance of sorrowful teares,' she asked forgiveness 'for bereving them of theire deare brother and friende'. They responded through their lawyer, who said they 'heartily' forgave her, and then all kneeled down together 'praying to GOD with hir and for hir, that hee also woulde remitte hir sinne'. Saunders next fell to lamenting the straits into which she had brought her children: a dead father and the shame of a felonious mother. Those of them who 'were of any capacitie and discretion', that is to say old enough to understand, she exhorted to learn from her plight how to avoid sin. She gave to each a book of meditations by John Bradford, and then sent them away so she could settle 'hir grieved heart' before she was hanged.[11]

Ann Drury was also suitably contrite and repentant. As she and Saunders were taken in a cart to execution she asked those lining the way to pray for her and openly admitted her guilt. At the gallows she knelt down facing the Earl of Bedford and other nobles, who were there on horseback, and made categorical denial that she had ever been involved in witchcraft or sorcery, or had accused certain merchants' wives of unchaste living, or had poisoned her late husband. Addressing the Earl of Derby, she protested that she was in no way responsible for his separation from his wife; and if, while in his service, she had given any offence through neglecting her duties, she begged his forgiveness: statements that suggest she had either had a sexual relationship with the Earl or his wife or had practised palmistry with deleterious effects. With the two women went to the gallows Trusty Roger. He too openly acknowledged his crime. Each of the three prayed separately with a preacher before the executioner drew away the cart on which they were standing, the method of hanging sometimes employed when the authorities wanted simultaneous executions.[12]

Earlier George Browne had also made a pious end. In jail he had admitted to a most ungodly life: he had followed 'the appetites and lustes of his sinfull flesh', never calling on God publicly or privately, never attending sermons, going to communion, or reading the scriptures or godly books. Nevertheless, says the writer approvingly, Browne finished his earthly existence with 'a marvellous apparence of heartie repentance' and 'willingnesse to forsake this miserable worlde'. At this point the narrative of the murder and punishment of the miscreants ceases and the author turns to demonstrating the theme in which he had the greatest interest, specifically, 'what is to be gathered of this terrible example, and how we oughte to apply the same to our owne behoofe'.[13]

This account of the murder of George Saunders, by Golding or some person unknown, appears to have provided not only the basis for the versions that appear in Holinshed and Stow but also the foundations for an Elizabethan play. The latter, entitled *A Warning for Fair Women*, was entered in the Stationers' Register in November 1599. The title page bears a note that it had been acted 'at diverse times' by the Lord Chamberlain's Men, but critics are not inclined, despite a reference to recent performance, to think that it was written near the end of the century. A date close to 1590 has been more popular, but there is much uncertainty and it may have been earlier still. It is possible that the publication of the second edition of Holinshed's *Chronicles* in 1587 reminded people of the murder and created new interest; hence, perhaps, the play. Some fifteen or twenty years after the event there must have been many persons in London who remembered the Saunders case well. The author of the play, therefore, would not knowingly have introduced into his play anything historically inaccurate. He would have been careful to write in accord with the popular memory, which in this case was likely still to be clear.[14]

In general the author of the play was very respectful of the existing factual account and reluctant to flesh out its bare bones with theatrical detail, unless such was absolutely necessary better to explain the plot. Important for the historian is the fact that the unknown author of the play had in his possession a few pieces of information that either were not available to the writer of *A brief discourse* or that the latter did not choose to include. The playwright's version of the murder, its aftermath, and the roles and relationships of those involved has the ring of truth; indeed, there is virtually nothing that can be pointed to as being historically unlikely. The only hint of thin historical ice comes at the very start of the play. Whereas *A brief discourse* and the accounts of Holinshed and Stow commence with George Browne receiving a letter bearing information concerning George Saunders's forthcoming visit to Woolwich, the opening scene of the play, once a bevy of moralising muses have left the stage, refers to a supper at which have been present the Saunders, man and wife, Ann Drury and Browne. The dialogue infers that at that event Browne talked about Ireland, where he claimed to be well known.[15] Since Mr Saunders asks Browne his name, we are left with the impression that the supper must have been at Ann Drury's house or elsewhere at her invitation, and that Browne had not previously met Saunders. The historicity of this episode becomes a subject of doubt when we remember that the pamphlet account states quite categorically that when Saunders was attacked by Browne he did not know him 'whatsoever report hath been made of former acqayntance betwixte them'.[16] This, however, can perhaps be explained as meaning that the author, who probably got much of his information from the Protestant ministers who comforted the culprits prior to their execution, when told Saunders did not recognise his assailant (which might well have occurred if the attack was an ambush, and they had met only once previously), took it to mean they had never met.

The intention of the dramatist, and indeed of the author of *A brief discourse* late on in that piece, seems to have been to imply that Ann Saunders met Browne initially in normal social intercourse – that is to say, she was not the initiator of the relationship by seeking to attract his attention. Her modesty and virtue are given particular emphasis, which is reinforced by the subsequent scene in the play in which Ann sits demurely at her door awaiting her husband's return from business and does not, on the face of it, appear to give any encouragement to George Browne when, passing by, he seeks to make conversation with her.[17] In the play Browne is clearly the initiator. He believes he can tempt her virtue successfully; he finds that she is affable, 'not coy nor scornfull, And may be wunne'. He feels she may be attracted to him. She is portrayed as being uncertain of her own emotions, a weakness that is attributed to her youth. Ann Drury says that Saunders is 'yong and faire. And may be tempred easily like waxe', a task she intends to undertake herself.[18]

The design of both sources is to portray Ann Drury as the fount of evil. Her servant Trusty Roger, who never minces his words, remarks to her that Saunders is only one of many she has 'wonne to stoope into the lewre, It is your trade'. The play puts considerable emphasis on Drury's reputation as a palmist and surgeon, occupations that were regarded as being only borderline in respectability. From various comments passed it seems her stock in trade was dealing with problems of a sexual nature, such as promoting adulterous relationships and treating sexually derived ailments. To encourage the first, as the case of Ann Saunders shows, she casts horoscopes through palm reading, the client being advised of an enticing amorous future if he or she will follow Drury's advice and reward her well for it. In this instance she advises both parties, for it is made clear from the outset of the play that Browne recognises Ann Drury as the key to the success of his lustful pursuit of Mrs Saunders. It is Drury's belief that Browne will pay her a large sum for her assistance (£100, so she can marry off her daughter), which instigates the whole enterprise. According to the play her first piece of practical advice to Browne was that he should attempt to entertain Ann Saunders in conversation at her door.[19]

Browne, seemingly a man driven by his sexual urges, is not portrayed with any sympathy. He is Drury's dupe. He is a 'gallant', possibly a 'captain' from Ireland, with vague Court connections. He dresses in white satin doublet and blue silk breeches. He is regarded as 'serviceable' by his superiors, but his readiness to kill George Saunders on several inappropriate occasions without thinking of the consequences does not suggest any great intelligence or mental balance. He appears to be totally at the mercy of his primal drives. When arrested, he tries to place much of the responsibility for the murder on Drury: he killed at her instigation on the understanding she would procure Ann Saunders's hand in marriage for him when the deed was done. He does, however, display a certain nobility of character by trying to shield Ann Saunders from the consequences of the crime.[20]

How Ann Saunders changed from being Saunders's apparently loyal wife to George Browne's lover receives no mention in A brief discourse, but the play is less reticent. The playwright tells us that Drury, when reading Ann Saunders's palm, informs her that she will soon be a widow. This, Drury emphasises, is God's design and must be accepted; indeed it is a piece of good fortune for her. She will soon remarry. She has already met her future husband and has spoken to him in the street; his name is George. Saunders, while protesting she would not be false to her spouse, says she will submit herself to whatever God has ordained. Drury quietly congratulates herself for kindling 'love fires' in Saunders's breast, adding that 'this will hammer so in her head . . . sheel wish the old were dead'. The details of how Ann Saunders became intimate with Browne are never revealed in the conversation of the human characters in the play. It is left to 'Tragedie', one of the periodically appearing Furies, to inform us in very short fashion that 'lawlesse Lust conducteth cruell Browne, He doth seduce this poore deluded soule' (that is, Saunders), and that Drury 'thrusts her forward to destruction'.[21]

Early on in both play and pamphlet Ann Saunders is portrayed as a mere pawn whose marital fate is decided for her by Drury and Browne. In fact she may well have played a much more active role both in the murder of her husband and in regard to her relationship with Browne. Most important here is the mention in *A briefe discourse* that, when on Saturday, 9 May, Ann came to believe she was to be hanged that very day, she confessed to one of the clergymen at Newgate jail not only her role in procuring her husband's death but also the 'unlawfull lust and liking' she had for Browne, and furthermore 'her sinfulness of life committed with him'.[22] This last statement may be taken as proof that there was a sexual relationship between the pair, possibly one extending over several months. Thus, when Drury cast Ann Saunders's horoscope and showed her God's design, she probably had strong suspicions Ann was seeking a way out of her marriage by fair means or foul, and, by providing her with the means, hoped to benefit herself financially.

Both the play and the pamphlet give a favourable report of George Saunders. He is wealthy, a merchant-tailor and citizen of London. Ann Saunders never complains of being ill-treated by him; rather the reverse. She is entrusted with making major purchases for the family. In her gallows confession she says, 'I had a good husband by whom I had manie children, with whom I lived in wealth.' She also refers to him as a good father. In the play we are told that George Saunders was of good appearance, 'handsome' and 'comely'.[23] If we seek clues as to why Ann Saunders was ready to dispense with this marital paragon, we find several in the play. One of the discoverers of his dead body refers to him as an 'ancient gentleman'. Since Ann is called young, it is possible the difference in years between husband and wife was a factor in her dissatisfaction with her lot. It may have been that her frequent pregnancies had alienated her. The play has it that she quarrelled with her husband over a purchase. When about to pay for linen she has ordered, she is unable to do so because her spouse, for a short time, needs all his funds for a financial transaction. Her discomfort is aggravated by her being told of this by a servant. She expostulates: 'I am a woman and in that respect, Am well content my husband shal controule me, But that my man should over-awe me too, And in the sight of strangers . . . do's grieve me to the heart.'[24] If George Saunders made a habit of giving instructions to his wife in this manner, it was bound to rankle, even in an age of strong patriarchal authority.

A more likely reason for Ann Saunders to want to be rid of her husband might have been her current pregnancy. At the time George Saunders was murdered, so *A brief discourse* tells us, she was about to give birth, which, in fact, she did a few days later. We are left to wonder if there was a direct and temporal connection between the two events. Was George Browne the father of the child, and did Ann fear her husband would disclaim paternity? If so, decisive action was imperative, for the fate of wives, should their husband decide to stomach the humiliation and admit to being cuckolded, could be unpleasant.[25]

Whatever the factors that alienated Ann Saunders from her husband, she fell in with Ann Drury's plan to have Browne kill him. She gave her agreement to a letter sent by Drury to Browne telling him to see the deed done as soon as possible. The play shows that the actions of the two women were later construed, in their indictments, as animating and procuring Browne to commit the murder. It is also in the play that Ann Saunders, sometime after the letter has been dispatched, expresses in an aside her concern that Browne may be intending harm to her husband. Presumably this is meant to suggest she was having second thoughts about the plan.[26] A successful attack on George Saunders was not easily accomplished. The difficulty lay in intercepting him when he was unaccompanied. Browne certainly tried. One attempt at ambush in London had to be aborted because Saunders met up with another gentleman just as Browne was ready to strike; another, at Billingsgate quay, was similarly fruitless because of the arrival of Ann Saunders at the crucial moment. Therefore Ann Drury's servant, Trusty Roger, was given the task of following George Saunders to discover when and where a suitable opportunity might present itself.[27] Roger's peregrinations are described in some detail by the playwright. Roger discovers that Saunders has been invited to a business meeting with a Mr Barnes at Woolwich. Next day Saunders goes to Woolwich and stays the night at Barnes's house. When he leaves next morning, accompanied by Barnes's servant John Bean, he is ambushed by Browne near Shooters Hill. Browne first cuts down Bean and then, despite Saunders's pleadings, stabs him in turn, repeatedly, killing him.

He dips his handkerchief in Saunders's blood, making as many holes in it as wounds he has inflicted, and sends it by Roger's hand (Roger has kept watch while the deed is done) to Ann Saunders. If the play is historically accurate here, and Ann had agreed to this method of communication and it was not simply the idea of a berserk Browne, it suggests that under her demure exterior there lay a very vicious streak. George Saunders does not survive the attack; however, the servant, John Bean, is discovered with ten wounds but still breathing. The finders are a local inhabitant, Old John, and Joan, his maid, who was apparently Bean's inamorata. Unluckily for Browne, Bean is able to describe the appearance of his assailant. To preserve it from the attention of animals, Saunders's corpse is temporarily deposited in a bush, and Bean is carried to Woolwich, where, in the ensuing search for the killer, the traditional hue and cry is raised.[28]

Meanwhile George Browne has made his way to the Court, which was then at Greenwich, only 2 miles away. This provides a scene in the play of particular significance, one that has no parallel in *A briefe discourse*. Browne takes a drink of ale in the buttery and exchanges greetings with a Master James, who remarks on Browne's bloodstained hose; but the latter tells a story about chasing hares on the way to Court to explain it. This Master James was possibly Martin James, registrar (keeper of the register of decrees and orders) of Chancery, but we cannot be sure. In the play he is later present at Browne's arrest at Rochester, when the dying Bean identifies Browne as the murderer, then when Browne confesses before the Council; he is also the gentleman whom Mell, the clergyman, approaches in an unsuccessful search for a pardon for Ann Saunders. It rather looks as if Master James was an important source of information about the case for the playwright.[29]

At this point the play cuts to Ann Saunders receiving the bloody and perforated handkerchief, which proves her husband's death, from Ann Drury and Trusty Roger. She wants to kill herself; Roger tells her to keep quiet or their guilt will be discovered. Ann admits that her lust is the cause of their predicament. She says murder cannot be concealed and spurns Browne on his return.[30] The story then moves to the Royal Court and to the 'Lords', who have just received notice by letter of the murder and the murderer. These 'Lords', presumably, are Privy Councillors, for it is they who, from this point, direct investigations. Already, apparently, the common rumour in London was that the victim was George Saunders and that George Browne was strongly suspected. Identification of the latter had been made by a waterman who

rowed Browne, in his bloody hose, back to London. This man noticed Browne
tried to hide stains on his clothing with his hat. He confirmed what Bean had
told his finders: the suspect was dressed in a doublet of white satin and a
large pair of blue silk breeches. Master James tells the Privy Councillors that
it was Browne dressed in that fashion whom he has seen and spoken to in the
Court buttery. Now the identity and dress of the suspect are known, the Privy
Council gives the order for his arrest. The ports are closed to all lacking its
warrant, and the sheriffs of London are to conduct a special search.[31]

Browne in the meantime is seeking money from his co-conspirators in
order to effect his escape. From the sale or pawning of their silver plate, the
two women raise £26. Lamenting his crime by now and claiming Ann Drury
has made him do it, Browne then flees to Rochester, where he obtains shelter
with another Browne, a butcher the play tells us, with whom he claims some
affinity by blood. He explains his desire for shelter as being caused by flight
from his creditors. There, however, he is soon arrested by the Mayor of
Rochester and Master James, the latter presumably sent by the Privy Council
for the purpose of identification and, more definitely, to escort the prisoner to
Woolwich for a confrontation with the dying John Bean. The latter, we are
told, is in a stupor from loss of blood and has not spoken for two days. In one
of the dramatic climaxes of the play Browne is shattered at finding Bean still
alive. Bean opens his eyes and his wounds begin to bleed again. When asked if
he recognises Browne, he answers, 'Yea, this is he that murdred me and
Master Sanders.' Thereupon, having asked God to forgive Browne and receive
his soul, he sinks down and dies. Master James then sends a report of the
successful identification to the Privy Council, and the Mayor, Mr Barnes and
he spend a short time reflecting on other murder cases they know of that
have contributed to their belief in the saying that 'murder will out'.[32]

When James's report reaches the Privy Council the messenger is asked by
way of assurance if Browne, at Woolwich, has denied the deed, to which the
answer is that he has not, but has rather lamented 'his hainous crueltie' with
tears. This is sufficient for the Privy Council to order the justices in London to
have an indictment drawn. The play continues with the Privy Councillors at
Greenwich examining Browne, who had been brought by boat from
Woolwich. He is asked whether there was 'any ancient quarrel' between him
and George Saunders, to which he answers in the negative. He also denies he
has killed in order to rob. When, however, it is put to him that he 'did affect'
Saunders's wife too much, he can only agree. A crucial point in the play is

reached when Browne is asked if Ann Saunders provoked him to murder her husband and promised to marry him if he did. This he strongly denies despite imprecations he should discharge his conscience.[33]

The Privy Council at this time received a letter from the sheriffs of London reporting that Ann Drury and Trusty Roger had admitted their guilt and confessed that Ann Saunders had given her consent to the murder. When this was put to Browne, however, he continued to protest her innocence, even claiming that all the £26 he had received towards his flight came from others. Of interest regarding Browne's status in the community are the words uttered by a Privy Councillor at this point that he was 'a man respected of us all, and noted fit for many services'. The play then has it that, following the interrogation, Browne was sent under escort to appear before the justices of the Queen's Bench at Westminster.[34] The interrogation episode is especially noteworthy for two reasons. It shows the Privy Council was quite ready to involve itself in the actual investigation of murder in particular cases. Additionally it demonstrates that the author of the play did not know or would not tell the whole story of the interrogation of Browne. From another source we have evidence to show that Browne's confession may have been elicited by threat of torture, a matter that will be dealt with in more detail below.[35]

We are next treated by the playwright to that very rare thing in early drama, an English common-law courtroom scene, namely George Browne's arraignment in the Queen's Bench at Westminster Hall. *A briefe discourse* is silent on virtually all the details of what happened on that occasion, but the play introduces several important features. We are told a small number of 'lords' had come from Court to observe the proceedings and that they sat on the bench, although whether this was out of curiosity or duty (sent by the Privy Council to overawe the jury should it be necessary) is not clear. As the trial begins the clerk of the court reads out the indictment: this includes the name, social status, place of habitation of the accused, date and time of the crime, and location and brief legal description of the crime and victims. The weapon or weapons used are not mentioned. To this charge Browne pleads guilty, whereupon the Lord Chief Justice, who is presiding, notes that a jury is therefore not needed and asks Browne what he can say in arrest of judgment – that is to say, why he should not be sentenced to death. Browne answers to the justices that they should let the guilty, meaning himself, Ann Drury and Roger, die, but take care to save the innocent Ann Saunders. The retort from the bench is that she 'should have no wrong', for which Browne thanks them. He asks also that after his execution his body should not be hanged in chains but be buried immediately. One of the justices concedes this, but when, immediately following, the court pronounces judgment, it is ordered that Browne is to be hanged until dead and that afterwards his body is to be 'at the prince's pleasure'.[36] This was a phrase that implicitly reserved the right to hang his corpse in chains wherever the Crown decided, which in this case was at the scene of the crime. All this occurred on Friday, 17 April 1573 and the execution was three days later.

The stage directions in the play at this point state, 'Browne is led out and Anne Sanders and Drurie brought in'; this was for their own trial. The playwright truncates events and joins the trial scenes together. In actual fact the women were arraigned not on 17 April but on 6 May, when Browne had been dead for more than two weeks. Furthermore, they were tried not in the Queen's Bench but at the London Guildhall. The play tells us they were indicted as both pre-facto and post-facto accessories to the crime, first enticing and procuring Browne to commit the murder, later aiding and abetting him when knowing his guilt. Both plead not guilty. Then Trusty Roger is brought in and asked, apparently as a witness for the prosecution, about the crucial letter. Who gave it to him, it is demanded. He says Drury has; and that she was the writer. The judges ask if Ann Saunders knew of it. To this vital question Roger responds that, 'she read it twise before the same was seald'. Thereupon Ann Saunders interjects: 'Did I thou wicked man? This man is hirde to betray my life.' At this point, according to the play, she was asked by the bench why she wore a white rose in her bosom. Her reply is that it was there as a token of her innocence. The presiding justice then asks Roger about the £26 given to Browne. Roger explains it was borrowed against Drury's and Saunders's plate, at which Saunders claims her plate has been stolen from her. Roger retorts, 'You gave it to me,' and adds bitterly, 'I did love you all too well.' A member of the bench asks Drury if the plate is part hers and part Saunders's and is told it is. He then asks once more if Ann Saunders was privy to the letter, to which Drury, after some prodding, answers in the affirmative.[37]

Drury adds that in addition to the letter Roger also carried a token, a handkerchief, from Ann Saunders to Browne that the latter later sent back soaked in George Saunders's blood. When Roger is asked to whom he delivered it on his return, he tells the court it was Ann Saunders. Ann strongly denies this, stating she was in 'childbed chamber at that time, Where t'was not meete that he or any man Should have accesse'. The presiding justice, continuing in the prosecutorial fashion the bench often adopted in this period, tells her bluntly she is lying. He adds that it is believed – he does not say by whom but the sense is by her London community – that 'You wrongd your husband with unchaste behaviour.' This has been taken as meaning she had had a child by Browne. The justice then sentences the two women and Roger to be hanged, there being no reference in regard to this trial of a jury, although such, and its verdicts, there must have been. Ann Saunders still protests her innocence, and as she is led away she accuses Drury of being responsible for her plight.[38]

The next scene of the play depicts George Browne on the way to his execution. His brother, Anthony, a felon in Newgate, who is to be hanged at York, is brought to speak with him and they exchange platitudes about the lot of the convicted felon. At the gallows a sheriff advises George to admit that Ann Saunders was an accomplice to her husband's death. He resolves, however, to confess his sins but to conceal that particular fact. He then admits to a life of evil living: drunkenness, blasphemy through 'monstrous oathes', never having read the Scriptures, never attending church, spending the Sabbath in the stews, gaming and perjury, and worship of vile fashions in dress. He urges that, 'All carelesse men be warned by my end, and by my fall', and then leaps off the gallows ladder to his death.[39] Presumably it was because he refused to admit Ann Saunders was a co-conspirator that his body was taken to Shooters Hill and hanged in chains there. The playwright took the whole of this episode concerning Browne out of chronological sequence, for, as we have seen, in fact his execution occurred sixteen days before the women were put on trial.

The remainder of the play tells of Ann Saunders's behaviour in jail prior to her execution. There she is visited by a clergyman whose name is not given but who A briefe discourse says was one Mell.[40] This cleric believes, or affects to believe, that Ann Saunders is innocent of the charges. When asked why so, he refers to her firm denial throughout and to a confession by Drury that she and Roger were the contrivers of the murder while Saunders was not. This confession had apparently been made while in jail; Drury, who at the trial had said Saunders had approved the vital letter, has now changed her story. On these grounds the minister begs Master James to try to obtain a pardon for Ann Saunders, adding that, if he can, 'sound recompense, Shal quit your paines'. James, however, will have none of it. He says he knows what Mell's real motivation is: to marry Saunders. The play, unlike *A briefe discourse*, which talks of his 'doting affection', does not say Mell has fallen in love with Saunders in so many words, but this is implied. Nor does it explain that Drury at one point had cleared Ann Saunders before several witnesses including the Dean of St Paul's, or that Mell had offered his 'own body and life' for her safety. For his 'bold offence' Mell was made to suffer. In the play it is Master James who tells him the pillory is to be the punishment for his 'impietie', whereas in the pamphlet, as we have seen, it is the Privy Council.[41]

Without providing a time frame, the play continues with a scene set outside Newgate jail, in which a carpenter explains to a fellow that he has been busy constructing a gallows large enough for the hanging of Saunders, Drury and Roger, an event scheduled for that very day. They are overheard by a fearful Ann Saunders, who asks to speak with Ann Drury. When they are together, Saunders asks the latter if she is still ready to clear her of the murder as she has promised, and take it upon herself. Drury says she is not: 'this is not the way to get remission, By joyning sinne to sinne,' she advises Saunders. She will confess her sins, and she suggests her fellow prisoner should do the same, otherwise 'our soules shal live In endlesse torments of unquenched fire'. These words have great effect on Saunders. She admits that to this point she never had any intention of confessing but 'at this instant I am strangely changed, And wil no longer drive repentance off'.[42]

Thereupon there enters a Protestant clergyman. He is all business: 'prepare your selves for death, The houre is nowe at hand, and mistris Sanders, At length acknowledge and confesse your fault, that God may be propitioner to your soule.' Saunders does so. She confesses to consenting to her husband's death and 'by wicked lust, and wilful sinne denying of the fault'; 'now I do repent and hate my selfe, Thinking the punishment prepared for me, Not halfe severe enough for my deserts'. The clergyman applauds this: 'done like a Christian and the childe of grace, pleasing to God, to angels, and to men, And doubt not but your soule shall find a place In Abraham's bosome, though your body perish.' The cleric then announces Saunders's children have come to receive her blessing. She abjectly apologises for the plight in which she is leaving them, and warns them that, if they enjoy 'dayes where you have wealth at wil, As once I had, and are well matcht beside: Content your selves, and surfet not on pride'. She gives to each child a book of 'holy meditations, Bradfords workes', kisses them, and is led off to the gallows. At this point the play ends except for a few, but important, lines spoken by the fury 'Tragedie', wherein it is claimed that the events in the play are historical: 'And should I adde, or else diminish aught, Many of these spectators then could say, I have committed error in my play.'[43]

In both the play and A briefe discourse there is a notable omission in the description they offer of events subsequent to the discovery of the murder. This concerns what happened to George Browne between 30 March, when he was brought before members of the Privy Council at Greenwich by the Mayor of Rochester, and his trial in the Queen's Bench on 17 April. We might assume that Browne confessed at Greenwich and that he was then sent to Newgate or the Marshalsea jail of the Queen's Bench while Ann Drury and Roger were examined and arrangements made for their trials. This was not in fact the case. From governmental records we learn that on 1 April the Privy Council sent letters ordering Browne to be taken to the Tower of London. There he was to be kept incommunicado and then examined by the Master of the Rolls and two judges, Southcote and Manwood (the first of the Queen's Bench, the second of the Court of Common Pleas), or any two of them. All other suspected 'contrivers' of Saunders's murder were also to be examined. The high rank of the examiners was unusual, as was the fact that the examination was to be conducted in the Tower. The reason for these measures was revealed in another instruction. The examiners were commanded to put Browne 'to tortures if they find cause'. To threaten a suspected murderer with the rack, the brake or the manacles, if he did not confess his guilt and supply the names of his confederates, was not common. The extant records of the Privy Council refer to only two previous instances (1553 and 1570).[44]

What seems to have been unique about this investigation is that when Browne and 'all others suspected' were examined the examination was to be based not on questions ('interrogatories') devised by the Privy Council or the examiners themselves but 'upon such instructions as shalbe given them by the brethern and frindes of the said Saunders'. Furthermore, the investigators were 'to admitte the brethern and frindes of Saunders to be presente at the examinacion, and to minister interrogatories if they finde cause', a provision without parallel in such cases.[45] Presumably, this employment of George Saunders's relatives and friends was to speed the investigation by obviating the need for a series of separate examinations of those who knew about Saunders's relations with his wife, her relationship with Browne, the influence and practices of Ann Drury, and similar. Whatever the aim, it was a startling development in conciliar criminal justice. It is not unlikely that George Saunders's brothers, their wives and his other kin, with whom, according to the pamphlet, Ann Saunders made her peace prior to execution, had requested they should be present when Browne was examined. Possibly 'Master Saunders, the lawyer', who spoke for the Saunders clan at the peace meeting with Ann, was responsible.[46] The co-option of the kin of the victim is suggestive of early medieval criminal law, and testimony to the inventiveness of the Tudor government in obtaining confessions in what it regarded as important cases. Noteworthy in a social sense is the fact that a case involving a member of the London merchant class was so considered.

The use of torture (that is, the employment of pain-giving instruments as distinct from duress by starvation or vile circumstances of imprisonment) was essentially a Tudor development, the formative years probably being the 1520s and 1530s. In Mary's reign torture was used on a wide variety of suspects: witches, robbers, horse thieves and rioters, as well as traitors. Common lawyers of the sixteenth and seventeenth centuries were wont to say torture was never practised under the common law, only on the fiat of the monarch, which might take the form of the command of his or her Council.[47] Since two of the professional judiciary were appointed to examine Browne, it is obvious this body knew of the use of torture and that some of its members approved. The two basic forms of torture in use in the Elizabethan period were the rack and the manacles; an instrument used less frequently was the brake. The rack was in use throughout the reign; the brake seems to have been retired in the early 1580s, while the manacles became an increasingly common resort after 1590.[48] The chronicle writers fail to mention the use of torture before the arrival of the Jesuits and seminary priests as part of the English mission around 1580. Then the practice, in regard to suspect traitors (as they were regarded) at least, became public knowledge for the first time and must have created alarm in some quarters, since a semi-official defence had to be drafted. The gist of this was that torture was employed only where the treason of the suspect was already manifest. Thus 'None was tormented to know whether he were gylty or no' but simply to discover the scope of the crime and the names of any accomplices.[49] The government's use of torture appears to have come under criticism not only in the early 1580s but again in the early 1590s. As a result, the practice had to be relinquished for short periods; but it was thought too valuable to surrender entirely and so was soon reinstated. There is no clear evidence that George Browne in the Tower actually suffered torture, although rather sinisterly the Privy Cuncil ordered a physician to be sent 'to loke unto him' after he had been there for two weeks.[50] From subsequent events we gather that, when examined, he placed the blame on himself as principal, and Ann Drury and Trusty Roger as accessories, exonerating Ann Saunders entirely. It appears that the Crown was satisfied with this statement from him and relied for its evidence against Ann Saunders on the depositions of Drury and Roger.

The government treated the murder of George Saunders as an important matter. This is proven not only by the use or threat of torture but quite as much by the employment of a notable lawyer as prosecutor for the Crown in court. In earlier times, and in lesser cases even in the later sixteenth century, the prosecution of felony cases seems to have fallen to the clerk of the court and the justices presiding, for the latter were allowed an inquisitorial capacity in their own court. In the Saunders case the prosecutor was 'Master Geffry', doubtless John Jeffrey, who was Queen's Serjeant from 1572, a Justice of the Queen's Bench from 1576, and Chief Baron of the Exchequer in 1577. He was described as being possessed of sharp invention, clear comprehension, good memory and judgement, and a prompt and ready delivery; clearly he was no legal lightweight.[51]

The stages of the trials as they appear in the play are of considerable interest to historians since precisely what occurred in a sixteenth-century criminal trial is still shrouded in mystery. The play, which combines the trial of Browne with the trial of Drury, Roger and Ann Saunders, has the Chief Justice of the Queen's Bench presiding throughout, although the Lord Mayor of London and four so-called lords were also present and seated on the bench. Whether these lords were members of the Privy Council or simply court nobility is not clear, but the former is more likely. In contrast with modern trials, the presiding judge and his fellows on the bench did not hesitate to question the accused directly. Roger was asked if Ann Saunders knew about the letter Drury had sent to Browne telling him how to proceed with the murder; Roger and Drury were asked about the plate on which £26 was raised to assist Browne's flight; and questions were put about the token (the handkerchief) Ann Saunders sent to Browne before he set out for Woolwich and which was later returned, bloodstained, by Roger. It is noticeable these questions from the bench provoked an altercation between Ann Saunders and Trusty Roger, which may have been the reason they were asked. For such a confrontation between the accused (several persons accused of the same crime might be tried on a single indictment at the same time, as here), or between accused and witnesses, was reckoned to be a great help in demonstrating guilt.[52] One lord on the bench found this episode so revealing that he told Ann Saunders that, since her guilt was obvious, she should not continue to deny it. The impact of such judicial opinions of guilt on the trial jurors can be imagined.

The ways in which the play and the pamphlet end are very different. In the former, Ann Saunders, having bade farewell to her children, is led off to the gallows. In the latter, Ann Drury's journey thither, her words to bystanders, Trusty Roger's speech on the same occasion, and, somewhat out of place, the confession by Browne, when in prison weeks earlier, of his sinful life, complete the narrative. There then follows a long homiletic address by the author and what purports to be the confession of Ann Saunders as she delivered it at the gallows. The address announces its purpose in clear tones: 'Nowe remayneth to shewe what is to be gathered of this terrible example and how we oughte to apply the same to our owne behoofe.' The writer's arguments centre on his view of the nature of man and of God's attitude to human sin. He has a low opinion of human nature: 'We be the impes of the old Adam,' he says, 'and the venim of sinne which he received from the olde serpent, is shedde into us all, and woorketh effectually in us all'. He believes that when men pay no regard to God he 'giveth them over to their own lustes', and 'when the measure of their iniquitie is filled up there is no way for them to escape the justice of God'. Even if they escape bodily punishment, 'the very hell of their owne conscience would prosecute them, and the sting of their minde would be a continuall prison, torment and torture to them'. This suggests the writer did not accept the contemporary maxim 'murder will out' as invariably true, at least not in the short term. God, he notes, sometimes allows sinners a long rein before he overthrows them; but he catches them in the end, amends them from their wickedness, and through their death blots out 'the stayne of their former filthe'. When God exposes wickedness to the world, the intention is not to entertain the watchers, or to shame the kinfolk of the criminal. The design, he believes, is that the terror of the example should make all men and women examine themselves, 'drive us to the inward consideration of ourselves'; this will 'provoke' repentance. He notes that those who reproach the repentant sinner or take a very severe view of other people's faults are usually blind to their own.[53]

The theme that God frequently caused a death that was murder, but unrecognised as such, to be revealed features quite extensively in the play at one point, although there are no such illustrations in *A briefe discourse*. In a conversation between Master James, the Mayor of Rochester and Mr Barnes on the topic 'God's justice hath bin stil myraculous', the Mayor recounts a murder case in which the corpse of a man, dead twenty years, was disinterred, a nail discovered 'knockt in the scalpe', and murder demonstrated. Barnes tells a story of a traveller who before he was slain told his murderer that the ferns that grew in that place would reveal him; and so it was, for seven years later a sprig of fern was carried by the wind into a room where the murderer was, causing him to confess the crime. James, in turn, relates how a woman attending a play at Lynn, in Norfolk, was so moved by a murderess on stage being haunted by her husband's ghost that she, in the audience, cried out that so it was with her also, and openly confessed.[54]

The hand of God in the discovery of a murderer was obviously a theme much favoured by clergy of the stronger reform variety. There was no lack of Protestant ministers who sought to give spiritual advice to the conspirators in the Saunders case, once they had been arrested and imprisoned. In addition to Mell, whose intentions may have been more physical than spiritual, the Dean of St Paul's (Alexander Nowell) and Masters Cole, Charke and Young exhorted Ann Saunders to clear her conscience and reconcile herself to God.[55] These clergymen, says the pamphlet writer, found Saunders, Drury and Trusty Roger 'very rawe and ignorant in all things perteyning to God and their soule health, yea and even in the principles of the Christen religion'.[56] However, we may suspect that it was as much the notoriety of the crime that attracted the ministers' attention, and a desire to demonstrate their skill in getting repentance.

Cases of infanticide and witchcraft apart, murder trials in which more than a single woman (but only women) conspired the crime were very rare, there being but two instances in extant Elizabethan assize files of Kent, Essex, Sussex and Hertfordshire. Doubtless this was another reason the inhabitants of London flocked to the executions of the two women on 13 May 1573. There were present 'many personages of honor and worship' and more people than had ever been seen at that execution site in living memory. The gallows were in Smithfield, where, the writer tells us, 'almoste the whole fielde, and all the way from Newgate, was as full of folke as coulde well stande one by another; and besides that, great companies were placed bothe in the chambers neere abouts (whose windowes and walles were in many places beaten down to looke out at) and also upon the gutters, sides and toppes of the houses, and upon the battlements and steeple of S. Bartholmewes'.[57]

Additional interest must have arisen from Ann Saunders's strong denial of guilt at her trial and a wish to see (as it was perhaps rumoured she might) if she would confess and repent at the gallows to murder, adultery or both. There must also have been some curiosity about what Ann Drury, clearly a woman of many parts, would say. Might she confess to the murder of her own late husband in addition to her role in the Saunders murder? Would she admit to misbehaviour while connected with the Earl of Derby's household?[58] There were sufficient matters in question powerfully to engage the public mind and make the Smithfield drama of death the popular event of the decade.

Appendix

A SUCCESSFUL MURDERESS? THE FORTUNES OF MARGERY FREEMAN, 1570–83

Margery Freeman, the daughter of Richard Freeman, 'a very poore man' of Oxford, was born in February 1559. John Hoare, or Hoer, was a servant of a canon of Christ Church, Oxford. He was to claim Margery was a 'gentlewoman born' and himself a gentleman. His date of birth we do not have, but he must have been considerably older than Margery, whom he married at Oxford on 30 April 1570, his bride being at that time a mere 11 years and 2 months of age. Margery's parents later claimed, though untruthfully, that she was the requisite 12 years old at the time.

We are told that the marriage was arranged by Margery's parents and friends in the belief that Hoare was 'of good ability'. However, within two months of the marriage Hoare is said to have broken into a chest in Margery's father's house, taken from it about £3 in money, pilfered other items and fled Oxford. He seems to have returned within a short time, but his young bride obviously had no high regard for him, since she then ran off herself. She returned a year later, started a rumour that Hoare had murdered her, and went into hiding in her mother's house. There she was eventually discovered hidden behind some boughs in the chimney, Hoare meanwhile having been imprisoned on suspicion. For her unseemly behaviour Margery was apparently examined about her 'abuse' of her husband by the Church authorities. She countered this charge by alleging that Hoare 'was not a man sufficient' that is, he was incapable of procreation. This led to a 'search' of Hoare, a physical examination, which resulted in the rejection of Margery's accusation, one probably aimed at securing the annulment of the marriage.

Soon after this Margery left her husband once again and went to London to look after an aunt, the wife of one Welby, who lived in Tuthill Street. Hoare appears to have followed Margery to London, but he may not have been successful at that point in locating her. Having, perhaps, given up hope of so doing, he took to wife in November 1571 a Maude Lewis, the marriage taking place at St Martin-in-the-Fields. Margery herself may have been partly responsible for this marriage, for, perhaps fearing discovery by Hoare, she had 'fayned herselfe to be deade' and caused her name to be entered in the church book of St Margaret's, Westminster, as being buried there after succumbing to the plague. Hoare eventually discovered Margery dwelling at a barber's house in King Street and 'challenged' her as his wife, but Margery refused him on the grounds of his marriage to Maude. This matter, we are told, was examined in the Dean's Court at Westminster and Hoare was ordered to be whipped through the local streets. This was done on 7 May 1574. An important factor in Hoare's marital commitments, namely Margery's age at the time of her marriage, was not, so a later note informs us, brought up at this time.

It was probably soon after this episode that Margery went off with a certain Jones, who seems to have been a waterman, to Henley-on-Thames, where he 'kept her . . . as his wieffe'. Once more Hoare discovered his first wife's whereabouts and again came and 'challenged' her. Jones, who was present, reached for a staff, intending to strike Hoare, but missed his footing, fell between two barges and was drowned. There is no hint in the source that Hoare was responsible for the death more directly. Although he had found his wife once more, Hoare was unable to make her live with him; she departed for a fourth time. This latest desertion coupled with the death of Maude Lewis at this time may well have prompted Hoare to begin cohabiting with Helen Buttress, or Richardson, of the London parish of St Andrew-by-the-Wardrobe. It was also at this time that Hoare, whose occupation is never stated in our sources, was summoned before the Mayor's Court for his practice of 'takinge upp younge poore children', making them 'loathsome' in order to move people to compassion (and charity) when he made them go begging for him. For this he was put in the pillory in Cheapside (April 1575) and then sent to the Bridewell for further punishment. There, when examined and the matter arose, he denied his Oxford marriage to Margery.

Two years later Margery was living in Colman Street, London, in the house of Henry Hungate, where she was employed as a maid. There she appears to have caught the eye of a wealthy upholsterer named Robert Whitehand, possibly a business associate of Hungate. We are told by one source simply that Whitehand became a suitor of Margery, while a parallel source states that she married Whitehand 'by the meanes of Hungate'. The marriage took place on 26 August 1577 but not before, as it was put, Margery had made known to Whitehand 'her incumbrance' with Hoare and Whitehand had asked the advice of many learned and godly preachers. These gave their opinion that Whitehand might lawfully marry Margery, since Hoare's subsequent marriage, to Maude, which was adulterous, had made the first, to Margery, 'voide'.

For his railing and abusing of Whitehand for marrying or being about to marry his first wife Hoare found himself in the Bridewell again and then committed by the Bishop of London to Newgate. Hoare's publicly voiced objections were probably the reason why Margery, doubtless through Whitehand, got herself divorced from Hoare at this point. A source hostile to Margery, compiled later on, notes that this divorce 'will not nowe be iustified'. The same source states that Margery and Whitehand were married by warrant from the Bishop of London, 'in consideration whereof' the Bishop 'is said to have received of them' a large coverlet of 'silke imagerie', 'one Bruxells Tyke of xii Quarters' and two Spanish blankets.

In his continuing quest Hoare was not without supporters. Two of his friends or associates entreated the Bishop of London on his behalf but found themselves committed, like Hoare, to Newgate. All were soon discharged, but Hoare was ordered to attend before the Court of High Commission, which he did for three terms. He was discharged having given a bond not to molest Margery or Whitehand, 'in consideration whereof and with condition' that he should marry Katherine Richardson 'dwellinge in the bishop's house'. For this undertaking Hoare was to receive £10 in cash with promise of £10 yearly during Margery's life. Where this money was to come from is not stated. The marriage took place in May 1578, but at some unspecified later date Hoare was separated from Katherine by the Bishop's order, no reason being provided by our sources. It might possibly have been connected with a law suit that Hoare now brought against Whitehand. Hoare was soon in prison again. Henry Hungate got him committed to the Bridewell once more and then set on the pillory in Cheapside through what Hoare and his supporters called 'forged accusations made to Mr Yonge the customer'. Hoare later claimed that evidence from a good number of inhabitants of St Bartholomew parish disproved the charges.

Thus far in the career of Margery Freeman there had been no violence or crime on her part. Now there was a change. We are told that after three years of marriage to Whitehand, that is, in mid-1580, Margery announced she would be rid of him and by any means possible. Her confidant was John Shawe, probably her lover. Just before his death Shawe confessed that Margery had consulted him about how to poison Whitehand. Later she prepared a dish of white herring for his dinner and warned Shawe, who was to dine with him, not to eat any himself. Whitehand ate the fish, complained, became sick, became 'swolne verie extremelie' and was dead in two days, though not before Shawe had noticed Margery 'conveying', as it was put, bags of money. Not liking what he saw, he made comment to Margery, but she answered only that Whitehand was 'sure enough', a remark that, if an intended pun, shows Margery had a dry wit, reminding Shawe that he was a co-principal in the crime.

In financial terms the murder was a great success. Whitehand died intestate and Margery, as widow, was able to benefit through her dower in the very large amount of £1,400 after arbitration with Whitehand's family. This must have made Shawe the more eager to marry her. He must have thought his suit was successful, for the day of the marriage was decided on and the licence was obtained. Unfortunately, before the nuptial knot was tied Margery went off to Yorkshire with a certain Blower, a servant, friend or associate of the Hungate family. There, doubtless by arrangement, she met Robert Hungate, a wealthy London mercer and brother of Henry, and married him (December 1580), thus disappointing not only Shawe but several gentlemen and citizens 'of good ability and credit' who were also suitors for her hand. Later on Shawe claimed that he had actually married Margery, and he was ready to give the day, month and year. He sued Margery in February 1581 in the Court of High Commission, but what happened there we are not told.

Shawe also vented his annoyance in a more public setting. He conducted a campaign of disparagement against Margery in her own London environment: it was said 'he raleth of her . . . in the open streets' so that she could not pass him by. Her new husband, Robert Hungate, retaliated by informing the Lord Chancellor that Shawe was a runagate, a masterless man and a common barrator, and obtained a writ out of Chancery that put Shawe in the Counter (April 1581). Although he was freed soon afterwards, he was compelled to provide sureties for his future good bearing towards Hungate and his wife. Fearing therefore to continue his 'lude and railing frenzies',

Shawe managed to persuade John Hoare and his wife Katherine to undertake the further slandering of Hungate and Margery. From this time Shawe and Hoare were allies. Thus on Sunday, 1 October 1581, dressed in Shawe's clothes, Hoare stood facing Margery in her pew in church for the length of the service and as she left the church he openly castigated her 'with public and vile speeches'.

Hoare's (via Shawe) harassment of Hungate and Margery then moved into the legal arena. He asked the local Church authorities to summon Hungate to answer for wrongly detaining his wife, meaning Margery. Accompanied by Shawe, he then complained to the Privy Council that Hungate was detaining from him his wife and £1,400 worth of his goods and, furthermore, was preparing to flee overseas. Hungate was sent for and denied the allegations before Sir Francis Walsingham. At that point Hoare and Shawe decided not to press the matter and pretended they were satisfied. They seem to have decided to bring charges instead before the Court of High Commission. The complaint made there at Michaelmas Term 1581 was basically the same: Hoare said Margery was his wife. Hungate in response referred to Hoare's slanders and general harassment. This court recognised that at the heart of the dispute was the validity of Margery's marriages and referred the issue to the Court of Arches, which, says one source sadly, 'to this days' it never proceeded with.

Simultaneously with the case before the Court of High Commission Shawe began another suit, in collusion with his ally Hoare, in a London common-law court. He sued Margery as Hoare's wife for jewels and other precious items that he had given her, presumably at the time he had been about to marry her. He was awarded damages against Margery and Hoare amounting to £44 13s 4d. On a writ of execution Margery was arrested but for some reason was soon free again. Then, in March 1582, continuing the pursuit at law, Hoare began an action against Robert Hungate of *mulier abducta cum bonis* in the Queen's Bench, the goods being valued again at £1,400, the amount Margery had acquired by arbitration on Whitehand's death. However, Hungate was able in June of the same year to get the Lord Chancellor to stay the Queen's Bench proceedings as well as the execution of the £44 13s 4d mentioned above. Chancery was now Hungate's court of resort: he had already brought a complaint there about the continuous vexation and 'confederacy'.

Hoare claimed later that it was at this point in the quarrel that Hungate and Margery plotted to use violence against his partner Shawe. He said that they procured Margery's brother-in-law John Nicolls, a shoemaker named Thomas Dresser and 'other lewd persons' to lie in wait for and murder Shawe. These conspirators discovered, however, that they could not safely accomplish the crime in London and therefore they served Shawe with process to make him appear in the Queen's Bench on the first day of Trinity Term 1582. Shawe appeared there, at Westminster, on the day, found no charges laid against him and made his way to Charing Cross. He was followed there by two other would-be assassins, Margery's brothers Richard and Thomas Freeman. These, says one source, murdered him there with their daggers, Shawe being weaponless.

The account of this affray given by Hungate and his wife, contrariwise, refuted the accusation that murder had been committed. It claimed that Richard and Thomas Freeman had met Shawe by chance and that then a sudden quarrel had erupted between them in which Thomas had 'lightly' hurt Shawe in the head with his dagger 'without peril or fear of damage'. This interpretation, which removed any suggestion of malice aforethought, turned the misdeed into killing in chance medley at worst, which was only manslaughter. Then the Hungate version diminished the offence still further. It claimed that Shawe had met Richard Freeman the next day and talked to him about the assault but had never caused him 'to be stayed or charged'. Furthermore, Shawe had gone about his business as usual with a kerchief keeping a plaster in place on his head for a whole fortnight and died only a week after that. Thus, the account stated, Shawe had died from God's visitation, not from the wound, and the depositions of two surgeons proved it. After the assault, the two Freeman brothers took refuge in Robert Hungate's house, and the constable who came to arrest them was denied entry until they had escaped. Later on one of the brothers, with John Nicolls, pursued Hoare with drawn swords when he was 'coming from his labour' at Moorgate but failed to injure him.

Hoare was now joined by a Robert Shawe and an unnamed brother of John Shawe in seeking justice against both the slayers and their confederates Hungate and Margery. When a coroner's inquest met to enquire into John Shawe's death, the Hoare–Shawe faction, so their opponents claimed, used 'rigorous proceeding' to induce the jurors to find them culpable but in fact they found only the two Freemans so. Therefore Hoare and the Shawes put forward a bill of indictment against Hungate and his wife as accessories at the next sessions at Newgate. Unsuccessful at that time, they 'pursued' the indictment at two further Newgate sessions. Unfortunately for them, although the last jury of indictment found the bill to be true, 'some of the bench' ended their attempt at prosecution by finding an error in it.

At this point the Hoare–Shawe group appear to have complained to the Privy Council. We are told by the hostile source that they persuaded Thomas Younge, 'a wicked and lewd man', whom they had corrupted with promise of great rewards, to testify on oath before Sir Owen Hopton and Sir Roland Haward, appointed by the Council to examine 'certain suggestions' provided by John Shawe's brothers. In his deposition Younge stated that Hungate and his wife had tried to get him to poison Hoare when the latter was languishing in the Counter prison. Margery, it was noted, had 'prescribed' to Younge two kinds of poison and given him £7 with a promise of a further £10 later. Unfortunately for the conspirators Hopton 'did so much favour the said Margerie that he would hardly hear anything against her nor suffer that which he heard to be put down'. The charges against Margery were designed, so Hungate and his wife claimed, to give 'presumption' that Margery had persuaded her brothers to attack John Shawe. Yet the tactics of her opponents produced results, for at the next local sessions of indictment Margery was successfully charged as an accessory in Shawe's death.

At this Margery surrendered herself to the authorities and asked to be tried forthwith. Her plan was apparently to get herself tried as an accessory before the two principals were arraigned, a move that, if successful, would greatly increase the chances of her being acquitted. The justices were ready to connive, arguing that Staunford's *Les Plees del Coron* permitted it in some circumstances. However, as she was about to be arraigned, Robert Shawe, who was present in court, drew a writ of certiorari, which he had just purchased, out of his pocket, causing the case to be moved into the Queen's Bench. In that court Margery, having given surety that she and her husband would be of good bearing towards Hoare, was allowed to go free.

Then it was that Margery and her husband Robert, in their turn, complained to the Privy Council, which referred the feud to the examination of several notables. The documents, our sources, whose content has been outlined above, were in fact the answers to articles/interrogatories that each side had compiled (1583) through its lawyers to accuse and gain admissions and evidence from the other. Unfortunately how the examiners and the Privy Council itself acted on the information thus garnered, as well as the later fortunes of the participants in the quarrels, is unknown.

The records that touch on the fortunes of Margery Freeman and her first husband John Hoare provide us with little information about their social milieu, their emotions and attitudes, or their exact motivation. This is largely because these records are solely of the legal variety: interrogatories (questions) and answers to them by witnesses offered by the two factions when their quarrel came ultimately before the Privy Council. The inter-rogatories were designed to elicit answers that showed the other side involved in some malpractice, to score legal points that would eventually produce a favourable decision by the Council. There is thus nothing resembling a continuous narrative to be discovered in these records, a deficiency that can be remedied only in small part by studying the legal strategies of the factions, their success or lack of it in a variety of courts, and by consideration of a number of passing remarks.

Many crucial matters remain unclear. Was the obsessed pursuer of Margery, John Hoare (whipped 1574, pilloried 1575 and 1578, and perhaps the first recorded stalker in English history), mentally unbalanced? Robert Hungate certainly told the Bishop of London that he was a madman, although the latter refused to have him committed to Bedlam. Was Hoare criminally inclined, as his thieving from Margery's father and his immoral begging by proxy seem to suggest? What was his occupation? How was he able to sue his adversaries so often and in so many courts? Was Margery, as it seems, a woman of notable sexual attractiveness, and if so what role did that quality play in gaining favourable verdicts and decisions before examiners and in courts of law? Did she actually marry John Shawe? Was he her lover when she was the wife of Robert Whitehand? How justified would we be in attributing Margery's misfortunes and apparent hardness of character to the arranged marriage she entered into when she was not yet 12? Were ecclesiastical officials and the officials of the Church courts easily bribed, or at least more easily bribed than their lay brethren? Some of these matters might have been elucidated had a pamphleteer or even a chronicler taken an interest in Margery's career. None did, doubtless because, as far as we know, she never went to open trial and thus there was no public revelation of her intriguing career and misdeeds. The protection and influence of a wealthy London mercer, her third husband, must also have been of assistance in that respect.

The deficiencies of the records in regard to the lives and personalities of people are compensated to some degree by the light they throw on several matters of law. A suit is brought in one court in order to circumvent a decision previously given in another and probably to obtain evidence for a prosecution in a third. Enquiry into a murder, we are shown, could be quickly stifled by interference in the workings of the coroner's inquest. Justices might be persuaded to try accessories before principals. It was probably a good defence for those who murdered by ambush to claim the deed was done in chance medley; or, if the victim of attempted murder happened to survive for several weeks, the miscreant might well claim the death came from natural causes. Additionally this group of records (TNA: PRO SP 12/158/ 35–7 and SP 12/235/ 47) shows the Privy Council as the ultimate investigative agency in a criminal case of some importance. This has also been demonstrated in the cases examined in depth above. It is an aspect of conciliar activity that, because the council after its enquiries frequently referred the cases to other courts for conclusion, has not been given sufficient prominence in historical writing. Certainly, in the current instance, the history of a young woman of relatively lowly status seeking to improve her lot and escape the bonds of a patriarchal society by fair means or foul, the documents compiled on the orders of the Privy Council are of more than passing interest.

NOTES

INTRODUCTION

1. T. Smith, *De Republica Anglorum*, ed. M. Dewar (Cambridge, 1982), p. 117; R. Holinshed, *Holinshed's Chronicles, England, Scotland and Ireland*, ed. H. Ellis (London, 1807–8), i, 313. Where this edition has been used below in this book, the abbreviation is 'Holinshed' *tout court*; where the first edition has been used, then 'Holinshed (1577)'.

2. These are my calculations from *Calendar of Assize Records, Sussex Indictments, Elizabeth I*, ed. J.S. Cockburn (London, 1975), *Cal. Assize Records, Kent Indictments, Elizabeth I*, ed. J.S. Cockburn (London, 1979), *Cal. Assize Records, Essex Indictments, Elizabeth I*, ed. J.S. Cockburn (London, 1979), *Cal. Assize Records, Hertfordshire Indictments, Elizabeth I*, ed. J.S. Cockburn (London, 1976), and The National Archives (TNA): Public Record Office (PRO), London, CHES 21/1 ff. 43–199.

3. On killing in chance medley, see J.G. Bellamy, *The Criminal Trial in Later Medieval England* (Toronto, 1998), pp. 61–6, which also covers felonies and their handling in much of the Tudor period.

4. The figures in this paragraph and the subsequent one are my calculations from *Cal. Assize Records, Indictments, Elizabeth I* for Sussex, Kent, Essex and Hertfordshire. The fifteenth-century Yorkshire evidence is in jail delivery rolls TNA: PRO JUSI 3/211 and 213.

5. See Chapter 2.

6. R. Wunderli, 'Pre-Reformation London Summoners and the Murder of Richard Hunne', *Journal of Ecclesiastical History*, 33 (1982), 218; S.F.C. Milsom, 'Richard Hunne's "Praemunire"', *English Historical Review*, 76 (1961), 80–2; E. Jeffries Davis, 'The Authorities for the Case of Richard Hunne, 1514–1515', *Eng. Hist. Rev.*, 30 (1915), 477–88. Hun's praemunire suit was contemporaneous with, and perhaps exacerbated, the incipient State-versus-Church quarrel over the scope of benefit of clergy. If Hun's demurrer at the King's Bench trial was a challenge to the validity of the canon law in England, then

his demise would undoubtedly have been to the Church's benefit: see the comments by J.D.M. Dennett in *The Complete Works of St. Thomas More*, ix, ed. J.B. Trapp (New Haven, 1979), pp. 222–5 and J.G. Bellamy, *Criminal Law and Society in Late Medieval and Tudor England* (New York, 1984), pp. 132–9.

7. *The Enquire and verdite of the quest panneld of the death of Richard Hune wich was founde hanged in Lolars tower* (Antwerp, n.d.); E. Hall, *The Union of the two noble and illustre families of Lancastre and Yorke*, ed. H. Ellis (London, 1809), pp. 572–80. *The Enquire and verdite* is virtually the same as the account in Hall except for occasional differences in spelling and its inclusion of about 300 words highly critical of the pre-Reformation Church and the betrayal of William Tyndal.

8. Hall, p. 580.

9. *Reports of Cases by John Caryll*, ed. J.H. Baker (Selden Society, 116, 2000), p. 686; Hall, p. 573.

10. Hall, pp. 573, 579.

11. *Ibid.*, pp. 573, 575.

12. *Reports of Caryll*, p. 686.

13. Hall, pp. 573–4.

14. *Ibid.*, pp. 575–6, 577–9. Joseph, who was a Church-court apparitor (summoner), had apparently been dismissed from his job soon after Hun was arrested because he would not deal with Hun in captivity 'cruelly', and as Horsey, the Chancellor, wanted. However, he was soon re-employed as Hun's gaoler: see Wunderli, 'Pre-Reformation London Summoners', 222–3. At one point Joseph gave his alibi about his whereabouts to the Council (Hall, p. 576), which shows the latter must have been monitoring the inquest's enquiries, and probably also conducting a parallel investigation of its own. The use of a wire in the slaying was perhaps intended to avoid leaving obvious wounds on the body rather than as a means of torturing: c.f. S.J. Smart, 'John Foxe and "The Story of Richard Hun, Martyr"', *Journal of Ecclesiastical History*, 37 (1986), 6.

15. Hall, pp. 574–5, 577–8.

16. *Ibid.*, pp. 579–80; J. Foxe, *The Acts and Monuments of John Foxe*, ed. G. Townsend (New York, 1965), iv, 196, 204. Hall's statement that Bishop Fitzjames requested Wolsey to have the King's Councillors investigate the case 'in the presence of the parties' could perhaps be taken as showing that the Council became involved through pressure by the Church. If this was in fact the case, the plan misfired when Joseph, probably through duress ('payne and duraunce', claimed Fitzjames) confessed to the slaying (see Hall, p. 579 and also below). Fitzjames, as Bishop of London, had Hun tried posthumously for heresy in what has been noted as a unique piece of ecclesiastical legal procedure; see A. Ogle, *The Tragedy in the Lollards' Tower* (Oxford, 1949), p. 85.

17. *Reports of Caryll*, pp. 691–2.

18. *A dialogue concerning heresies* in *The Complete Works of St Thomas More*, vi, ed. T.M.C. Lawler, G. Marc'hadour and R.C. Marius (New Haven, 1981), p. 326; Foxe, ed. Townsend, iv, 198.

19. *A dialogue concerning heresies*, pp. 318, 323, 326.

20. *Letters and Papers, Foreign and Domestic, Henry VIII*, iii, no. 3062/4; *A dialogue concerning heresies*, p. 325. More's lack of any reference to Joseph's confession is the more noticeable in that he could have implied, as did Fitzjames, that it had been obtained by duress. When More wrote *A dialogue* doubtless his political aspirations also contributed to his denying Hun's death was murder and to his offering arguments that were general to the point of fatuity.

21. In one of the depositions taken by the coroner's inquest Joseph was noted as having said that the Mayor of London 'taketh this matter whotte (hot)': *The Enquire and verdite*; Hall, p. 576.

22. Hall, pp. 575, 579.

23. The information, which Joseph gave 'of hys awne free wyll', was recorded, says Hall, by members of the coroner's jury. This suggests they were present at Joseph's examination by the Council in the Tower: Hall, p. 575. For 'putting to pain' in the Tower (of thieves in this case), which shows the practice was not uncommon, see e.g. *Letters and Papers, Henry VIII*, iv (ii) no. 3702.

24. Says Foxe, 'the cause was then brought into the parliament house'. There 'the truth was laid so plain before all men's faces'; to no avail: Foxe, ed. Townsend, iv, 197.

25. Davis, 'Richard Hunne', 481.

26. The writing of the pamphlet, *The Enquire and verdite*, may have been connected with the efforts (*c.* 1536–9) of Hun's daughter Margaret and her husband Roger Whaplod to obtain possession of Hun's lands and tenements as granted to them in 1523: *Letters and Papers, Henry VIII*, xv, no. 1029/65. The introduction to the pamphlet laments religious persecutions, and pillories the English clergy as being totally unrepentant for their 'old abominations'; they cling to their possessions, 'abhore chast matrimony' and 'daylie . . . commit whoredome'.

27. For examples and details of the various themes in the murder accounts, see Chapter 2.

28. See L.B. Wright, *Middle-Class Culture in Elizabethan England* (Ithaca, NY, 1958), pp. 468–78.

29. On reginal adultery as high treason, see Bellamy, *The Tudor Law of Treason: An Introduction* (London, 1979), pp. 40–1.

30. On the increase in the number of felons who gained benefit of clergy, see Bellamy, *Criminal Trial*, pp. 136–7 and id., *Criminal Law and Society*, pp. 156–8.

A few pamphlet writers address women directly, using the second-person plural; see Chapter 2.

31.   For the equivocal position in law of sorcery/witchcraft/necromancy cases in the medieval period and their absence from the records of the common-law courts, see Bellamy, *Criminal Trial*, pp. 191–2. However, in the fifteenth century, suggestive of rising concern about these offences, there were a few cases in which the King's death was intended, where they were construed as treason: see id., *The Law of Treason in England in the Later Middle Ages* (Cambridge, 1970), pp. 126–8. The first contemporary account of an infanticide case seems to have been that in the pamphlet *Sundrye strange and inhumaine murthers lately committed* (1591), sig. B1: see Chapter 2.

32.   On the involvement of servants, the Ardern, Stourton, Saunders, Lincoln, Beast and Page cases are particularly instructive: see Chapters 2, 4, 5 and 6.

33.   The horror with which sixteenth-century people viewed murder by poison is well demonstrated by Henry VIII's statute (22 Henry c. 9) making the penalty, as Harrison puts it, 'to be boiled to death': Holinshed, i, 311.

34.   Such transmogrification or cruentation was reported in the Hobson (1581), Lincoln (1590), Lord Bourke (1591) and Uppingham (1591) cases: see Chapter 2.

35.   See the Beech/Winchester, Kynnestar and Saunders cases: see Chapters 2 and 6.

36.   These are the Beast, Hobson and Brewen cases: see Chapter 2.

37.   The Meaphon and Robson cases and other comments on the matter are in Chapter 2.

38.   In order, these are the Lincoln, Meaphon and Saunders cases: see Chapter 2.

39.   These are the Chambers and Greenoll cases: see Chapter 2.

40.   There are no references to the use of bloodhounds in the pursuit and detection of murderers, although they were used in at least one Elizabethan case of witchcraft. Nor do we encounter any specific mention of what might be called third-party informers about murder (i.e. bringers of information to law officers about covert murder).

41.   These are noticeable features of the Lincoln, Meaphon and Beech/Winchester cases: see Chapter 2.

42.   See A. Fitzherbert and R. Crompton, *L'Office et Auctoritie de Justices de Peace* (London, 1972), f. 75; see also Chapter 1.

43.   These are the Robson, Beech/Winchester and Saunders cases.

44.   However, one of the cases studied at length, that concerning the Witherick family, suggests marital abuse might be considered by those investigating to be worth enquiring about. There was no contemporary account produced of this case; only legal and governmental records survive: see Chapter 3.

45. Smith, ed. Dewar, p. 108.

46. These pieces of drama are based on the Ardern, Saunders and Beech/ Winchester cases.

47. *Acts of the Privy Council of England*, ed. J.R. Dasent (London, 1890–1907), vols ii–xxxii.

CHAPTER I: MURDER AND THE LAW

1. *Tractatus de Legibus et Consuetudinibus Regni Anglia qui Glanvilla vocatur*, ed. G.D.G. Hall (London, 1965), p. 174; *Henrici de Bracton de Legibus et Consuetudinibus Angliae*, ed. G.E. Woodbine, rev. S.E. Thorne (Cambridge, Mass., 1968), ii, 298, 340–1, 378; *Britton*, ed. F.M. Nichols (Oxford, 1865), pp. 34–8.

2. See Bellamy, *Criminal Trial*, pp. 57–61.

3. *Ibid.*, pp. 63–4.

4. *Reports from the Lost Notebooks of Sir James Dyer*, ed. J.H. Baker (Selden Soc., 109–10, 1993–4), ii, 404; A. Fitzherbert, *La Graunde Abridgement* (1515), f. 249v.

5. *Early Treatises on the Practice of the Justices of the Peace in the Fifteenth and Sixteenth Centuries*, ed. B.H. Putnam (Oxford, 1924), p. 379. Marowe was drawing attention to a case in *Year Books*, 15 Edward II Pasch., f. 463.

6. A. Fitzherbert and R. Crompton, f. 17.

7. *Ibid.*, ff. 17, 18v; *English Reports*, Dyer 128b; *ibid.*, Moore 87.

8. Fitzherbert and Crompton, f. 18.

9. *English Reports*, Plowden, 474a.

10. Fitzherbert and Crompton, f. 19; 13 Richard II st. 2 c. 1.

11. *Tudor Royal Proclamations*, ed. P.F. Hughes and J.F. Larkin (New Haven, Conn., 1964–9), i, 262–3.

12. *Reports of Dyer*, ed. Baker, ii, 417. It is possible that the doubt may have lain in the status of the slain posse member.

13. *English Reports*, 9 Coke 65b–70a; M. Dalton, *The Countrey Justice* (London, 1619), p. 218.

14. W. Staunford, *Les Plees del Coron* (1557), f. 37v; Fitzherbert and Crompton, f. 34v; *Year Books*, 35 Henry VI Mich, pl. 24. Apparently there was a discussion by the professional judges at Lincoln's Inn in 1549 on the nature of the crime when a man who had been robbed pursued the felon and recovered his goods but allowed the robber to go free. It was agreed he was guilty of concealment and was not an accessory to felony: F. Moore, *Cases and Collect. . . . per Sir Francis Moore* (London, 1663), p. 8.

15. Dalton, p. 260. Staunford (f. 37v) refers his readers to *Year Books* 2 Richard III Mich. pl. 22, where there is comment on erasing legal records and the enrolling of non-found bills with 'true' bills of indictment.

16. As Holinshed's *Chronicles* tells us in regard to the murder of Arthur Hall by Martin Bullocke in 1572, 'The truth of the matter' came to light 'by the good providence of God, the revealer of such evill facts': Holinshed, iv. 266; see also Chapter 2.

17. For example, the emphasis in pamphlets on detective work by the magistrates and lawyers of Rye in the Robson case, by the victim's sister in the Page murder, by the coroner in the Meaphon case, as well as the successful long-distance pursuits in the Randolph murder. The plays concerned with the Saunders and Beach murders are even more emphatic in this regard. See Chapter 2.

18. Holinshed, i, 314. In the Randolph case an inhabitant of Aylesbury, who had met Randolph and was able to describe his assailants, accompanied the hue and cry, which was probably a major reason for its success: see Chapter 2. Townships could be fined for failure to arrest murderers.

19. For the Brewen and Meaphon cases, see Chapter 2.

20. See Bellamy, *Criminal Trial*, pp. 43–4.

21. *Year Books*, 2 Henry VII Pasch. pl. 1.

22. See Chapters 2 and 3.

23. See Chapter 2.

24. *Year Books*, 21 Edward IV Mich. pl. 49; 1/2 Philip and Mary c. 13. Thomas Smith seems to imply that the members of the coroner's inquest were allowed time to canvass the neighbourhood for the names of suspects and persons knowledgeable about the crime: Smith, ed. Dewar, p. 108.

25. Smith offers only about twenty or so words on examination: *ibid.*, pp. 107, 109, 113.

26. A good example is the examination of Henry Robson; see also the Brewen case: for both see Chapter 2. Although contemporary writers do not dwell on the point, it is clear that the vast majority of murderers mentioned in this book confessed or were compelled to confess when they were examined. One threat used for this purpose seems to have been that of being hanged in chains.

27. See Bellamy, *Criminal Trial*, pp. 142–3.

28. Fitzherbert and Crompton, f. 75.

29. C.R. Unsworth, 'Witchcraft Beliefs and Criminal Procedure in Early Modern England', pp. 94–5, in *Legal Record and Historical Reality*, ed. T.G. Watkin (London, 1989); *Acts of the Privy Council*, iv, 201, and *ibid.*, vii, 367–8.

30. See Chapters 5 and 6.

31. *Acts of the Privy Council*, xi, 158; *ibid.*, xxvii, 187. On 'manacles', see Bellamy,

Tudor Law of Treason, pp. 113–14.

32. See Bellamy, *Tudor Law of Treason*, pp. 116–17; W.D. Cooper, 'Further Particulars of Thomas Norton and of State Proceedings in Matters of Religion in the Years 1581 and 1582', *Archaeologia*, 36 (1855), 116.

33. As stipulated by the statute 2/3 Philip and Mary c. 10, which was probably confirming existing practice.

34. On the practices and mechanics of indicting, and the form of the indictments themselves, see Bellamy, *Criminal Trial*, pp. 24–30. Indicting sessions before the justices of the peace where felony was at issue seem to have taken place before, or simultaneously with, the jail delivery/assize sessions in the later sixteenth century. Evidence might on occasion be produced in a murder case at the indicting sessions by a law officer of the Crown: see e.g. *Letters and Papers, Henry VIII*, iv (ii), no. 3926. On grand jurymen in witchcraft cases, see R. Bernard, *Instructions for Grand Jury Men* (1627), pp. 228–40.

35. J.S. Cockburn, *Calendar of Assize Records, Home Circuit Indictments, Elizabeth I and James I, Introduction* (London, 1985), pp. 102–3.

36. See P.G. Lawson, 'Lawless Juries? The Composition and Behaviour of Hertfordshire Juries, 1573–1624', in J.S. Cockburn and T.A. Green (eds), *Twelve Good Men and True* (Princeton, 1988), pp. 119–21, 124–5. Cockburn in 'Twelve Silly Men? The Trial Jury at Assizes, 1560–1670', prefers, however, to emphasise the illiteracy and ignorance of trial jurors: *ibid.*, pp. 159, 162. Early in the trial the accused had the opportunity to challenge (i.e. object to and have removed) particular jurors, but few ever did. The statute 23 Henry VIII c. 13 had made men whose goods were worth £40 eligible for service on trial juries. This was obviously aimed at those in commerce.

37. See Chapter 6. Thus the play provides us with a description of justices' behaviour that other records, literary and legal, hint at but do not demonstrate. When Trusty Roger, a witness for the Crown, is brought to face the accused, Ann Saunders, they have an altercation, a way favoured by the justices for getting at the truth: see also Bellamy, *Criminal Trial*, pp. 109–10.

38. See Bellamy, *Tudor Law of Treason*, pp. 142–5.

39. Bellamy, Criminal Trial, pp. 113–14. See also Cockburn, 'Twelve Silly Men?', pp. 177–8. It has been argued that the accused were tried in batches so that the overburdened jurors would be more dependent on the judges' direction: *ibid*.

40. Bellamy, *Criminal Trial*, p. 116.

41. On the conduct of the justices in their management of the trial, see Bellamy, *Criminal Trial*, pp. 110–12.

42. TNA: PRO ASSI 35/1–44; *Cal. Assize Rec., Sussex Indictments, Elizabeth I*, pp. 1–431; TNA: PRO CHES 21/1, ff. 43–199; *Cal. Assize Rec., Kent Indictments, Elizabeth I*, pp. 1–504. The modern murder conviction rate is over 90 per cent.

43.   *Acts of the Privy Council*, xiv, 300; *Lancashire and Cheshire cases in the Court of Star Chamber*, ed. R. Stewart-Brown (Lancashire and Cheshire Record Society, 71, 1916), pp. 113, 122–3; *Calendar of State Papers, Domestic, 1601–1603*, p. 213.

44.   The sole exception, a practice appearing late in Elizabeth's reign, was the punishment of galley service for a number of years. There are a number of references to murderers so dispatched: see Cockburn, *Assize, Introduction*, p. 127, and Bellamy, *Criminal Trial*, p.151. One Kent assize record (July 1591) announces circumspectly that a woman who has murdered her husband is to be executed in the manner appropriate to the crime, a phrase suggesting either distaste for the penalty among the lawyers or popular opposition to it.

45.   The Tudor legal commentator Edmund Plowden states quite clearly that persons were reprieved from sessions to sessions so they could purchase a pardon: E. Plowden, *The Commentaries or Reports of Edmund Plowden* (London, 1816), p. 475.

46.   On the substantial topic of pardons for felony, see Bellamy, *Criminal Trial*, pp. 137–48.

47.   *Cal. Pat. Rolls, 1555–1557*, pp. 13–14, 182, 308, 357, 484.

48.   *Ibid., 1558–1560*, pp. 20, 328, 429.

49.   4 Henry VII c. 13; 4 Henry VIII c. 2. The statute 12 Henry VII c. 7 forbade the privilege where the slaying was petty treason; 4/5 Philip and Mary c. 4 forbade it for those who ordered or plotted murder.

50.   See Bellamy, *Tudor Law of Treason*, pp. 189–203, for the complexities of the execution scene. Where the crime was murder, the proceedings were similar but less elaborate and, unfortunately, much less well documented. Thus we lack, for the most part, reliable figures on the size of the crowds and detailed reports of murderers' last words. We have little about the behaviour of those clergy who had accompanied the condemned person to the gallows, nothing on whether questions were put to the latter and by whom, or whether there were any last-minute bargains struck, such as benefits for spouse or children in return for a complete confession.

51.   Holinshed, i, 311.

52.   *John Calvin*, ed. J. Dillenberger (New York, 1971), p. 491.

CHAPTER 2: WRITING ABOUT MURDER

1.   On indictments and appeals see Bellamy, *Criminal Trial*, and Chapter 1 above.

2.   See the Introduction.

3.   See *Records of Some Sessions of the Peace in Lincolnshire, 1360–1375*, ed.

R. Sillem (Lincoln Record Society, 30, 1936), pp. lxx–lxxiv; R. Virgoe, 'The Murder of Edmund Clippesby', *Norfolk Archaeology*, 35, pt 3 (1972), 302–7. See also S.J. Payling, 'Murder, Motive and Punishment in Fifteenth Century England: Two Gentry Case-Studies', *English Historical Review*, 113 (1998), 1–17 on the murders of Sir John Basynges (1446) and John Chaworth (1464). Perhaps the most detailed reconstruction of a late-medieval English murder is of the slaying of Nicholas Radford, a distinguished Devonshire lawyer, by Sir Thomas Courtenay, son of the Earl of Devon, in October 1455. In this instance the details in the indictment can be fortuitously fleshed out by a petition to parliament and a contemporary letter: see R.L. Storey, *The End of the House of Lancaster* (London, 1966), pp. 168–70.

4. *Knighton's Chronicle 1337–1396*, ed. G.H. Martin (Oxford, 1995), p. 49. The wife was assisted by a servant 'and others who conspired with them'. The most extensive account of a non-political murder in a medieval chronicle compiled by a cleric seems to be that by John Amundesham concerning the violent death of William Grys at Norwich at Christmas 1423; even so, it runs to only 100 words: *Annales monasterii S.Albani a Johanne Amundesham*, ed. H.T. Riley (Rolls ser., 28, 1870–1), p. 16. Yet there is a good deal of detail about several fourteenth-century murders in a feud between gentry to be found in what appears to be a sixteenth-century ballad version of a lost medieval account: see 'The Eland Tragedy: Revenge upon Revenge', in Holroyd, *Collection of Yorkshire Ballads*, ed. C.F. Forshaw (Barnsley, 1974), pp. 196–210. This is critically assessed by J.M. Kaye in 'The Eland Murders, 1350–1: A Study of the Legend of the Eland Feud', *Yorkshire Archaeological Journal*, 51 (1979), 61–79.

5. *Gregory's Chronicle* in *The Historical Collections of a Citizen of London*, ed. J. Gairdner (Camden Soc., 2nd ser., 17, 1876), pp. 163–4, 182, 184; *The Brut*, ed. F.W.D. Brie, Early English Text Society, *OS* 131, pp. 445, 472, 474; *ibid.*, *OS* 136, pp. 479–83. It is *The Brut* that remarks that murder cannot be concealed for ever: 'murdour woll com oute'; however, the first appearance of this dictum seems to be in Chaucer's *Nun's Priest's Tale*, line 232 ('modre wol out').

6. The murderers or murder victims, unlike a good percentage of those in chronicles of pre-fifteenth-century origin, were usually members of the commercial and lower classes.

7. Hall, p. 815. Hall himself does mention briefly that in 1512 a yeoman of the guard 'slew wilfully' a servant of Lord Willoughby in Westminster Palace and was hanged there, his body being left on the gallows for two days: *ibid.*, 526. He also refers to the poisoning by Richard Roose of several members of the Bishop of Rochester's household, which led to the statute 22 Henry VIII c. 9 and Roose being 'boyled . . . to the death': *ibid.*, 780–1.

8. *Ibid.*, pp. 824, 827, 842.

9. *Ibid.*, p. 842; R. Grafton, *Chronicle at large unto the First yere of Q. Elizabeth* (London, 1569), pp. 1224, 1235, 1238, 1253.

10. J. Stow, *Annales of England* (1605), pp. 821, 833, 942, 979–80, 1020, 1067.

11. Holinshed, iii, 172, 524, 531.

12. *Ibid.*, iii, 803. Perhaps censorship was involved in the Wolfe case.

13. *Ibid.*, iii, 819, 821–2.

14. TNA: PRO KB 8/13 mm. 4, 8; Holinshed (1577), pp. 1581–2. There had been bad blood between Henry VIII and the Fiennes (Dacre) family since the 1520s. Some thought that Dacre's failure to obtain a pardon was because various courtiers were manœuvring to have his lands; but, since Dacre's indictment implied his crime even touched on treason, it is obvious that the King intended his death. See also Bellamy, *Criminal Trial*, p.143, and id., *Bastard Feudalism and the Law* (London, 1989), pp. 135, 168.

15. Holinshed, iii, 1022. The legal record of the trials is TNA: PRO KB 8/17/4, mm. 1, 3, where the name of the principal murderer is given as Charles de Guevara, gentleman. Surprisingly Holinshed (1577), like Stow and Hall, but in contrast with the second edition, omits the case of Margaret Davie, who, for causing the deaths of four people in three different households where she had lived, was boiled to death at Smithfield in March 1543 under the statute of 1530: see C. Wriothesley, *A Chronicle of England*, i, ed. W.D. Hamilton (Camden Soc., NS 11, 1875), pp. 134–5; Holinshed, iii, 824.

16. Holinshed, iii, 1024–31.

17. *Statutes of the Realm* (Record Commission, 1810–28), iv (i), 5–8, 72. On witnesses and their testimony at this time, see Bellamy, *Criminal Law and Society*, ch. 3. On conviction rates for felony in Edward VI's reign, see Bellamy, *Criminal Trial*, pp. 68–9, 123.

18. *The Diary of Henry Machyn*, ed. J.G. Nichols (Camden Soc., 42, 1848), p. 4; R. Grafton, *An abridgement of the Chronicles of England* (1562), f. 147. The developing debate in print on the qualities of womanhood has been studied by Wright, *Middle-Class Culture*, pp. 468–72, who notes that the publisher Robert Copland encouraged such works as being particularly profitable to him. Interest in husband-murder seems to have been strong when there was active Protestantism and when there were accusations of witchcraft. The three cases of murder in Henry VI's reign (mentioned above) appear in London chronicles in years when Lollardy was still strong and troublesome, and when there were several reports of witchcraft.

19. Holinshed, iv, 85. This may or may not have been murder. The *Chronicles* adds that the victim, William Whitrents, was 'in great peril of death'. It does not say he died, yet Carpenter was certainly hanged: *Machyn* (p. 121) says he was hanged 'all night naked'. There was no trial as such; since the deed was done

in court a judgment was automatically recorded. Mere intent to murder without overt deed was no offence unless the intended victim was a Privy Councillor. The *Chronicles* also reports that a Spaniard who killed an Englishman was hanged for it at Charing Cross in October 1554, but this may have been chance medley (manslaughter) not murder: *ibid.*, iv, 64. Holinshed and the compilers of the second edition both omit the murder in 1556 of Giles Rufford by two hirelings of Benett Smyth. The two murderers were hanged in chains near Huntingdon, and Smyth in Buckinghamshire: *Machyn*, p. 102.

20. Holinshed (1577), p. 1766; Stow, *Annales*, p. 1067; Wriothesley, i, p. 137. Grafton says the punishment was severe because the Queen and her Council feared similar occurrences: Grafton (1562), f. 162.

21. J. Hunter, *South Yorkshire: The History and Topography of the Deanery of Doncaster* (London, 1828–31), i, 173–7. Lewis and Edmund West were ambushed by John and George Darcy when returning from a fair on 25 May 1556. Machyn notes that the West party numbered eight and their ambushers forty: *Machyn*, p. 107.

22. Holinshed, iv, 262, 330. Thomas Chamber was poisoned by a dish of roseacre mixed with milk, and died two days later: see *Cal. Assize Rec., Kent Indictments, Elizabeth* I, p. 104.

23. Holinshed (1577), p. 1862. This seems to have been the original 'body in a trunk' murder in English history.

24. See the detailed studies of these two murders in Chapters 4 and 6.

25. *A briefe discourse of the late murther of master George Saunders, a worshipfull Citizen of London* (London, 1573), pp. 224–6; *A Warning for Fair Women: A Critical Edition*, ed. C.D. Cannon (The Hague, 1975), pp. 161–70.

26. *A briefe discourse*, pp. 236–8. See Chapter 6. Charles Stourton said a few words and a prayer before execution: *Transactions of the Bibliographical Society*, iv (1898), 66–7.

27. *A true reporte or description of an horrible, wofull and most lamentable murther doen in the citie of Bristowe by one Jhon Kynnestar, a sherman* (London, 1573), sigs A2–A3. The murder occurred in August 1572 and Kynnestar was hanged the same month. For the only other well-documented instances of wife-murder in Elizabeth's reign, the Meaphon and Robson cases (1595 and 1598), see pp. 70–3.

28. *Ibid.*, sigs A4–A5. The writer names four witnesses to the veracity of his account.

29. *Ibid.*, sigs A6–A7.

30. Holinshed, iv, 343, 345, 426, 494; Stow, *Annales*, p. 1163. The Worcester brothers, Stow notes, were of Spanish ancestry.

31. A. Munday, *A view of sundry examples*, in J.P. Collier, *John a Kent and John a Cumber* (London, 1851), pp. 80–96. Half of Munday's victims are women, but there are no instances of husbands murdering their wives (or vice versa).

32. *Ibid.*, p. 87.

33. *Ibid.*, pp. 89–91, 97.

34. The interference of the devil figures in several places, however: *ibid.*, pp. 81, 87, 92.

35. *Ibid.*, pp. 93–6. The words uttered by Bourn's ex-mistress were damning: 'I wil have him hewed as small as flesh to the pot' (p. 94). It is the first detailed recording in literature of evidence given at a coroner's inquest since Hall provided depositions concerned with the death of Richard Hun.

36. *A true report of the late horrible murder committed by William Sherwood, prisoner in the Queenes Bench for the possession of Popery the 18 of June 1581* (London, 1581), sigs A2–A5. Richard Hobson was a young man born of good parentage in the Isle of Wight. Sherwood was a gentleman 'born to some land' near Beverley, Yorkshire. When his money was exhausted, he had been removed to the 'common' part of the gaol. Hobson appears to have defrayed his prison charges (sig. A3). Sherwood stabbed Hobson with a knife and tried to escape. He was caught and brought before Hobson's corpse. The blood 'which was settled' then 'issued out afreshe' (sig. A4). The indictment shows the crime was committed on 28 June 1581: *Calendar of Assize Records, Surrey Indictments, Elizabeth I*, ed. J.S. Cockburn (London, 1980), p. 221.

37. *A true report*, sigs A6–A7. The crowd attending the execution was vociferous, crying out 'hang him, hang him, there be none here of his profession'. The fact that Sherwood proclaimed the Pope supreme head of the universal Church and Christ's vicar on earth doubtless added to the hostility of the onlookers. The writer concludes by saying how boldly Sherwood 'imbraced forraine jurisdiction', adding 'all they which be Papistes harteley doo the like', and therefore each needs to be 'well cougeled at the fyrste' like a 'sheepwerier'.

38. *A briefe discourse of two most cruell and bloudie murthers committed bothe in Worcestershire and bothe unhappily in the yeare 1583* (London, 1583). The first murder was committed during the night of 31 December 1582/1 January 1583, the second in the following June.

39. The writer visited Smith in jail and was told by him that, after the blows to Greenoll's head, he stabbed him to the heart. He covered the grave in the cellar with bales of flax, dry vats and chests; then he washed himself and the house. It was, of course, known that Greenoll had visited Smith that night. Smith was 'both hansome and well featured a young man', and his father was 'one of the chief in Esam'. Smith had been married only eight weeks; his wife was visiting friends on the night of the murder. Interestingly, the writer laments the shock Smith's crime must have caused for his wife: 'I commit it to

the judgement of all virtuous women what a greefe it was to her when first she heard of these unhappy newes': *ibid.*, sigs A6–A7, B1.

40. Tomson resisted his lover's imprecations to murder her husband for 'a great while' but eventually 'solemly at the eating of a Posset the night before he did the deed, he promised faithfully to accomplish her will': *ibid.*, sigs B2–B3.

41. *Ibid.*, sigs B1, B3, B4. Mrs Beast was burned just outside Evesham; Tomson hanged at Cotheridge, the scene of the crime. The writer tells us, 'I beheld the death of one of the parties.'

42. *Ibid.*, sigs A3, B3.

43. See P. Lake, 'Deeds against Nature: Cheap Print, Protestantism and Murder in Early Seventeenth-Century England', in K. Sharpe and P. Lake (eds), *Culture and Politics in Early Stuart England* (Basingstoke, 1994), pp. 262–8.

44. Stow, *Annales*, pp. 1263, 1271.

45. T. Kyd, *The trueth of the most wicked and secret murthering of Iohn Brewen, Goldsmith of London, committed by his owne wife* (London, 1592), pp. 6–8.

46. *Ibid.*, pp. 8–12.

47. *Ibid.*, pp. 12–14. The arresting detail and direct speech in this section of Kyd's account is matched in the many reports of sixteenth-century murder only by parts of Holinshed's account of the conspiracy against Thomas Ardern.

48. *Ibid.*, pp. 14–15.

49. Kyd tells us the executions took place 'on wednesday last', so he must have composed the piece in the following week.

50. *Sundrye strange and inhumaine murthers lately committed* (1591), sig A2. The writer also argues revenge should be left to God and emphasises the guilt of accessories: 'In murther the consenter is as evil as the deed doer.'

51. Failing to pursue one's suit like this at felony trials must have been fairly frequent in cases of robbery, burglary and grand larceny, as the statute 21 Henry VII c. 11 suggests. It is the indictment that shows that Lincoln's Christian name was Nicholas and the labouring man was Thomas Hayton, a husbandman from Hastings: *Cal. Assize Rec., Kent Indictments, Elizabeth I*, pp. 314–15.

52. *Sundrye strange murthers*, sig. A3. The three children murdered were Nicholas, John and Phoebe; the date was 5 December 1590.

53. *Ibid.*, sig. A4. The account must have been written between the end of February and August 1591, since the author talks of Lincoln being condemned at 'the last' assizes.

54. Following this case the author, very briefly, tells of a slaying at Uppingham 'not long ago' where the corpse bled when the murderer came before it. Furthermore, one of the eyes opened and stared at the miscreant whenever he was brought in as if to say, 'stay him, my blood asketh for vengeance': *ibid.*, sig.

A4. There follows what is probably the first extended account of an infanticide. 'Of late', Alice Shepheard of Salisbury, her mother, grandmother and a midwife, broke the neck of the male child of which she had just been delivered and buried it in the churchyard, but it was soon discovered. Alice was greatly suspected, so the four women were examined by a justice. They all took an oath that the child was stillborn and were discharged. However, the midwife as she left reproached herself for her false oath and was overheard. The four were examined again and 'after a faint denial they generally confessed' and were sentenced to death at the next assizes: *ibid.*, sig. B1.

55. *Ibid.*, sig. B2. Mrs Page's maiden name was Eulalia Glanfield (sig. B3). Her lover Strangwich/Strangwidge had London connections, which probably accounts for the writer's interest and knowledge.

56. *Ibid.*, sig. B3.

57. We are not told whether Mrs Page was burned at the stake or hanged.

58. See P. McGrath, *Papists and Puritans under Elizabeth I* (New York, 1967), pp. 360–3.

59. *The most horrible and tragicall murther of the right honorable, the virtuous and valorous Gentleman, John Lord Bourgh, Baron of Castle Connell* (1591) in J.P. Collier, *Illustrations of Early English Literature* (London, 1863), i, 3–6; Stow, *Annales*, p. 1270.

60. *The Arraignment, Examination, Confession and Iudgement of Arnold Cosbye* (London, 1591), sigs A2–B4.

61. *Ibid.*, sigs B3v–B4.

62. *The manner of the death and execution of Arnold Cosbie for murthering the Lord Bourke*, in Collier, *Illustrations*, i, 15–20. To kill in a duel was held by the Crown to be murder, not manslaughter. This was because the parties came to the contest with a relatively long-standing intent to kill. If two men met by chance, exchanged insults and decided to fight a duel then and there, a resulting death was only manslaughter since the slaying was done in hot blood, not at an agreed meeting place sometime after the challenge. See Chapter 1.

63. *A world of wonder, A masse of murthers, A covie of cosonages* (London, 1595), sigs F1–F4.

64. *Two notorious murders. One committed by a tanner on his wives sonne nere Hornechurch in Essex. The other on a Grasier nere Ailsburie in Buckinghamshire. With these is intermixt another murdrous intending fellonie at Rislip in Middlesex. All done this last month* (London, 1595), pp. 4–5. The stepson was Thomas Chambers, 'a young man of great towardnes, of condition gentle, of body well proportioned'. His sister's husband was John Graygoose of Epping, a husbandman. If Thomas Chambers died before Christmas 1595, £200 in cash

and £30 a year in land left to him by his father was to go to his sister, Graygoose's wife. John Graygoose was the instigator of the murder, which occurred at Rush Green near Hornchurch. The fate of Wright may be given erroneously in the pamphlet. Assize records have been taken as showing he was acquitted, at least for this crime: see *Cal. Assize Rec., Essex, Elizabeth I*, p. 441. However, this particular record is damaged.

65. *Two notorious murders*, pp. 7–9. Randolph was an older man 'of gentle nature and verye open'. Dernley and his two confederates, Parry of Shoreditch and Richardson of Knightrider Street (London), had ridden from London. The inhabitant of Aylesbury, Tayler, who issued the warning, suspected Parry and Richardson of villainy because of how they were 'horsed and weaponed'. He it was who identified the body ('by the apparel better than the face').

66. *Ibid.*, p. 10. There may have been general disbelief that Parry and Richardson could be robbers and murderers. The planner of the murder knew them better: 'For had they not been exercised to robbery and spoyle howe durst Dernley have broke so hainous a matter to them, or if he had not before time so purpost how could he so sodainly have found them for his purpose': *ibid.*

67. *Ibid.*, p. 6.

68. *A most horrible and detestable Murther committed by a bloudie minded man upon his owne Wife: and most strangely Revealed by his Childe that was under five yeares of age* (London, 1595), sigs A3–A4; *Cal. Assize Rec., Sussex, Elizabeth I*, p. 295. The murder was committed on 1 October 1594.

69. *The Examination, confession and condemnation of Henry Robson, Fisherman of Rye, who poysoned his wife in the strangest maner that ever hitherto hath bin heard of* (1598), sigs A3, A4.

70. *Ibid.*, sigs A4, B1. The physicians obtained permission to 'rip' from 'the officers', presumably the magistrates of the town.

71. 'Well then I perceive (sayd Robson) you glut after my blood, and if it will pleasure you you shall have it': *ibid.*, sig. B2. He does not appear to have received any favour from the magistrates.

72. R. Yarington, *Two Lamentable Tragedies* (London, 1601), sig. A3: 'The most here present, know this to be true, / Would truth be false, so this were but a tale.' The play had probably been first performed in the mid-1590s: A. Harbage, *Annals of English Drama, 975–1700* (London, 1964), pp. 60–1.

73. *Two Lamentable Tragedies*, sigs A3–C4. Merry tells his sister that the boy has already been killed by someone else: *ibid.*, sig. C4v. Robert Beech, a chandler, is called honest and said to live a 'harmlesse' life: *ibid.*, sig. D3.

74. *Ibid.*, sigs D3, D3v. The surgeons who had been called said each of the seven wounds was a mortal one.

75. Williams was well aware that the knowledge he had of Beech's murder might

lead Merry also to kill him. This was the reason he left Merry's employ. Temporarily he slept in a hayloft at the Three Cranes inn. The cloak and money for a visit to the fair were presumably a bribe by Merry: *ibid.*, sigs C1, D3v. It is possible that 'Master Cowley' was Thomas Cowley the stationer.

76. The watermen found the bag near Baynard's Castle stairs: *ibid.*, sig. G.

77 . *Ibid.*, sigs Gv–G4.

78. *Ibid.*, sigs. H3–H4. William's slip was to blurt out, 'What? Shall I then betray my maisters life?' How he knew Merry had killed Winchester we are not told. On failing to report murder, see Chapter 1.

79. *Ibid.*, sigs I2–I2v. The constable's words of arrest to Merry, who was in bed, were, 'In the Queenes name I doo commaund you rise, / And presently to goe along with us'.

80. *Ibid.*, sigs Kv–K2v. Merry also said that Rachel was 'never privie' to the murders, 'But onelie helpest me when the deede was done, / To wipe the blood and hide away my sinne.' Typically the officer supervising the hangings, probably one of the London sheriffs, wanted the gallows speeches to cease: 'I pray make hast, the hower is almost past.' The denial of guilt by Rachel was an uncommon occurrence, as we have seen. Coupled with her exoneration by Merry, it may have made the crowd restive. The person to be hanged usually stood on the steps of a ladder that, on the sheriff's signal, the hangman turned over.

81. The theme of the Italian murder was a sensitive one for the upper classes, namely envy about inheritance. The uncle was to have possession of the nephew's lands and goods until he came of age. The uncle made sure there was no coming of age.

82. *Ibid.*, sigs E2v, K3.

83. *Ibid.*, sigs G4, Iv.

84. Legal counsel for those accused of a felony was not available in the sixteenth century, at least not overtly, as we have seen.

85. A feature of the Merry murders that must have drawn much attention was the sight of a young woman going to execution in recalcitrant mood and denying her guilt, the latter being, it seems, the only recorded example in regard to murder in the Tudor era (witchcraft cases apart).

86. *Ibid.*, sigs D3–D3v, Gv–G3v.

87. *The manner of the cruell outrageous murther of William Storre M.A.* (Oxford, 1603), sigs A2–A2v.

88. *Ibid.*, sigs A3–A3v.

89. *Ibid.*, sigs A4.

90. *Ibid.*, sigs A4–B2.

91. *Three Bloodie Murders* (London, 1613), sigs Bv–B2.

92. *The Life, Confession and Heartie Repentance of Francis Cartwright, Gentleman* (London, 1621), sigs A2–D2.

93. See J.H. Langbein, 'The Origins of Public Prosecution at Common Law', *American Journal of Legal History*, 17 (1973), 327.

94. For a survey of those features, see M. Gaskell, *Crime and Mentalities in Early Modern England* (Cambridge, 2000), esp. chs 6 and 7.

95. And even secure enough to get a thrill from reading about the criminal underworld. They may also have felt comfortable enough to allow their emotions freer rein. A sexually charged atmosphere among theatre audiences has been suggested: see P. Lake with M. Questier, *The Antichrist's Lewd Hat* (New Haven, 2002), pp. 448–54.

CHAPTER 3: THE BILDESTON MYSTERY

1. B. McClenaghan, *The Springs of Lavenham* (Ipswich, 1924), pp. 6, 29–30; *Letters and Papers, Henry VIII*, iii (i), no. 529.

2. TNA: PRO SP 1/131, ff. 203, 206, 212.

3. *Ibid.*, ff. 206, 206v, 208.

4. *Ibid.*, ff. 202, 206v, 208.

5. *Ibid.*, ff. 207, 208, 212.

6. *Ibid.*, ff. 202, 208v, 212, 212v, 215. John Spring had made a name for himself when he quieted the dissidents protesting the collection of the 'amicable' grant at Lavenham in 1528.

7. See below. For an assessment of Bourchier's career, see S.J. Gunn, 'Henry Bourchier, Earl of Essex (1472–1540)', in G.W. Bernard (ed.), *The Tudor Nobility* (Manchester, 1992), pp. 134–79. There are some comments on the Witherick case at pp. 149–50.

8. TNA: PRO SP 1/131, ff. 208v, 209, 209v.

9. TNA: PRO SP 1/242, f. 12. However, Margery Witherick on examination said Gawger 'made' her son accuse his father: TNA: PRO SP 1/131, f. 210.

10. TNA: PRO SP 1/131, f. 204. This is the first example I have met of reference to law officers 'planting' evidence so as to make certain of conviction.

11. *Ibid.*, ff. 209v, 210, 212, 212v. What Witherick's 'costs' were is not clear. The Earl of Essex was at Hoddesdon, Hertfordshire, at this time: *ibid.*, f. 213.

12. *Ibid.*, ff. 200v, 210, 213; TNA: PRO SP 1/242 f. 12.

13. TNA: PRO SP 1/131, fos. 200v, 201, 213, 213v.

14. *Ibid.*, ff. 200, 213v.

15. *Ibid.*, ff. 210v, 214.

16. *Ibid.*, ff. 210v, 211.

17.	The behaviour of this justice of the peace, George Colte, at Witherick's trial suggests that one of the tasks allotted to these local justices as they sat with the professional judges at the assizes was to ensure the flow of suitable evidence for the Crown. It has been argued (A. Bevan, 'The Henrician Assizes and the Enforcement of the Reformation', in R. Eales and D. Sullivan (eds), *The Political Context of Law* (London, 1987), pp. 61–76) that the assize judges were unable, until the late 1530s, to make their own enquiries into the crimes of the suspects who came before them at jail delivery; and that then this was corrected by the awarding of 'circuit' (general) commissions of oyer and terminer, first enrolled in July 1538, to them. The argument offered by Bevan is that this was necessary for dealing with cases of treason. But did the Witherick case play a part?

18.	TNA: PRO SP 1/131, ff. 214, 214v.

19.	*Ibid.*, ff. 200, 215v. Presumably the indictment on which Philip Witherick was arraigned was based on the evidence provided by his son's initial examinations. There is no indication the court was nonplussed by the lack of a corpse. The Council was apparently suspicious of the trial jury: Thrower, the constable, was asked directly if he knew any of the jurors and whether 'any labor was made to them'. He answered in the negative: *ibid.*, f. 214v.

20.	*Ibid.*, f. 202. The Witherick case has similarities with the better-known Campden case of 1660. In this, William Harrison, the steward of Viscountess Campden, disappeared while collecting rents in August 1660 and reappeared late in 1662, claiming to have been kidnapped and sold into slavery in Turkey. By that time his servant, John Perry, had been hanged for his murder, as had Perry's brother and mother, both of whom he had accused as the slayers of his master: see *A True and Perfect Account of the Examination, Confession, Tryal, Condemnation and Execution of Joan Perry and her two Sons John and Richard Perry for the Supposed Murder of William Harrison, Gent.* (London, 1676).

21.	TNA: PRO SP 1/131, f. 202.

22.	Prittlewell is now part of Southend. We are not told whether 'Wakering' was modern-day Great or Little Wakering.

23.	TNA: PRO SP 1/131, ff. 202v, 203, 207v.

24.	John Purtche and Roger Coley, two inhabitants of Bildeston who had assisted the bailiff and the constables, were also examined: *ibid.*, f. 200; TNA: PRO SP 1/242 f. 12. The Council deputed the task of examining (on its own interrogatories) some of those involved in the case to local justices of the peace. Others seem to have had to appear before the Chancellor (i.e. the Council).

25.	TNA: PRO SP 1/242, ff. 13–14.

26.	TNA: PRO SP 1/131, f. 199.

27.	*Ibid.*

28. *The Reports of Sir John Spelman*, ed. J.H. Baker (Selden Soc., 93–4, 1976–7), i, 60.

29. TNA: PRO SP 1/131, f. 199.

30. *Ibid.*, f. 203. It seems quite likely that Thompson encouraged Ambrose to flee and not return. Did they intend to share a 'finding' fee?

31. *Ibid.*

32. *Ibid.*, f. 204.

33. *Ibid.*, f. 207.

34. *Ibid.*, f. 211.

35. The recent statute 25 Henry VIII c. 6 had made buggery 'with mankind or beast' a felony without any benefit of clergy for offenders. Hitherto this offence, *contra naturam*, had been dealt with by the ecclesiastical courts.

36. It is quite possible, of course, that Gawger and his allies had plotted with Ambrose for him to disappear from Bildeston and never return. Gawger's involvement in a murder a year later certainly points in this direction; see pp. 108–9.

37. *Letters and Papers, Henry VIII*, vi, nos 1272, 1273; Gunn, pp. 167–8. Cranmer sought to have the Earl allow Stainsby's grievances to be settled by arbitration. Why he should particularly concern himself with Stainsby's woes is not apparent. We may wonder if the latter's religious beliefs engaged Cranmer's sympathies. The quarrel was not solely concerned with rights in Bildeston. In March 1534 the Council ordered the Earl to restore to Stainsby certain lands he and his ancestors had held in Essex that the Earl had taken from him: *Letters and Papers, Henry VIII*, vii, no. 375.

38. D.N.J. MacCulloch, *Suffolk and the Tudors* (Oxford, 1986), pp. 150, 163.

39. TNA: PRO SP 1/131, f. 207.

40. TNA: PRO SP 1/242, f. 12; TNA: PRO SP 1/131, ff. 212v, 213, 214.

41. *Reports of Spelman*, i, 60. Spelman was in Norfolk with the Duke of Norfolk in April 1538 and thus in a good position to ascertain the facts: *Letters and Papers, Henry VIII*, xiii (i), no. 742.

42. TNA: PRO KB 27/1118 Rex m. 4. The murder occurred 12 March 1539.

43. *Ibid.*

CHAPTER 4: THE MURDER OF THOMAS ARDERN

1. Holinshed, iii, 1024–31; J. Taylor, *The unnaturall father: or a cruel murther committed by one J. Rowse*, in J. Taylor, *All the Workes of J. Taylor the Water Poet* (London, 1630), sigs S2v–S3.

2. Holinshed, iii, 1024.

3.   *Ibid.*

4.   British Library, Harleian MS 542, f. 34. This account of the murder is similar to that in Holinshed; it may have been the basis for his report or both may have derived from a common source; E. Jacob, *The History of the Town and Port of Faversham in the County of Kent* (London, 1774), p. iv. A third account of the murder is to be found in the wardmote book of Faversham, ff. 59–60; this has been printed in *The Tragedy of Master Arden of Faversham*, ed. M.L. Wine (London, 1973), pp. 160–3.

5.   *The House of Commons, 1509–1558*, ed. S.T. Bindoff (London, 1982), ii, 328–9; W.C. Richardson, *A History of the Court of Augmentations, 1536–1554* (Baton Rouge, 1961), pp. 155, 280–1.

6.   *Letters and Papers, Foreign and Domestic, Henry VIII*, xv, no. 831/17; *ibid.*, xvii, no. 71/48.

7.   *Ibid., Addenda*, i (ii), no. 1514; *ibid.*, xix (ii), no. 800/36. However, Cheyne bought a lot of land in the Faversham area in 1550 (£2,000 worth) including some that had belonged to the monastery: *Cal. Pat. Rolls, 1549–1551*, pp. 342–3.

8.   *Letters and Papers, Henry VIII*, xxi (ii), no. 241/7; *ibid.*, xx (i), no. 465/79.

9.   *Machyn*, p. 4.

10. *Letters and Papers, Henry VIII*, xxi (ii), nos. 475/8, 475/55; *Cal. Pat. Rolls, 1549–1551*, p. 345. In 1539 a relative of Alice Ardern considered purchasing, or at least bidding for, the customership of Sandwich; the sum he had in mind was £300: *Letters and Papers, Henry VIII*, xiv (ii), no. 231.

11. *House of Commons, 1509–1558*, ii, 329; Holinshed, iii, 1027.

12. *House of Commons, 1509–1558*, ii, 329; *Letters and Papers, Henry VIII*, xxi (i), no. 149/33. Jacob credits Ardern with procuring a new charter for the town when the abbey was dissolved: Jacob, p. iv.

13. Holinshed, iii, 1030.

14. *The Complete Peerage of England*, ed. G.E. Cokayne (London, 1910–59), ix, 651. His wife Alice's first husband John Brigendon had been a client or associate of Thomas Cromwell: *Letters and Papers, Henry VIII*, xiii (ii), no.1184; *ibid.*, vi, nos. 822, 1574; *ibid.*, vii, no. 630.

15. *House of Commons, 1509–1558*, ii, 22–3; *Court of Augmentations*, p. 189.

16. *Letters and Papers, Henry VIII*, xx (i), no. 125/14; *House of Commons, 1509–1558*, ii, 329. Perhaps North had heard that because of their marital difficulties Ardern was intending to leave all his wealth to his daughter. It will be remembered that at about the same time (22 December) Ardern lost his position as a 'jurat' of Faversham. The house was the one Ardern had built east of the abbey gate *c.* 1545. In the seventeenth century it was known locally as a 'great house': L.C. Orlin, 'Man's House as his Castle in Arden of

Faversham', *Medieval and Renaissance Drama in England*, 2 (1985), 69.

17. BL, Harleian MS 542, f. 34.

18. Holinshed, iii, 1024–5; *Arden of Faversham*, ed. Wine, p. xxxvii; *The Roxburgh Ballads*, ed. J.W. Ebsworth (Hertford, 1895) iii (pt i), 47. An earlier eighteenth-century chapbook states Ardern was 59 when he married Alice (1543 or 1544): Orlin, p. 86.

19. Holinshed, iii, 1024; BL, Harleian MS 542, f. 34.

20. BL, Harleian MS 542, f. 34; Holinshed, iii, 1024–5.

21. Jacob, p. v; *Arden of Faversham*, ed. Wine, p. 160; BL, Harleian MS 542, f. 34.

22. Holinshed, iii, 1024–5; *House of Commons, 1509–1558*, ii, 329.

23. Holinshed, iii, 1025. It has been stated that Ardern's daughter Margaret married a John Blackborne, whose Christian name, entered erroneously, was *recte* William (i.e. the painter): see J.H. Marshburn, *Murder and Witchcraft in England, 1550–1640* (Norman, Oklahoma, 1971), p. 21.

24. Holinshed, iii, 1025; *Court of Augmentations*, p. 155; *Letters and Papers, Henry VIII*, xx (i), no. 557. Sir Anthony Ager (or Aucher) of Dover, Kent, held a receivership in the Court of Augmentations for the counties of Kent, Surrey and Sussex. He was also Victualler of the Works at Dover, Chief Victualler of Boulogne, Marshal of Calais, and Master of the King's Jewels: *Court of Augmentations*, pp. 221, 281; *Cal. Pat. Rolls, 1547–1548*, p. 151.

25. *Letters and Papers, Henry VIII*, xxi (i), no. 149/33; *Cal. Pat. Rolls, 1549–1551*, p. 183. The play *Arden of Faversham* (ed. Wine, p. 36) tells us that Greene, although it gives him the name 'Dick', was a religious man, which gives some support to this identification. Jacob calls him John.

26. Holinshed, iii, 1025. The Faversham wardmote book states that Will was, in fact, summoned from Calais; it refers to him as 'Blackwyll of Calyce': *Arden of Faversham*, ed. Wine, p. 160. Holinshed does not provide Black Will's surname, but another Black Will, the servant of the two sons of Edward IV when they were incarcerated in the Tower in 1483, was named William Slaughter.

27. Ardern was staying at a parsonage he possessed in London.

28. Holinshed, iii, 1026; BL, Harleian MS 542, f. 35.

29. Holinshed, iii, 1026–7.

30. Shakebag is called Losebagg in the wardmote book: *Arden of Faversham*, ed. Wine, p. 161.

31. Holinshed, iii, 1027.

32. *Ibid.*

33. *Ibid.*, iii, 1027–8.

34. According to Holinshed the neighbour was one 'Dumpkin'. He was, in fact, probably the Thomas Dunkyn (then mayor) to whom in August 1545 Ardern sold a messuage and an acre of land in Faversham: *Letters and Papers, Henry*

VIII, xx (ii), no. 2.

35.   Holinshed, iii, 1028. The Faversham wardmote-book account says that Will was paid at the house of Cicely Pounder and that the sum was £8: *Arden of Faversham*, ed. Wine, p. 161. The book states that Will used a napkin to strangle Arden; then Mosby struck him with his pressing iron and cut his throat: *ibid.*

36.   Holinshed, iii, 1028.

37.   *Ibid.*, iii, 1028–9. The Faversham wardmote book says that the field where the body was deposited was called 'the Amory croft': *Arden of Faversham*, ed. Wine, p. 161. It is difficult to construe the intent of the murderers at this juncture; they may have hoped the dead Ardern would be thought to have been slain while investigating some disturbance in the 'Amory croft' or pursuing someone who had trespassed on his property.

38.   Holinshed, iii, 1028.

39.   *Ibid.*, iii, 1029–30.

40.   *Ibid.*, iii, 1030; Jacob, p. v. The wardmote book says they were indicted and arraigned at Faversham; a later hand has inserted the words 'in the Abbey Halle which the said Ardern purchased': *Arden of Faversham*, ed. Wine, pp. 161–2.

41.   Holinshed, iii, 1030.

42.   The wardmote book says Greene was captured in Cornwall, which seems more likely: *Arden of Faversham*, ed. Wine, pp. 161–2.

43.   Holinshed, iii, 1030.

44.   Widow Cooke may have been the relict of Henry Cooke, merchant-tailor of London, co-grantee with Ardern in September 1543 of various marshes along the south bank of the Thames in Kent, which belonged to Lyesness Manor: *Letters and Papers, Henry VIII*, xviii (ii), no. 241/7.

45.   Holinshed, iii, 1030–1.

46.   *Letters and Papers, Henry VIII*, xx (ii), no. 266/36; *Acts of the Privy Council*, iii, 229–30, 285, 319.

47.   *Acts of the Privy Council*, iii, 221, 306. Black Will may, in fact, have been captured by Godolphin at Boulogne but then escaped from there to the Netherlands.

48.   *Calendar of State Papers, Foreign, 1553–1558*, p. 279.

49.   *Ibid.*; Holinshed, iii, 1030. A marginal note appended to the account in the wardmote book states that Black Will committed several murders at Flushing 'and so was scorched or half burned to deth': *Arden of Faversham*, ed. Wine, p. 163.

    There is little in print on the early history of extradition relative to England, although I have written on it in regard to fugitives whom the crown considered traitors; see Bellamy, *The Tudor Law of Treason*, pp. 88–91. The Edwardian government deported a French murderer back to France in November 1551. There seems to have been an understanding between certain countries that notorious criminals seeking refuge should be returned to their homeland when there was no political element to the crime: see *Acts of the Privy Council*, iii, 407.

50. Although the authorship of the second edition (1587) of Holinshed's *Chronicles* is still a subject of debate, there seems little doubt that Raphael Holinshed himself compiled the original work, which was published in 1577, and was thus responsible for the inclusion of the Ardern murder.

51. Holinshed, iii, 1024.

52. *House of Commons, 1509–1558*, iii, 494–5; *Dictionary of National Biography* (s.v. Twyne). In the 1530s Twyne gave lectures at Sandwich on heresy, though whether he still travelled there when Ardern was customer is not known: *Letters and Papers, Henry VIII*, vii, no. 1608.

53. *House of Commons, 1509–1558*, i, 634–8; *Cal. Pat. Rolls, 1549–1551*, pp. 290–3; *ibid., 1550–1553*, pp. 342–3; Holinshed, iii, 856–8; *ibid.*, iv, 157–8.

54. *House of Commons, 1509–1558*, iii, 601; *Complete Peerage of England*, iii, 192–3.

55. The letter from the Privy Council to Sir Philip Hoby of 12 May 1553 seems to indicate that Cheyne sent a posse of his own servants in pursuit of Black Will to the Netherlands. By their 'procurement' he was 'staied' at Flushing. The implication is that Cheyne had done this on his own authority, which suggests his personal involvement in seeking out the principal murderer: *Cal. State Papers, Foreign, 1547–1553*, p. 279.

56. *House of Commons, 1509–1558*, i, 547. Certainly Holinshed mentions the deeds of Sir Nicholas Burdet, killed in the Hundred Years War (in 1439), but he also mentions his son being executed for treason in 1477, which is not what a patron would want to read: Holinshed, iii, 145, 159, 195.

57. Holinshed, iv, 86.

58. *Ibid.*, iii, 1022; *ibid.*, (1577), pp. 1581–2.

59. Thus some examples of Holinshed's 'low' history are the murder of a woman by a stranger-vagabond to whom she had given shelter (iii, 172), a woman who produced quadruplets (iv, 329), a sighting of a very large star (iv, 320) and a woman who voided upwards 'with horrible stinke' (iv, 329). Women figure prominently in this 'low' history.

60. See the comments on the trial in Bellamy, *Tudor Law of Treason*, *passim*.

61. *Ibid.*, pp. 171–3; Holinshed, iii, 1030.

62. On the definition and earlier history of petty treason, see Bellamy, *Law of Treason in England in the Later Middle Ages*, pp. 225–31. The murder of

husbands by wives in the later Tudor period has attracted the attention of a good number of specialists in English literature. A useful exposition of what may be called the literary commentary on the Ardern case that also draws attention to the many other contributors in the field is to be found in the paper by R. Helgerson, 'Murder in Faversham: Holinshed's Impertinent History', to be found in D.R. Kelley and D.M. Sacks (eds), *The Historical Imagination in Early Modern Britain* (Cambridge, 1997), pp. 133–58.

63. *Cal. Assize Rec., Surrey, Elizabeth I*, n. 3044. There must also have been other instances in the counties of the home circuit, where the sessional records have not survived. Holinshed notes one such case in Kent (1576) and Stow two more (1592 and 1594). In two of these three cases the miscreant was a woman accused of poisoning her husband, and all were sentenced to be burned: Holinshed, iv, 262, 330; Stow, *Annales*, pp. 1271, 1275.

64. In an examination of extant jail delivery records of all the English circuits for the period 1388–99, Kathleen Garay found that only 211 of the accused felons (out of some 5,600) were women. Of these, 22 were sentenced to death, including 3 for the murder of their husbands: K.E. Garay, 'Women and Crime in Later Mediaeval England: An Examination of the Evidence of the Courts of Gaol Delivery, 1388 to 1409', *Florilegium*, 1 (1979), 87–109. The extant Yorkshire records for the period 1399–1407 show 44 out of 396 persons accused of felony were charged with homicide (i.e. manslaughter or murder); there is but a single instance of a woman accused of murdering her husband: see TNA: PRO JUST 3/ 191 mm. 19, 19d. She was convicted and burned. For a woman burned at Tower Hill in 23 Henry VI for killing her husband see *Historical Collections of a Citizen of London*, p. 184.

65. TNA: PRO JUST 3/ 212 mm. 6, 7.

66. E. Powell, *Kingship, Law and Society* (Oxford, 1989), p. 264.

67. *Complete Peerage of England*, vi, 652.

68. Referring to a misapplication of the felony law at Rye in 1547, Holinshed writes: 'Such conclusions are manie times made in the ports who sometimes use the privilege of their liberties not as they ought but as they list': Holinshed, iii, 893.

69. The joint cost to the city of Canterbury of the burning of Alice and the hanging of Bradshaw was a substantial 43 shillings: *Historical Manuscripts Commission, Ninth Report* (London, 1883–4), p. 154. Since the price of a halter with which to hang a person was sixpence, and the payment to the man who did the hanging was a shilling, burning someone who had been sentenced to the stake appears to have been inordinately expensive: *ibid.*, p. 156. Either the executioner got a special fee for burnings or the combustibles used were of an exceptional type.

70. *House of Commons, 1509–1558*, iii, 22; D. E. Hoak, *The King's Council in the Reign of Edward VI* (Cambridge, 1976), pp. 252–3. The setback was the loss of the chancellorship of the Court of Augmentations to Richard Sackville.

71. The conviction rate for felony was noticeably greater in Middlesex (the only southern county for which records survive) in Edward VI's reign than under Queens Mary and Elizabeth I: *Middlesex County Records*, ed. J.C. Jeaffreson (London, 1886–92), i, 245–87.

72. *Acts of the Privy Council*, iii, 229.

73. However, Ardern's will, dated 20 December 1550, suggests North was concerned with protecting his stepdaughter's interests at that time.

74. There are no signs of pardons for petty treason in Edward VI's reign.

75. *House of Commons, 1509–1558*, i, 329.

76. *Acts of the Privy Council*, iii, 229–30.

77. *Ibid.*, iii, 319.

78. There were procedural reasons for the higher conviction rate for felony in addition to social and economic ones. The matter of the severity of the Tudor age I have addressed elsewhere. See Bellamy, *Criminal Trial*, chs 3 and 4.

79. The statute was 22 Henry VIII c. 9. Burning as the prescribed punishment for female perpetrators of petty treason continued into the seventeenth century.

80. Similarly propelled by sexual desire was a London merchant's wife, Ann Saunders, who in 1573 conspired with Ann Drury and George Browne (the actual killer) to slay her husband: see *A briefe discourse of the late murther of master George Saunders, a worshipfull Citizen of London* (London, 1573), *passim*; see also Chapter 6. This was surely a case fresh in mind when Holinshed wrote.

81. See above.

82. *Arden of Faversham*, ed. Wine, pp. 5, 7, 107.

83. *Ibid.*, pp. 41, 43, 81, 83, 133, 136; *The Elizabethan Underworld*, ed. A.V. Judges (London, 1930), *passim*.

84. *Arden of Faversham*, ed. Wine, p. 32.

85. *Ibid.*, pp. 4, 6, 41, 43, 44, 83, 88, 125.

86. *House of Commons, 1509–1558*, ii, 24–5; *Dict. Nat. Biog.* (s.v. George Clifford, Henry Clifford, Roger North, Thomas North); *Complete Peerage of England*, ix, 652–3. George Clifford, the third Earl, had married, and separated from, Margaret Russell, a daughter of the Earl of Bedford, who was suspected of witchcraft.

87. *Arden of Faversham*, ed. Wine, pp. 49, 56–71. The episode of the shutters together with Ardern's alleged visiting 'whores' in London shows that a ballad of 1633 on Alice's 'lamentation' is based on the play and not on Holinshed's account.

88. *Ibid.*, pp. 4, 130–3.

89. Holinshed, iii, 1028; *Arden of Faversham*, ed. Wine, pp. 18, 24, 126, 137–8.

90. *Arden of Faversham*, ed. Wine, pp. 5, 22–3, 124.

91. *Complete Peerage of England*, xi, 548–9, xii (ii), 852–4. On the mid-sixteenth-century financial embarrassment of Earl William, see W.R.B. Robinson, 'Sir William Herbert's Acquisition of Offices in Wales on the Death of Henry, Earl of Worcester in 1549', *Historical Research*, 69 (1996), 279. The Earl was in financial difficulties at the time of the marriage, and Edward North seems to have used much of his own wealth to rescue him. Christiana gave birth to Earl William's son, Edward, on 20 March 1551: P.S. Allen, 'The Birth of Thomas North', *English Historical Review*, 37 (1922), 566.

92. A vital point made in the accounts and in the play is that Alice (like another husband-murderer, Ann Saunders) was 'fair' – that is to say, was a belle of her sex.

93. Holinshed, iii, 1029; BL Harleian MS 542, f. 37v.

94. As suggested by A. Patterson, *Reading Holinshed's Chronicles* (Chicago, 1994), p. 7. I regard what Patterson refers to as 'the representing of diversity of opinion' or 'multivocality' as being designed for the very practical end of avoiding recrimination when politics changed, and, more importantly, a move to ensure the interest of the largest purchasing public. Registering the views of the middle class and below I see as being to a considerable degree a marketing device, and Holinshed and his continuators supposed interest in constitutional and legal rights similarly. There was also, of course, a patriotic element in the work.

95. *Letters and Papers, Henry VIII*, xvii, no. 71/48.

96. *Ibid.*, xix (i), no. 610/14; *ibid.*, xv, no. 611/26.

97. *Abstract of the bailiffs accounts of monastic and other estates in the county of Warwick*, trans. W.B. Bickley, Dugdale Society, 2 (1923), 111, 125. In July 1543 Whorwood and Walter obtained a grant of land in Charlecote in the tenure of William Lucy; *Letters and Papers, Henry VIII*, xviii (i), no. 981/30.

CHAPTER 5: LORD STOURTON AND THE HARTGILLS

1. BL Harleian MS 590, ff. 76, 76v.

2. BL Lansdowne MS 3, ff. 102–105v.

3. The results of his investigations are in J.E. Jackson, 'Charles, Lord Stourton, and the Murder of the Hartgills', *Wiltshire Archaeological and Natural History Society Magazine*, 8 (1864), 242–341. Jackson, a Wiltshire clergyman and antiquary, was rector of Leigh Delamere with Sevington, and vicar of Norton Coleparte.

4. J.C. Wedgewood and A.D. Holt, *History of Parliament, 1439–1509, Biographies* (London, 1936), pp. 422–3.

5. *Cal. Pat. Rolls, 1461–67*, p. 24; *ibid., 1476–85*, pp. 10, 403, 456, 491, 1083. From May 1483 Edward Hartgill shared the office of carrying the rod before the King at Windsor on St George's day: *ibid.*, p. 348. Another yeoman of the Crown at this time was a Thomas Hartgill (d. 1505): Thomas, too, had a connection with Mere, but his relationship with Edward is unknown.

6. *House of Commons, 1509–1558*, ii, 309–10.

7. Jackson, 328–9.

8. *Letters and Papers, Henry VIII*, vi, no. 299.

9. *Wiltshire. The Topographical Collections of John Aubrey, FRS, AD 1659–70*, ed. J.E. Jackson (Devizes, 1862), p. 393. Potter added that 'when he came into his family the Lord Stourton gave the next Sunday ten groates to the Priest of the Parish to say a Masse for him at Church, for the expiation of Hartgill's sin in killing the man': *ibid.*

10. *Letters and Papers, Henry VIII*, xv, no. 391.

11. *Topographical Collections*, p. 393.

12. *House of Commons, 1509–1558*, iii, 391; *Complete Peerage*, xii (i), 305–8.

13. *Cal. State Papers, Foreign, 1547–53*, p. 329; Jackson, 296, 299. Charles Stourton's letters, where they are not totally arrogant, breathe fire and brimstone.

14. *Letters and Papers, Henry VIII*, xix (i), no. 80/25; Jackson, 262.

15. *Topographical Collections*, p. 393; Jackson, 263, 265.

16. Jackson, 266, 276–7. The extant correspondence involving Charles Stourton is printed *in extenso* in Jackson.

17. *Ibid.*, 245, 276.

18. Bellamy, *Tudor Law of Treason*, pp. 217, 240. Agnes's mother was Lady Katherine Howard, daughter of Thomas Howard, the third Duke of Norfolk. Agnes must have been about twenty-five years younger than Lord William Stourton. Rhys ap Gruffydd was notoriously wealthy. He was said to have land worth £10,000 a year and personal property worth £30,000: *Dictionary of Welsh Biography down to 1940* (Oxford, 1959), p. 847. How much of this wealth ended up in the King's hands is unclear. The act that attainted Rhys (21 Henry VIII c. 34) excepted from forfeiture the lands held to Katherine's own use or to the use of herself and Rhys jointly.

19. Jackson, 243; *Complete Peerage*, xii (i), 306.

20. Stourton Caundle (Dorset) is about 12 miles south of Stourton. After Rhys's death Katherine married Henry Daubeney, Earl of Bridgewater, but was living apart from him for some time prior to his decease in April 1548: *Complete Peerage*, ii, 311.

21. Jackson, 245, 335. Despite her son's efforts to intimidate her, Elizabeth did in fact marry. By mid-1550 she had become the wife of Edward Ludlowe of Maiden Bradley (Wilts.).

22. There was nothing exceptional in this; it was not an uncommon practice: see R.A. Houlbrooke, *Church Courts and the People during the English Reformation* (Oxford, 1979), p. 94.

23. *Acts of the Privy Council*, iii, 321.

24. Jackson, 287–8. Agnes was still embroiled with Charles Stourton in regard to the administration of his father's estate (a debt owing to it) in 1553: *ibid.*

25. *Ibid.*, 269, 308, 328. Charles Stourton himself had a close connection with the Protector: in April 1547 Lord William thanked the latter for taking his son into his service: *Cal. State Papers, Foreign, 1547–1553*, p. 328.

26. On 'good lordship', see Bellamy, *Bastard Feudalism*, pp. 58–9, 96–7; Jackson, 296.

27. See Bellamy, *Bastard Feudalism*, especially chs 3 and 4.

28. The details of this case are in two letters printed in Jackson, 290–2. Hartgill's ability to manœuvre to advantage where the law was concerned is amply displayed here; his tactics were masterly.

29. It is noticeable that both Charles Stourton and William Hartgill set considerable store by being present in person among their servants when confrontation with the enemy, and resulting violence, were expected. On peace commissions, see Bellamy, *Bastard Feudalism*, pp. 17–19.

30. Jackson, 300–2, 304–5. On the attractions of Star Chamber as the court of resort for parties in dispute, see Bellamy, *Bastard Feudalism*, pp. 132–3.

31. The correspondence involving Thynne is printed in Jackson, 293, 295, 297–8, 299–300, 320.

32. The date is given in a lawyer's draft entitled 'Certen Articles to be objected against Charles Lord Stourton on the behaulf of Sr John Thynne and Sr John Bonham, Knights', printed in Jackson, 319–20. Stourton admitted to delaying for only seven days.

33. *Ibid.* Stourton was able to put one of his antagonists' allies, Sir John Thynne, in the wrong because the latter had refused to allow a servant of Stourton's to proclaim Queen Mary at Warminster (Wilts) on about 20 July. Thynne had so acted because he was steward of the town and believed it was his privilege to publish the proclamation, especially as he had not been formally told of Stourton's appointment to the lieutenancy: *ibid.*, 311.

34. *Ibid.*, 315–17. There is no report of the duel taking place, but Thynne and Bonham brought an action for slander against Stourton: *ibid.*, 319.

35. *Acts of the Privy Council*, iv, 315, 323; J. Aubrey, *Lives of Eminent Men*, ed. A. Clark (Oxford, 1898), ii, 479.

36. Letter from Stourton to the Sheriff of Wiltshire in Jackson, 318.

37. Letter from Humphrey Molsley, Thynne's lawyer, to his client in Jackson, 321.

38. *Acts of the Privy Council*, v, 55–7; Jackson, 323.

39. The indictment is printed in translation in Jackson, 323–4; *Acts of the Privy Council*, vi, 31.

40. BL Lansdowne MS 3, f. 102.

41. *Ibid.*, ff. 102–105v.

42. To ensure the compliance of his fellow justices of the peace Stourton must surely have related some tale of a felony recently committed by the Hartgills.

43. Fitzjames and Chaffyn, the latter once an ally of William Hartgill, presumably insisted that the normal procedure in cases of arrest for felony be followed.

44. Fitzjames and Chaffyn, because they left the Hartgills still in Stourton's custody, were thus partially responsible for their ultimate fate. The gist of the narrative is that they were overawed by Stourton. Social rank counted even among fellow members of peace commissions.

45. The servant who struck John Hartgill was William Farre, and the one who clubbed William was Henry Symmes; so says the indictment: TNA: PRO KB 8/36 m. 11.

46. Stourton's response to the servant is also recorded in English in the indictment.

47. *Acts of the Privy Council*, vi, 43. Stourton was moved to the Tower on 28 January 1557: *Machyn*, p. 125.

48. BL Harleian MS 2143, f. 5.

49. *Ibid.* Of the four men involved in the conveying of the Hartgills from Bonham to Stourton, one, Roger Gough, fled to Wales and was still being searched for, on the Privy Council's orders, in mid-February: *Acts of the Privy Council*, vi, 50.

50. BL Harleian MS 2143, f. 5v.

51. *Acts of the Privy Council*, vi, 72.

52. BL Lansdowne MS 3, f. 105v.

53. *Machyn*, p. 126.

54. TNA: PRO KB 8/36 mm. 11, 12.

55. *Ibid.*

56. Fitzherbert, *Graunde Abridgement*, f. 249v.

57. *Acts of the Privy Council*, vi, 58, 66.

58. TNA: PRO KB 8/36 m. 11; *Machyn*, pp. 126–7. On 'pressing', originally called 'peine forte et dure', see Bellamy, *Crime and Public Order in England in the Later Middle Ages* (London, 1973), pp. 141–2.

59. TNA: PRO KB 8/36 mm. 4, 11. Machyn says, 'he was cast by ys owne wordes to be hangyd': *Machyn*, p. 127.

60. *Acts of the Privy Council*, vi, 57, 66; *Machyn*, p. 127.

61.   *Transactions of the Bibliographical Society, 67; Topographical Collections*, p. 394.

62.   Jackson, 257–8; *Acts of the Privy Council*, vi, 66.

63.   *Topographical Collections*, p. 393.

64.   G. Burnet, *History of the Reformation of the Church of England*, ed. N. Pocock (Oxford, 1865), iii, 448–9.

65.   Jackson, 260.

66.   The Hartgills may have refused Stourton's offer because they imagined that, since their arrest had been made in the presence of justices of the peace, Stourton would not dare to harm them.

67.   Bellamy, *Criminal Trial*, ch. 4.

68.   *Cal. Pat. Rolls, 1555–57*, pp. 14, 308, 357, 484.

69.   Burnet, *History of the Reformation*, ii, 560–1. We may wonder if Privy Chamber connections played any part in the failure of Stourton to obtain a pardon. Was William Ryse, a Groom of the Chamber, whose wife was a Lady-in-Waiting and an intimate of the Queen, related to Agnes Ryce? Grafton says the Queen and Privy Council feared that clemency would encourage other similar murders: Grafton, *An abridgment*, f. 162.

70.   Agnes Hungerford compiled an exhaustive inventory of her goods before her execution, perhaps to ensure they all went, as required, to the king and did not fall into her stepson's hands: *Letters and Papers, Henry VIII*, iii (ii), no. 2861.

71.   TNA: PRO KB 8/12 mm. 4, 8; Holinshed, iii, 821–2. See Chapter 2.

72.   See Bellamy, *Bastard Feudalism*, pp. 135–6. By any standard Stourton's crime appears much more heinous than Dacre's.

73.   See *Middlesex County Records*, ii, 245–7.

74.   *Acts of the Privy Council*, v, 68. Judges held their offices at the monarch's will and were instantly removable.

75.   See Bellamy, *Criminal Law and Society*, pp. 25–6.

76.   *State Trials*, ed. W. Cobbett and T.B. Howell (London, 1809), i, 887–8.

77.   See Bellamy, *Tudor Law of Treason*, pp. 112–17.

78.   *Acts of the Privy Council*, iv, 201, 284; *ibid.*, v, 145, 202; *ibid.*, vi, 124–31. Torture might be used even for boulting out riot and 'disorder', mere trespasses: *ibid.*, 130. The 1555 commission did not prevent the Privy Council from appointing other examiners with power to torture on an ad-hoc basis. The 1555 commission seems to have been a development of the commission to examine prisoners in the Tower, using torture where expedient, of November 1551: *ibid.*, iii, 407.

79.   *Letters and Papers, Henry VIII*, xiv (i), no. 1211.

80.   Jackson, pp. 333–4.

81.   Walter's reason may have been that she had had him cut out of Sir Edward's will.

82. *Complete Peerage*, vi, 625.

83. *Letters and Papers, Henry VIII*, xv, no. 1029/34.

84. Holinshed, iii, 818; *Letters and Papers, Henry VIII*, xv, nos 498, 926. The act that attainted Walter Hungerford stated that he had committed buggery with William Maister, Thomas Smith and others of his servants.

85. Was the 'outrage' referred to by Lord William Stourton in July 1539 connected with the sexual activities of Walter Hungerford?

86. Jackson, pp. 327–8; *Cal. Pat. Rolls, 1557–58*, pp. 261–2.

87. Jackson, pp. 330–1; *Cal. Pat Rolls, 1557–58*, p. 306

CHAPTER 6: A FEMALE CONSPIRACY

1.   See Chapter 2.

2.   Holinshed, iv, 323, 330, 345, 426; Stow, *Annales*, pp. 1143, 1152.

3.   As recognised by the dramatist who produced the play based on the crime, *A Warning for Fair Women*: see pp. 174–7. It has been suggested that George Saunders was a son of William Saunders of Welford, Northamptonshire, and thus a cousin both of Sir Edward Saunders, Chief Baron of the Exchequer and Sir Christopher Hatton's mother; and that Ann Saunders was from the well-known Newdigate family of Surrey and Middlesex: E. St J. Brooks in *Notes and Queries*, 174 (12 March 1938), pp. 182–4. A note in the first edition of *A briefe discourse* appears to support these connections: see J.H. Marshburn, 'A cruell murder donne in Kent', *Studies in Philology*, 46 (1949), p. 137. Such connections and the fact the crime was committed, so to speak, on its own doorstep, would help explain the privy council's interest.

4.   He tells us that the murderer, when under the gallows, leapt voluntarily off the ladder instead of delaying his death, as was the normal practice, until the hangman turned the ladder over: Stow, *Annales*, p. 1142.

5.   Holinshed, iv, 323.

6.   *A briefe discourse*, p. 221.

7.   *Ibid.*, pp. 222–4. The pamphlet fails to tell us, though the plea rolls do, that Browne found shelter initially (on 26 March and later) at the home of a Robert Symes: see *Middlesex County Records*, i, 82.

8.   *A briefe discourse*, pp. 225–6.

9.   *Ibid.*, pp. 226–7.

10. *Ibid.*, pp. 228–9.

11. *Ibid.*, pp. 230–1. Presumably John Bradford's book was his *Godlie Meditations on the Lordes Prayer, the Beleefe, and Ten Commandements* (1562). Bradford was burned at Smithfield in July 1555: *Machyn*, p. 90.

12. *A briefe discourse*, pp. 231–2. The Earl of Derby's wife, who had a distant claim to the throne, was Margaret Clifford; she was thought a spendthrift and overinterested in magic, and the couple separated. The two earls may have been present in part so that they could instantly refute any slanderous accusations raised against them by Ann Drury in her last words under the gallows.

13. *Ibid.*, pp. 232–3.

14. *Ibid.*, p. 209; *Warning for Fair Women*, p. 10. 'Tragedie', in the play's epilogue, says that it is an accurate historical account; that nothing fictional has been introduced nor any actual event deliberately omitted.

15. *Warning for Fair Women*, pp. 100–1.

16. *A briefe discourse*, p. 223. The pamphlet's statement, however, may have been intended to imply that Saunders had no knowledge of his wife's liaison with Browne.

17. It is, of course, quite possible that sitting at her doorstep was not a modest act in a woman (theoretically awaiting her husband's return) but a way of engaging in gossip or even attracting male attention. If there had been sexual attraction between Ann and Browne at the supper, she might have been expecting him to walk by.

18. *Warning for Fair Women*, pp. 110, 111.

19. *Ibid.*, pp. 101, 110, 116.

20. *Ibid.*, pp. 123–4, 131, 146, 159.

21. *Ibid.*, pp. 116–17, 119–20.

22. *A briefe discourse*, p. 230.

23. *Ibid.*, pp. 236–7; *Warning for Fair Women*, pp. 111, 140.

24. *Warning for Fair Women*, pp. 114–16.

25. *A briefe discourse*, p. 225. Wriothesley tells us that in August 1551 a London adulteress was accused by 'six honest and substantiall persons' of her ward, on whose 'book' (bill) she was indicted by the wardens' inquest and then arraigned before the Lord Mayor. On conviction she was 'carted ymediatlie' in a 'raye' hood with a white rod in her hand, 'according to the ould lawes of the cittie', and banished thence: C. Wriothesley, *A Chronicle of England during the Reigns of the Tudors, II*, ed. W.D. Hamilton (Camden Soc., NS 20, 1877), p. 52.

26. *Warning for Fair Women*, pp. 121, 131, 135, 164. Having Ann Saunders express concern was probably intended to show she was ambivalent in her support for Drury's plan. The statement also adds a degree of mystery to the play; doubtless this was by design.

27. *Ibid.*, pp. 123, 130–1.

28. *Ibid.*, pp. 132, 135–40. The pamphlet states that Bean, unable to stand, crept away from the scene of the crime on all fours. He died five days later: *A briefe*

discourse, p. 223.

29. *Warning for Fair Women*, pp. 140–1; *Cal. Pat. Rolls, 1566–69*, p. 385; *ibid., 1575–78*, p. 4.

30. *Warning for Fair Women*, p. 142

31. *Ibid.*, pp. 146–7. One of the Lords of Council remarks that Browne, who apparently is well known to them, is 'faire and fat'. These were probably flattering terms in the sixteenth century.

32. *Ibid.*, pp. 147–9, 151–7.

33. *Ibid.*, pp. 158–9.

34. *Ibid.*, pp. 159–60. Browne's confession was supposedly sent with him.

35. The author of *A briefe discourse* is similarly silent on this matter.

36. *Warning for Fair Women*, pp. 160–3. There is a short scene set in court in a common-law felony case in *Nice Wanton*: see *Specimens of Pre-Shakespearean Drama*, ed. J.M. Manly (New York, 1897), pp. 471–5.

37. *Warning for Fair Women*, pp. 164–5. The trial of the two women was delayed until Ann Saunders had given birth.

38. *Ibid.*, pp. 165–7.

39. *Ibid.*, pp. 168–9.

40. *A briefe discourse*, p. 227.

41. *Warning for Fair Women*, pp. 170–1; *A Briefe discourse*, pp. 227–8.

42. *Warning for Fair Women*, pp. 171, 173.

43. *Ibid.*, pp. 174, 176, 177. There is no mention in the play of Ann Saunders seeking forgiveness from her husband's relatives.

44. *Acts of the Privy Council*, viii, 94; *ibid.*, iv, 201; *ibid.*, vii, 367–8.

45. *Ibid.*, viii, 94.

46. *A briefe discourse*, p. 230.

47. On the rise and practice of torture in sixteenth-century England in general, see Bellamy, *Tudor Law of Treason*, pp. 110–21, 260–2. The references to Tudor torture that appear in *Acts of the Privy Council* are collected in the appendix of J. Heath, *Torture and English Law* (Westport, 1982).

48. See *ibid.*, pp. 112–15, 261 for examples of the employment of these instruments.

49. *Archaeologia*, 36 (1855), 116.

50. *Acts of the Privy Council*, viii, 96.

51. *The House of Commons, 1558–1603*, ed. P.W. Hasler (London, 1981), ii, 374.

52. On the behaviour, in the sixteenth century, of presiding judges at arraignment and the role of the altercation between accused and victim or witnesses, see Bellamy, *Criminal Trial*, pp. 109–11, 113. See also Chapter 1.

53. *Warning for Fair Women*, pp. 175–7; *A briefe discourse*, pp. 232–4.

54. *Warning for Fair Women*, pp. 156–7.

55.   The most distinguished of these was Nowell, who in 1572 had visited the Duke of Norfolk, then a prisoner for treason in the Tower, several times; he later attended him at his execution; *Cal. State Papers, Domestic, 1547–1580*, pp. 434, 438–40. Cole was probably Robert Cole, rector of St Mary-le-Bow, 1559–76, and of All Hallows, Bread St, 1569–76: see J.W. Martin, *Religious Radicals in Tudor England* (London, 1989), p. 217. It is noteworthy that such prominent clergy took an active interest in the case. Presumably such attendance, where it was connected with confession and repentance, was a feather in their caps and an aid to ecclesiastical promotion and public popularity.

56.   *A briefe discourse*, pp. 229–30.

57.   *Ibid.*, p. 226.

58.   The author of the pamphlet devotes almost a page to the execution speech of Ann Drury. She had announced her guilt even as she travelled by cart to the gallows, and, in contrast with Ann Saunders, 'with great lowlinesse and reverence'. *A briefe discourse*, p. 232.

INDEX